Time
FOR
GRAMMAR

Fourth Edition

EXPERT

CONTENTS

Grammar Basics 문법 기초 지식 **6**

CHAPTER 01 Sentence Patterns 문장의 형식

UNIT 01 S + V & S + V + C 1형식과 2형식 **10**

UNIT 02 S + V + O & S + V + I.O. + D.O. 3형식과 4형식 12

UNIT 03 S + V + O + O.C. 5형식 14

CHAPTER 02 Perfect Aspect 완료시제

UNIT 01 Present Perfect 현재완료 **24**

UNIT 02 Past Perfect / Future Perfect 과거완료 / 미래완료 26

CHAPTER 03 Modals 조동사

UNIT 01 can, may, must, should 조동사의 종류와 용법 **36**

UNIT 02 Other Expressions with Modals 38
조동사의 관용적 표현

CHAPTER 04 Passives 수동태

UNIT 01 Passive Voice 수동태의 형태와 시제 **48**

UNIT 02 Passives of S + V + I.O. + D.O. / S + V + O + O.C. 50
4형식·5형식 문장의 수동태

UNIT 03 Other Passive Forms 주의해야 할 수동태 52

CHAPTER 05 To-infinitives to부정사

UNIT 01 Substantive To-infinitives to부정사의 명사적 용법 **62**

UNIT 02 Adjective & Adverbial To-infinitives 64
to부정사의 형용사적·부사적 용법

UNIT 03 Subject, Tense, and Voices of To-infinitives 66
to부정사의 의미상의 주어, 시제, 태

UNIT 04 Infinitives as Object Complements 68
목적격 보어로 쓰이는 부정사

UNIT 05 Common Structures of Infinitives 70
to부정사의 주요 구문

CHAPTER 06 Gerunds 동명사

UNIT 01 Functions and Usage of Gerunds **80**
동명사의 역할과 쓰임

UNIT 02 Gerunds vs. To-infinitives 동명사와 to부정사 82

CHAPTER 07 Participles 분사

UNIT 01 Functions of Participles 분사의 기능 **92**

UNIT 02 Participle Clauses 분사구문 94

UNIT 03 Various Participle Clauses 다양한 분사구문들 96

CHAPTER 08 — Comparisons 비교

UNIT 01 Comparisons Using the Positive Degree **106**
원급을 이용한 비교

UNIT 02 Comparisons Using Comparatives 108
비교급을 이용한 비교

UNIT 03 Comparisons Using Superlatives 110
최상급을 이용한 비교

CHAPTER 09 — Conjunctions 접속사

UNIT 01 Subordinating Conjunctions **120**
종속접속사

UNIT 02 Correlative Conjunctions / Indirect Questions 122
상관접속사 / 간접의문문

CHAPTER 10 — Relatives 관계사

UNIT 01 Relative Pronouns 관계대명사 **132**
UNIT 02 Relative Adverbs 관계부사 134
UNIT 03 Nonrestrictive Relative Clauses 136
관계사절의 계속적 용법
UNIT 04 Compound Relatives 복합관계사 138

CHAPTER 11 — Subjunctive Mood 가정법

UNIT 01 Subjunctives 가정법 **148**
UNIT 02 I wish/as if/It is time + Subjunctive 150
I wish/as if/It is time + 가정법
UNIT 03 Implied Subjunctive / Leaving Out *if* 152
if절 대용어구 / if의 생략

CHAPTER 12 — Agreement & Narration 일치와 화법

UNIT 01 Number Agreement 수일치 **162**
UNIT 02 Tense Agreement 시제 일치 164
UNIT 03 Indirect Speech 간접화법 166

CHAPTER 13 — Sentence Arrangement 기타 구문

UNIT 01 Emphasis, Negation, & Parallel Structure **176**
강조, 부정, 병렬 구조
UNIT 02 Apposition, Inversion, & Ellipsis 178
동격, 도치, 생략

GRAMMAR POINT

Unit에서 배워야 할 문법을 대표 예문과 함께 체계적으로 제시하여
쉽게 학습할 수 있도록 구성하였습니다.

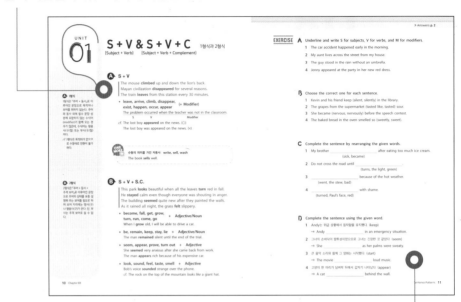

EXERCISE

해당 Unit에서 배운 내용을 다양한 유형의 문제들
을 풀어 보며 확인하고 익힐 수 있습니다.

WRITING CONNECTION

Step 1에서는 문법 개념을 확인하고, Step 2에서는 문법 사항을 활용한 문장 쓰기 연습을
하고, Step 3에서는 주어진 우리말에 맞게 영작하고 단어를 배열해 보도록 구성하였습니
다. 학습한 문법 사항을 작문에 적용해 봄으로써 문법의 실제적 쓰임을 익히고 문장을 완
성하는 연습을 할 수 있습니다.

ACTUAL TEST

> Answers p. 3

[1-2] 빈칸에 들어갈 말로 알맞은 것을 고르시오.

1 They add some sugar when their coffee tastes _____.

① sweetly　② bitter
③ bitterly　④ bitterness
⑤ sourness

2 My sister _____ me to close the window so that she did not have to.

① had　② asked
③ turned　④ watched
⑤ smelled

[3-4] 빈칸에 들어갈 수 없는 것을 고르시오.

3 What they said about the new restaurant _____ false.

① happened　② seemed
③ appeared　④ proved
⑤ turned out

4 If the weather is fine, Sally and Jack _____ to go surfing this weekend.

① plan　② want
③ enjoy　④ hope
⑤ agree

[5-6] 밑줄 친 부분이 어법상 옳은 것을 고르시오.

5 ① I pushed the button on the wall, but nothing <u>was happened</u>.
② Even though the plane shook hard, the passengers remained <u>calmly</u>.
③ The new gym around the corner <u>looks</u> a pyramid.
④ The man wearing the black suit <u>disappeared</u> into the crowd.
⑤ He seemed <u>foolishly</u> when he nodded off during the class.

6 ① They <u>discussed about</u> the topic for a couple of hours.
② Mario <u>married with</u> Sue last year.
③ The lady <u>entered the room</u> with a tray full of cookies.
④ I <u>resemble with</u> my mom a lot, so I have her eyes.
⑤ The citizens have to <u>obey to</u> the laws.

7 주어진 문장을 3형식으로 알맞게 전환한 것은?

Alex got his mother a chair from the garage.

① Alex got a chair of his mother from the garage.
② Alex got his mother for a chair from the garage.
③ Alex got a chair for his mother from the garage.
④ Alex got to his mother a chair from the garage.
⑤ Alex got a chair his mother from the garage.

Sentence Patterns **19**

WRITING

> Answers p. 4

22 빈칸에 공통으로 들어갈 알맞은 말을 쓰시오.

· I got Tom _____ check my e-mail for me as I was outside.
· Sally showed how to do a magic trick _____ us.

→

23 두 문장이 같은 의미가 되도록 빈칸에 알맞은 말을 쓰시오.

The students gave the teacher their attention.
= The students gave _____

24 우리말 뜻을 참고하여 어법에 맞게 문장을 다시 쓰시오.

The nurse asked the age for the patient.
(간호사는 그 환자에게 나이를 물었다.)

→

[25-26] 다음 글을 읽고, 물음에 답하시오.

My friend Sarah and I planned to go to the amusement park on the weekend. (A) 우리는 버스 정류장에서 만나기로 결정했다. However, I got up late. (B) I made her waits for me for a long time. I felt sorry and apologized.

25 (A)의 우리말을 영어로 쓰시오. (to부정사를 사용할 것)

26 (B)를 어법에 맞게 고쳐 쓰시오.

22 Chapter 01

[27-28] 우리말에 맞게 주어진 단어를 바르게 배열하여 문장을 쓰시오.

27 그는 내가 그와 함께 도서관을 가도록 설득했다.
(to the library, with him, me, he, persuaded, to go)

→

28 내 컴퓨터가 작동하지 않아서 나는 많은 돈이 들었다. (money, did not work, cost, as, me, my computer, a lot of, it)

→

🎯 CHALLENGE!

Write your own answer to the question.

01 What does your friend or your parents advise you to do? (Use *advise . . . to*.)

02 Have you ever prepared a special event for someone? What did you do?
(Use *made (somebody) (something)* . . . .)

ACTUAL TEST

해당 Chapter에서 학습한 문법 사항을 총정리 할 수 있도록 다양한 유형의 문제로 구성하였습니다.

WRITING

서술형 문제를 수록하여 학교 내신 시험의 서술형 문항에 완벽히 대비할 수 있도록 했습니다.

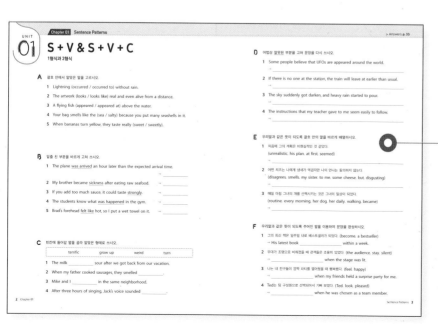

Chapter 01 Sentence Patterns

> Answers p. 33

UNIT 01 S + V & S + V + C
1형식과 2형식

A 괄호 안에서 알맞은 말을 고르시오.

1 Lightning (occurred / occurred to) without rain.
2 The artwork (looks / looks like) real and even alive from a distance.
3 A flying fish (appeared / appeared at) above the water.
4 Your bag smells like the (sea / salty) because you put many seashells in it.
5 When bananas turn yellow, they taste really (sweet / sweetly).

B 밑줄 친 부분을 바르게 고쳐 쓰시오.

1 The plane <u>was arrived</u> an hour later than the expected arrival time.
2 My brother became <u>sickness</u> after eating raw seafood.
3 If you add too much sauce, it could taste <u>strongly</u>.
4 The students know what <u>was happened</u> in the gym.
5 Brad's forehead <u>felt like</u> hot, so I put a wet towel on it.

C 빈칸에 들어갈 말을 골라 알맞은 형태로 쓰시오.

terrific　　grow up　　weird　　turn

1 The milk _____ sour after we got back from our vacation.
2 When my father cooked sausages, they smelled _____.
3 Mike and I _____ in the same neighborhood.
4 After three hours of singing, Jack's voice sounded _____.

2 Chapter 01

D 어법상 잘못된 부분을 고쳐 문장을 다시 쓰시오.

1 Some people believe that UFOs are appeared around the world.
→
2 If there is no one at the station, the train will leave at earlier than usual.
→
3 The sky suddenly got darken, and heavy rain started to pour.
→
4 The instructions that my teacher gave to me seem easily to follow.
→

E 우리말과 같은 뜻이 되도록 괄호 안의 말을 바르게 배열하시오.

1 처음에 그의 계획은 비현실적인 것 같았다.
(unrealistic, his plan, at first, seemed)
2 어떤 치즈는 나에게 냄새가 역겹지만 나의 언니는 동의하지 않는다
(disagrees, smells, my sister, to me, some cheese, but, disgusting)
3 매일 아침 그녀의 개를 산책시키는 것은 그녀의 일상이 되었다.
(routine, every morning, her dog, her daily, walking, became)

F 우리말과 같은 뜻이 되도록 주어진 말을 이용하여 문장을 완성하시오.

1 그의 최신 책은 일주일 내에 베스트셀러가 되었다. (become, a bestseller)
→ His latest book _____ within a week.
2 무대가 조명으로 비춰졌을 때 관객들은 조용히 있었다. (the audience, stay, silent)
→ _____ when the stage was lit.
3 나는 내 친구들이 깜짝 파티를 열어줬을 때 행복했다. (feel, happy)
→ _____ when my friends held a surprise party for me.
4 Ted는 팀 구성원으로 선택되어서 기뻐 보였다. (Ted, look, pleased)
→ _____ when he was chosen as a team member.

Sentence Patterns **3**

WORKBOOK

본 교재에서 익힌 문법 사항을 반복 연습할 수 있는 워크북입니다. Unit별 두 쪽으로 더 많은 문제를 풀어보며 배운 내용을 완벽하게 익힐 수 있습니다.

1 품사
Parts

영어에는 8개의 대표적인 품사가 있다.
명사, 대명사, 동사, 형용사, 부사, 전치사, 접속사, 감탄사이다.

명사
Noun

사람, 사물, 장소, 개념 등의 이름을 나타내는 말이다.
문장에서 주어, 목적어, 보어로 쓰인다.
Sally likes homemade **food**.
Tony is my best **friend**.
The **boys** are playing **baseball**.

대명사
Pronoun

명사를 대신하는 말이다. 문장에서 주어, 목적어, 보어로 쓰인다.
They are **his** kittens.
This book is **yours** and that is **hers**.
I love **my** parents.

동사
Verb

사람 혹은 사물의 움직임이나 상태를 나타내는 말이다.
Brian **is** my best friend.
Kelly **drinks** milk every day.
We **play** basketball after school.

형용사
Adjective

명사의 성질, 수량, 모양, 크기, 색깔 등을 묘사하는 말이다.
명사나 대명사를 꾸며 주거나 보어로 쓰인다.
The **tall** man is my uncle.
Sally has **many** relatives.
Your dog is **cute**.

부사
Adverb

장소, 시간, 방법, 정도, 빈도 등을 나타내는 말이다. 동사, 형용사,
다른 부사, 또는 문장 전체를 꾸며 준다.
Lucy studies **hard**.
The weather is **so** nice.
Finally, we arrived at New York.

전치사
Preposition

명사나 대명사와 함께 쓰여 장소, 시간, 목적 등을 나타내는 말이다.
Someone is **at** the door.
There is a computer **in** the room.
I take tennis lessons **on** Tuesdays.

7 접속사 Conjunction

단어와 단어, 구와 구, 절과 절을 연결하는 말이다.

Andy wants salad **and** soup.

My sister sings well, **but** I don't.

Eric takes a nap **after** he has lunch.

8 감탄사 Interjection

기쁨, 슬픔, 놀람 등의 감정을 나타내는 말이다.

Oh, it's already 7 o'clock.

Wow, you look great today!

Oops, I forgot my purse.

2 문장의 성분
Sentence Elements

1 주어 Subject

모든 문장에는 주어와 동사가 있다. 주어는 동작의 주체가 되는 사람이나 사물을 나타내는 말로, 문장에서 '누가'에 해당한다. 주로 문장의 맨 앞에 온다. 주어가 될 수 있는 것은 명사(구/절)와 대명사이다.

The sun shines brightly on leaves.

We should respect other people.

2 동사 Verb

주어의 상태나 행동을 나타내는 말로, 문장에서 '~이다, ~하다'에 해당한다. 주로 주어 뒤에 온다.

She **is** our English teacher.

It **snows** heavily in the forest.

3 목적어 Object

동사가 나타내는 동작의 대상이 되는 말로, 문장에서 '무엇을'에 해당한다. 주로 동사 뒤에 온다. 목적어가 될 수 있는 것은 명사(구/절)와 대명사이다.

I read **a magazine** about fashion design.

His rude words made **her** angry.

주어나 목적어를 보충 설명해 주는 말이다. 주로 동사나 목적어 뒤에 온다.
보어가 될 수 있는 것은 명사(구/절), 대명사, 형용사(구)이다.
People call him **Gentleman**.
The winner of the contest is **her**.
You look **happy** this morning.

문장의 주요 성분인 주어, 동사, 목적어, 보어를 수식하는 말로 상세하게
의미를 더해 준다.
The man **in the picture** is my grandfather.
We took a rest **for ten minutes**.
I found this movie **very** interesting.

3 구와 절
Phrases & Clauses

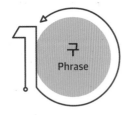

둘 이상의 단어들이 모여서 문장에서 명사, 형용사, 부사처럼 쓰이는 것을 말한
다. '주어+동사'를 포함하지 않는다.

- 명사구: 명사처럼 문장에서 주어, 목적어, 보어로 쓰인다.
  She married **a famous singer**.
  His dream is **to become a scientist**.
- 형용사구: 형용사처럼 문장에서 명사를 수식하거나 보어로 쓰인다.
  Is there anything **to eat** in the fridge?
  The girls **in the park** are my friends.
- 부사구: 부사처럼 문장에서 동사, 형용사, 다른 부사, 문장 전체를 수식한다.
  Brian goes to school **by bike**.
  They study hard **to pass the exam**.

'주어+동사'를 포함한 여러 단어가 모여 문장 내에서 명사, 형용사, 부사처럼 쓰이
는 것을 말한다.

- 명사절: 명사처럼 문장에서 주어, 목적어, 보어로 쓰인다.
  I know **that you are smart**.
- 형용사절: 형용사처럼 문장에서 명사를 수식한다.
  Do you remember the girl **who called me yesterday**?
- 부사절: 부사처럼 문장에서 동사, 형용사, 다른 부사를 수식한다.
  Write it down on paper **before you forget it**.

CHAPTER 01

Sentence Patterns
문장의 형식

UNIT 01

S + V & S + V + C

1형식과 2형식

UNIT 02

S + V + O & S + V + I.O. + D.O.

3형식과 4형식

UNIT 03

S + V + O + O.C.

5형식

UNIT 01

S + V & S + V + C 1형식과 2형식

(Subject + Verb)   (Subject + Verb + Complement)

Ⓐ **1형식**

1형식은 「주어 + 동사」로 이루어진 문장으로 목적어나 보어를 취하지 않는다. 주어와 동사 외에 필수 문장 성분에 포함하지 않는 수식어 (modifier)가 함께 오는 경우가 많은데, 수식어는 형용사(구/절) 또는 부사(구/절)이다.

cf. 1형식은 목적어가 없으므로 수동태로 전환이 불가하다.

Ⓐ S + V

The mouse **climbed** up and down the lion's back.
Mayan civilization **disappeared** for several reasons.
The train **leaves** from this station every 30 minutes.

♦ **leave, arrive, climb, disappear, exist, happen, occur, appear** (+ Modifier)

<u>The problem</u> <u>occurred</u> <u>when the teacher was not in the classroom.</u>
　　　S　　　　　V　　　　　　　　　Modifier

cf. The lost boy **appeared** on the news. (○)
　　The lost boy was appeared on the news. (×)

수동의 의미를 가진 자동사: write, sell, wash
The book **sells** well.

Ⓑ **2형식**

2형식은 「주어 + 동사 + 주격 보어」로 이루어진 문장으로 주어의 상태를 보충 설명해 주는 보어를 필요로 하며 보어 자리에는 명사(구)나 형용사(구)가 온다. 단, 부사는 주격 보어로 쓸 수 없다.

Ⓑ S + V + S.C.

This park **looks** beautiful when all the leaves **turn** red in fall.
He **stayed** calm even though everyone was shouting in anger.
The building **seemed** quite new after they painted the walls.
As it rained all night, the grass **felt** slippery.

♦ **become, fall, get, grow, turn, run, come, go** + **Adjective/Noun**
When I **grow** old, I will be able to drive a car.

♦ **be, remain, keep, stay, lie** + **Adjective/Noun**
The man **remained** silent until the end of the trial.

♦ **seem, appear, prove, turn out** + **Adjective**
She **seemed** very anxious after she came back from work.
The man **appears** rich because of his expensive car.

♦ **look, sound, feel, taste, smell** + **Adjective**
Bob's voice **sounded** strange over the phone.
cf. The rock on the top of the mountain *looks like* a giant hat.

EXERCISE

A Underline and write S for subjects, V for verbs, and M for modifiers.

1 The car accident happened early in the morning.

2 My aunt lives across the street from my house.

3 The guy stood in the rain without an umbrella.

4 Jenny appeared at the party in her new red dress.

B Choose the correct one for each sentence.

1 Kevin and his friend keep (silent, silently) in the library.

2 The grapes from the supermarket (tasted like, tasted) sour.

3 She became (nervous, nervously) before the speech contest.

4 The baked bread in the oven smelled so (sweetly, sweet).

C Complete the sentence by rearranging the given words.

1 My brother _____ after eating too much ice cream.
(sick, became)

2 Do not cross the road until _____.
(turns, the light, green)

3 _____ because of the hot weather.
(went, the stew, bad)

4 _____ with shame.
(turned, Paul's face, red)

D Complete the sentence using the given word.

1 Andy는 위급 상황에서 침착함을 유지했다. (keep)

   → Andy _____ in an emergency situation.

2 그녀의 손바닥이 땀투성이였으므로 그녀는 긴장한 것 같았다. (seem)

   → She _____ as her palms were sweaty.

3 큰 음악 소리와 함께 그 영화는 시작했다. (start)

   → The movie _____ loud music.

4 고양이 한 마리가 담벼락 뒤에서 갑자기 나타났다. (appear)

   → A cat _____ behind the wall.

UNIT 02

S + V + O &
(Subject + Verb + Object)

S + V + I.O. + D.O.
(Subject + Verb + Indirect Object + Direct Object)

3형식과 4형식

Ⓐ 3형식

3형식은 「주어 + 동사 + 목적어」로 이루어진 문장으로, 3형식 동사는 보어 없이 목적어를 필요로 한다.

cf. '-을/를'로 해석되지 않아 자동사로 생각해서 전치사가 필요할 것이라고 착각하기 쉬운 타동사

Ⓐ S + V + O

Henry **caught** a big fish with his new fishing rod.
They **hope** to attend the graduation ceremony.
I **finished** making a welcome card for the exchange student.

- **hope, want, agree, promise, plan, expect, refuse, decide** + **To-infinitive/Noun**
  She **wanted** to go to the summer camp with her friends.

- **finish, start, stop, enjoy, avoid, suggest, quit, hate, give up** + **Gerund/Noun**
  He **enjoys** walking along the beach right before the sunset.

cf. **attend, discuss, enter, obey, resemble, marry, explain** + **Object**
  My sister Jina **resembles** my grandmother very much. (○)
  My sister Jina resembles with my grandmother very much. (×)

Ⓑ 4형식

'…에게 ~을 해 주다'라는 의미로 쓰이는 수여동사가 간접목적어와 직접목적어 두 개의 목적어를 취하는 문장이 4형식이다.

cf. envy, forgive, cost 등의 동사는 4형식 문장에서 3형식 문장으로 전환이 불가하다.

Ⓑ S + V + I.O. + D.O.

Jack **built** his dog a new house after the tornado.
The police **showed** the man a picture of a suspect.
Can you **tell** me where I can get a train ticket?

- 「S + V + I.O. + D.O.」 → 「S + V + O + Modifier」
  My father **bought** us what we need.
  → My father bought what we need *for* us.

  <Preposition Usage>
  (1) to: give, send, pass, write, show, teach, tell, read, bring, lend, owe, offer
  (2) for: buy, get, make, build, cook, find, leave, sing, prepare
  (3) of: ask, inquire

cf. **envy, forgive, cost + I.O. + D.O.**
  She **envies** Tom his success. (○)
  She envies his success to Tom. (×)

EXERCISE

A Underline and write I.O. for indirect objects and D.O. for direct objects.

1 David brought me a glass of water when I went into his house.

2 My teacher told us the news about the field trip.

3 When should I show my dad his birthday present?

4 The doctor wrote her patient a prescription for her stomachache.

B Correct the underlined part.

1 I hope <u>seeing</u> the opening ceremony of the Olympics. → _____

2 Karen suggested <u>to make</u> a pizza for dinner. → _____

3 Nick plans <u>saving</u> more money to buy the latest cellphone. → _____

4 The student <u>discussed about</u> some ways to recycle. → _____

C Rewrite the sentence with a modifier.

1 Andy told me a horror story.

→ Andy told a horror story _____.

2 They made their children a tree house.

→ They made a tree house _____.

3 Jessy wrote her friend a Christmas card.

→ Jessy wrote a Christmas card _____.

4 Jenny asked her teacher some questions about the earthquakes.

→ Jenny asked some questions about the earthquakes _____.

D Complete the sentence using the given words.

1 연극이 시작한 후에는 그 홀에 들어갈 수 없다. (the hall)

→ You cannot _____ after the play starts.

2 그는 그의 생일에 나에게 케이크 한 조각을 줬다. (a piece of)

→ He gave _____ on his birthday.

3 그녀는 하루 종일 전화를 받지 않았다. (answer, the phone)

→ She did not _____ all day.

4 Kevin은 나에게 냅킨을 건네주었다. (pass, a napkin, to)

→ Kevin _____.

UNIT 03

S + V + O + O.C. 5형식
(Subject + Verb + Object + Object Complement)

A 5형식 (목적격 보어가 명사)

5형식은 「주어 + 동사 + 목적어 + 목적격 보어」 구조의 문장이다. 동사에 따라 목적격 보어로 명사(구)가 오며, 이때 목적어와 목적격 보어는 동격이다.

B 5형식 (목적격 보어가 형용사/분사)

5형식 문장은 동사에 따라 목적격 보어로 형용사(구) 또는 분사(구)가 온다. 형용사(구) 목적격 보어는 목적어의 상태를 설명하며, 분사(구) 목적격 보어는 목적어의 진행되는 상황을 강조한다.

• 일부 지각동사와 사역동사는 목적어와 목적격 보어의 관계가 능동일 때는 목적격 보어로 현재분사를, 수동일 때는 과거분사를 취한다.

C 5형식 (목적격 보어가 to부정사/원형부정사)

5형식 문장은 동사에 따라 목적격 보어로 to부정사(구)가 오며, 이때 to부정사는 명사 역할을 한다. 지각동사와 사역동사는 목적격 보어 자리에 일반적으로 원형부정사가 온다.

cf. 준사역동사 get은 목적격 보어로 to부정사(구)가 온다.

A S + V + O + O.C. (Noun)

| When the man rescued a boy, people **called** him *a hero*.
| We **appointed** Tim *our team leader* because of his leadership.
| After many experiments, doctors **named** it *the placebo effect*.

◆ **name, elect, call, consider, appoint** + O + Noun

After Mike read my poem, he **considered** me *a great poet*.

B S + V + O + O.C. (Adjective/Participle)

| She **finds** Jack *funny* as he is good at telling funny stories.
| He **watched** the sun *rising* through his room window.

◆ **make, keep, find, think, leave, prove** + O + Adjective

The silence in the room **made** us *uncomfortable*.

◆ **see, hear, make, have** + O + Present/Past Participle

I **saw** a man *picking up* trash in the park.
I **had** the machine *fixed* by a skilled worker.

C S + V + O + O.C. (To-infinitive/Bare infinitive)

| Our captain **encouraged** us *to play* the game without fear.
| Susan **had** her mother *pull out* her wisdom tooth.
| He **saw** his friend *score* a goal in the last minute.

◆ **want, ask, tell, advise, expect, allow, order, remind, force, persuade, encourage** + O + To-infinitive

He **forced** us *to put down* what we had in our hands.

◆ **see, hear, listen to let, have, make,** + O + Bare infinitive

Reading comic books always **makes** me *laugh*.

cf. Her mother **got** her *to finish* her homework before dinner. (○)
Her mother got her finish her homework before dinner. (×)

EXERCISE   **A**   **Complete the sentence by rearranging the given words.**

1   Since many of his songs are popular, people _____.
(him, a pop star, consider)

2   Our teacher tried to _____.
(better people, us, make)

3   The president _____.
(the defense minister, Mr. Smith, appointed)

4   Since John did not suffer any injuries, he _____.
(the accident, called, a miracle)

B   **Choose the correct one for each sentence.**

1   When I feel upset, eating sweets makes me (happy / happily).

2   He finds the movie (interesting / interestingly) because of its plot.

3   Anna heard someone (knocked / knocking) on the door.

4   I had my dog (wash / washed) after we got back from the walk.

C   **Complete the sentence using the correct form of the word in the box.**

clean	change	ask	get

1   The coach allowed the players _____ some rest after practice.

2   The professor let the audience _____ questions about the lecture.

3   We tried to persuade him _____ his decision.

4   My mom made my sister and me _____ our room on the weekend.

D   **Complete the sentence using the given words.**

1   우리가 해변에 도착했을 때, 우리는 많은 사람들이 수영하는 것을 보았다. (see, swim)

→ When we arrived at the beach, we _____.

2   추웠기 때문에 나는 Tim에게 두꺼운 재킷을 입을 것을 상기시켰다. (remind, wear)

→ I _____ a thick jacket because it was cold.

3   대부분의 학생들이 기말고사가 어렵다고 여겼다. (find, the final exam, difficult)

→ Most of the students _____.

4   그녀는 파이를 굽는 동안 아이들끼리 놀도록 했다. (have, the children)

→ While she baked a pie, she _____ by
themselves.

WRITING CONNECTION

1 Grammar Check-up

A Choose the correct one.

1 Strangely, Harry _____ without saying anything to his friends.

ⓐ left   ⓑ leaving   ⓒ left at   ⓓ to leave

2 The old lady stays _____ because she exercises every morning.

ⓐ healthy   ⓑ healthily   ⓒ health   ⓓ unhealthily

3 Sally quit _____ junk food because of her doctor's advice.

ⓐ eat   ⓑ eaten   ⓒ eating   ⓓ to eat

4 We expect _____ home around midnight because of the traffic jam.

ⓐ arrive   ⓑ arriving   ⓒ arrived   ⓓ to arrive

5 Simon sometimes asked strange questions _____ Tina.

ⓐ to   ⓑ of   ⓒ for   ⓓ on

6 My parents encourage us _____ our opinions.

ⓐ express   ⓑ expressed   ⓒ to express   ⓓ expressing

B Circle the inappropriate one between ⓐ and ⓑ. Then correct it.

1 The restaurant's food mostly tastes <u>sweetness</u>, so I <u>do not like</u> it there. _____
                                                   ⓐ   ⓑ

2 When I <u>look at</u> Jake's family, Jake <u>resembles with</u> his father a lot. _____
                        ⓐ   ⓑ

3 A letter <u>was arrived</u> last night, and I <u>put it</u> on the table. _____
                   ⓐ   ⓑ

4 My aunt offered some cookies <u>of me</u>, but I was <u>too full</u>. _____
                              ⓐ   ⓑ

5 As Sam hates <u>lending</u> things, he did not let me <u>to use</u> his headphone.
                      ⓐ   ⓑ _____

2 Phrases to Sentences

A Complete the sentence by referring to the Korean translation.

1 일기예보는 다음 주에 큰 태풍이 발생할 것이라고 예측한다. (occur)

→ The weather forecast predicts that a big typhoon _____ next week.

2 Bob은 항상 웃고 있기 때문에 친절해 보인다. (seem)

→ Bob _____ as he always smiles.

3 나의 사촌이 방문했을 때, 나는 그를 위해 방을 준비했다. (prepare, a room)

→ When my cousin visited, I _____.

4 네가 그 책을 다 읽은 후에 그 책을 나에게 빌려줄 수 있니? (lend)

→ Can you _____ after you read it?

5 나는 Janice가 공원에서 네 잎 클로버를 찾고 있는 것을 보았다. (search for)

→ I _____ a four-leaf clover in the park.

6 나의 아빠는 나에게 캠핑을 갈 때 여분의 신발을 가져가라고 조언하셨다. (advise, take)

→ My dad _____ spare shoes when I go camping.

B Underline the error and rewrite the sentence.

1 A sandstorm was occurred, so we could not see anything from the window.

→ _____

2 Andrew went to New York because he had to attend to a seminar.

→ _____

3 I apologized to Serena, and she forgave my mistake to me.

→ _____

4 We had our picture taking by the best photographer in town.

→ _____

5 Nick sent some flowers of me when I was in the hospital.

→ _____

6 She proved the information wrongly by doing a search on the Internet.

→ _____

3 Sentence Practice

A Translate the Korean into English using the given words.

1 a. 선수들은 경기에서 공정하게 경쟁하기로 동의했다. (compete)

→ The athletes _____ fairly in the race.

b. 면접관은 내일 나를 만나는 것에 동의했다. (the interviewer, agree, tomorrow)

→ _____

2 a. 나의 할아버지는 나에게 타인을 존중하는 것에 대한 교훈을 가르쳐 주셨다. (a lesson)

→ My grandfather _____ about respecting others.

b. 그의 도움 때문에 나는 그에게 저녁을 빚졌다. (owe, because of)

→ _____

3 a. Vicky는 비록 아직 완성되지 않았지만 내가 그녀의 에세이를 읽도록 해 주었다. (let)

→ Vicky _____ her essay although it was not finished.

b. Amy는 내가 그녀가 좋아하는 가수의 노래를 듣도록 했다. (have, listen to)

→ _____

4 a. 나는 내 선물이 그녀를 행복하게 만들길 바란다. (make)

→ I hope my present _____ .

b. 내 생각에 그 영화는 Jenny를 슬프게 만들 것이다. (make, sad)

→ _____

B Unscramble the words to make a sentence.

1 그 정장 때문에 너는 성숙해 보인다. (the suit, mature, look, because of, you)

→ _____

2 나는 이 기계를 끄고 싶지만, 어떻게 끄는지 모른다.

(to, how, but, turn off, I, I, this machine, know, want, do not)

→ _____

3 Tony가 나가기 전에, 그는 탁자 위에 나에게 메시지를 남겼다.

(before, on, Tony, a message, went out, left, he, the table, me)

→ _____

4 학생들은 Joe를 반장으로 선출했다. (elected, the class president, Joe, the students)

→ _____

ACTUAL TEST

> Answers **p. 3**

[1-2] 빈칸에 들어갈 말로 알맞은 것을 고르시오.

1
> They add some sugar when their coffee tastes _____ .

① sweetly ② bitter
③ bitterly ④ bitterness
⑤ sourness

2
> My sister _____ me to close the window so that she didn't have to.

① had ② asked
③ turned ④ watched
⑤ smelled

[3-4] 빈칸에 들어갈 수 없는 것을 고르시오.

3
> What they said about the new restaurant _____ false.

① happened ② seemed
③ appeared ④ proved
⑤ turned out

4
> If the weather is fine, Sally and Jack _____ to go surfing this weekend.

① plan ② want
③ enjoy ④ hope
⑤ agree

[5-6] 밑줄 친 부분이 어법상 옳은 것을 고르시오.

5
① I pushed the button on the wall, but nothing <u>was happened</u>.
② Even though the plane shook hard, the passengers remained <u>calmly</u>.
③ The new gym around the corner <u>looks</u> a pyramid.
④ The man wearing the black suit <u>disappeared</u> into the crowd.
⑤ He seemed <u>foolishly</u> when he nodded off during the class.

6
① They <u>discussed about</u> the topic for a couple of hours.
② Mario <u>married with</u> Sue last year.
③ The lady <u>entered the room</u> with a tray full of cookies.
④ I <u>resemble with</u> my mom a lot, so I have her eyes.
⑤ The citizens have to <u>obey to</u> the laws.

7 주어진 문장을 3형식으로 알맞게 전환한 것은?

> Alex got his mother a chair from the garage.

① Alex got a chair of his mother from the garage.
② Alex got his mother for a chair from the garage.
③ Alex got a chair for his mother from the garage.
④ Alex got to his mother a chair from the garage.
⑤ Alex got a chair his mother from the garage.

8 어법상 문장 전환이 옳지 <u>않은</u> 것은?

① Jim lent me his comic book.

   → Jim lent his comic book to me.

② The reporter asked the actress some questions about her new movie.

   → The reporter asked some questions about her new movie of the actress.

③ My mom baked us a cake yesterday.

   → My mom baked a cake for us yesterday.

④ The engineer offered Anne the job.

   → The engineer offered the job of Anne.

⑤ The hotel prepared them a nice room.

   → The hotel prepared a nice room for them.

[9-10] 주어진 문장과 문장 형식이 <u>다른</u> 것을 고르시오.

9

> His decision made me feel upset.

① Nothing makes him happy.

② My mom got us some hot chocolate.

③ The typhoon caused the house to be flooded.

④ I watched several ducks floating on the water.

⑤ Eating a lot of vegetables keeps us healthy.

10

> Charlie seems tired because of his hard work.

① Tobby kept silent saying nothing.

② Some roses in the garden smell wonderful.

③ They got excited about going to the zoo.

④ A hiker reached the top of the mountain.

⑤ Paul stayed awake last night.

11 어법상 <u>어색한</u> 문장은?

① Jack suggests recycling used bottles.

② He stopped working when it got dark.

③ I avoided riding a bike without a helmet.

④ She quit to learn Spanish as it was hard.

⑤ They gave up persuading Joe to change his mind.

[12-13] 문장의 형식이 <u>다른</u> 하나를 고르시오.

12 ① The police arrived at the site quickly.

② The car accident occurred yesterday.

③ He cooked a nice meal for his brother.

④ The wind blows lightly.

⑤ Changes happen slowly.

13 ① We called him a captain.

② The teacher considers Joe a smart student.

③ I call him Dumbo since his ears are big.

④ They appointed Julie the new manager.

⑤ Sam showed me his new laptop.

14 두 문장을 한 문장으로 바르게 연결한 것은?

> I saw the package. It was delivered to you.

① I saw the package deliver to you.

② I saw the package delivers to you.

③ I saw the package to deliver to you.

④ I saw the package delivering to you.

⑤ I saw the package delivered to you.

[15-16] 우리말과 일치하도록 빈칸에 들어갈 알맞은 말을 고르시오.

15
> 그 남자는 일꾼들에게 마을에 우물을 파도록 했다.
> → The man _____ a well in the village.

① got the workers dig
② let the workers to dig
③ got the workers to dig
④ got the workers digging
⑤ made the workers to dig

16
> 그는 하늘에 많은 드론이 날아다니는 것을 보았다.
> → He _____ in the sky.

① saw many drones flown
② saw many drones to fly
③ saw many drones to flying
④ saw many drones flying
⑤ saw many drones flew

[17-18] 빈칸에 들어갈 말이 알맞게 짝 지어진 것을 고르시오.

17
> • Sue bought a souvenir ____(A)____ me in Paris.
> • The teacher expects the students ____(B)____ do well on the test.

   (A) (B)　　　　(A) (B)
① for – to　　② of – for
③ to – for　　④ to – to
⑤ for – of

18
> • The mayor wants ____(A)____ build a bridge over the river.
> • The workers ____(B)____ the workshop to improve their knowledge.

   (A)　(B)　　　　(A)　(B)
① to – attended to　② to – attended
③ for – attended to　④ for – attended
⑤ of – attended

[19-20] 빈칸에 공통으로 들어갈 말로 알맞은 것을 고르시오.

19
> • I _____ a doll hanging from his backpack.
> • My parents _____ me play the violin in the school orchestra.

① saw　　② let　　③ showed
④ helped　　⑤ got

20
> • The lady had many wrinkles on her face. She _____ old.
> • The passengers _____ angry about the delay of the train.

① found　　② seemed　　③ existed
④ owed　　⑤ refused

21 어법상 올바른 문장의 개수는?

> • Kate taught me how to cook the traditional dish of her country.
> • The airplane crash was occurred near the top of the mountain.
> • He appears calmly when he does not talk.
> • My brother always encourages me challenge myself in any situation.
> • I do not want him to give up singing as he has a great voice.

① 1개　② 2개　③ 3개　④ 4개　⑤ 5개

22 빈칸에 공통으로 들어갈 알맞은 말을 쓰시오.

> • I got Tom _____ check my e-mail for me as I was outside.
>
> • Sally showed how to do a magic trick _____ us.

→ _____

23 두 문장이 같은 의미가 되도록 빈칸에 알맞은 말을 쓰시오.

> The students gave the teacher their attention.
> = The students gave _____
>
> _____ .

24 우리말 뜻을 참고하여 어법에 맞게 문장을 다시 쓰시오.

> The nurse asked the age for the patient.
> (간호사는 그 환자에게 나이를 물었다.)

→ _____

[25-26] 다음 글을 읽고, 물음에 답하시오.

> My friend Sarah and I planned to go to the amusement park on the weekend. (A) 우리는 버스 정류장에서 만나기로 결정했다. However, I got up late. (B) I made her waits for me for a long time. I felt sorry and apologized.

25 (A)의 우리말을 영어로 쓰시오. (to부정사를 사용할 것)

_____

26 (B)를 어법에 맞게 고쳐 쓰시오.

→ _____

[27-28] 우리말에 맞게 주어진 단어를 바르게 배열하여 문장을 쓰시오.

27
> 그는 내가 그와 함께 도서관을 가도록 설득했다.
> (to the library, with him, me, he, persuaded, to go)

→ _____

_____

28
> 내 컴퓨터가 작동하지 않아서 나는 많은 돈이 들었다. (money, did not work, cost, as, me, my computer, a lot of, it)

→ _____

_____

🎯 CHALLENGE!

Write your own answer to the question.

01 What does your friend or your parents advise you to do? (Use *advise . . . to.*)

_____

_____

02 Have you ever prepared a special event for someone? What did you do?
(Use *made (somebody) (something) . . . .*)

_____

_____

Perfect Aspect

완료시제

UNIT

01

Present Perfect
현재완료

UNIT

02

Past Perfect / Future Perfect
과거완료/미래완료

UNIT 01

Present Perfect 현재완료

A Present Perfect

I **have** just **finished** my homework. <completion>
She **has been** a teacher since 2020. <continuation>
I **have** never **met** Helen before. <experience>
They **have moved** to Jejudo. <result>

- ◆ **Words used in present perfect**
  - **just, finally, already, yet** (completion)
    Someone **has** *already* **eaten** my soup.
    I **have** not **decided** on my position *yet*.

  - **since, for, so far, until now** (continuation)
    How long **have** they **been** married?
    – They **have been** married *for* 20 years.

  - **ever, never, before, once, three times** (experience)
    Have you *ever* **been** to Japan?
    – Yes, I **have been** to Japan *twice*.

- ◆ **Words NOT used in present perfect: finished-time words**
  - **yesterday, ago, last, then, just now, in 2019, when** (interrogative)
    I took a trip to Europe last summer. (○)
    I have taken a trip to Europe last summer. (×)

B Present Perfect Progressive

I It **has been raining** for a month.

e.g. Charlie **has been going out** with Alice.
We **have been waiting** here since 6 o'clock this morning.
What **have** you **been doing** since summer vacation started?

Past vs. Present Perfect
- 과거: 동작이 일어난 과거 시점에 초점이 있고, 현재와의 연관성은 없다.
- 현재완료: 과거에 일어난 일이 현재에 계속되고 있거나 영향을 미치는 것을 나타내며, 현재와의 연관성에 초점이 있다.

I **lost** my car key. (과거에 잃어버렸고, 지금은 찾았는지 알 수 없음.)
I **have lost** my car key. (과거에 잃어버렸고, 지금도 잃어버린 상태임.)

EXERCISE

A Choose the correct one for each sentence.

1 We (have bought, bought) a new sofa last Sunday.

2 I (was, have been) looking for members of the school club these days.

3 She (has been, has gone) to China, and she has not come back yet.

4 My dad (just finished, has just finished) washing the dishes.

5 I (have visited, visited) my uncle in Boston twice so far.

6 They (have been staying, are staying) with us since last week.

B Fill in the blanks of the dialogue using the given words.

1 A: Where have you been?

B: I _____ just _____ to the supermarket. (be)

2 A: Have you ever seen the Eiffel Tower?

B: No, I _____ never _____ it. (see)

3 A: Where is Julia? I have been looking for her since yesterday.

B: Didn't you know? She _____ _____ to Paris. (go)

C Fill in the blanks so that the two sentences have the same meaning.

1 I started waiting for you two hours ago. I am still waiting.

= I _____ for you for two hours.

2 Mike started running an hour ago. He is still running.

= Mike _____ for an hour.

3 It is snowing now. It started snowing three days ago.

= It _____ for the past three days.

D Complete the sentence using the given words.

1 그들은 이미 그 신발을 수선했다. (already, repair)

→ They _____ the shoes.

2 Ethan은 그의 백팩을 잃어버려서 그의 형의 것 중 하나를 빌려야 한다. (lose)

→ Ethan _____ his backpack, so he has to borrow one of his brother's.

3 나는 전에 태국 음식을 먹어 본 적이 없다. (eat)

→ I _____ Thai food before.

4 나의 삼촌은 대학을 졸업한 후 지금까지 여행 중이다. (travel)

→ My uncle _____ since he graduated from college.

UNIT 02

Past Perfect / Future Perfect 과거완료/미래완료

A 과거완료

「had + p.p.」 형태로, 과거의 어느 시점보다 더 앞서 일어난 일이 과거 시점에 영향을 미칠 때 쓴다.

Ⓐ Past Perfect

I **had** just **put** the phone down when the doorbell rang.
<completion>
He **had worked** at the company for nine years before he got a promotion. <continuation>
I thought she **had** never **been** to Thailand. <experience>
She **had lost** her passport and purse before she got to the airport. <result>

B 미래완료

「will have + p.p.」 형태로, 현재에 진행 중인 일이 미래의 어느 시점에 완료되거나, 계속, 경험, 결과를 나타낼 때 쓴다.

Ⓑ Future Perfect

I can go out with you tonight. I **will have finished** my homework by then. <completion>
I **will have lived** in Korea for 10 years by the end of the year.
<continuation>
I **will have visited** Turkey three times by the end of this trip.
<experience>
By the time you read this letter, I **will have left** this country.
<result>

◆ **Expressions used in future perfect**
 • by then, by next year, by the end of this year, by the time S + V
  I **will have spent** all my money *by the end of the week*.

C 과거완료진행/미래완료진행

과거의 일정 기간 동안 행동이 계속될 때 과거완료진행 「had been + v-ing」을 쓰고, 미래의 어느 시점까지 현재의 행동이 계속될 때 미래완료진행 「will have been + v-ing」을 쓴다.

Ⓒ Past/Future Perfect Progressive

I **had been waiting** for her for two hours when she finally arrived.
By next year, she **will have been living** here for 20 years.

e.g. She **had been crying** until you came.
   It **will have been raining** for a month tomorrow.

EXERCISE

A Choose the correct one for each sentence.

1 We (will have, have) known each other for 10 years by next month.

2 They (has, had) arrived before it became too dark.

3 She (will have, has) graduated from high school by February next year.

4 I could not open my car. I (have, had) left my car key in it.

B Complete the sentence by rearranging the given words.

1 I _____ eating lunch when you come home this afternoon.
  (have, will, finished)

2 He _____ for two hours when you come back at 12 p.m.
  (sleeping, been, will, have)

3 I wanted to sit down because I _____ at work all day.
  (standing, been, had)

4 She _____ to drive a car until she moved to L.A.
  (able, not, had, been)

C Fill in the blanks using the given word.

1 Mira was not at home. She _____ to the bookstore. (go)

2 By the end of this year, I will _____ reading 50 books. (finish)

3 Selena _____ a new job when I met her. (start)

4 I heard he _____ English for a year. (study)

5 We will _____ about the topic until this evening. (talk)

D Complete the sentence using the given words.

1 우리는 Jim이 다른 도시로 이사 가기 전까지 잘 지내고 있었다. (get along well)

  → We _____ until Jim moved to another city.

2 Peter는 어떤 수업에도 참석하지 않았기 때문에 기말시험에서 낙제했다. (attend)

  → Peter failed the final exam because he _____ any classes.

3 우리가 그녀를 만날 때쯤이면, 그녀는 숙제를 다 했을 것이다. (finish)

  → By the time we meet her, she _____ her homework.

4 내년이면 Jack은 수의사로 오 년째 일하고 있을 것이다. (work)

  → Jack _____ as a vet for five years by next year.

WRITING CONNECTION

1 Grammar Check-up

A Choose the correct one.

1 How long _____ you been studying German?

ⓐ did   ⓑ have   ⓒ do   ⓓ had

2 I _____ made dinner before Sue arrived at my house.

ⓐ have   ⓑ did   ⓒ had   ⓓ do

3 I think we have _____ this film already.

ⓐ see   ⓑ saw   ⓒ seen   ⓓ seeing

4 Sara lost her watch. She _____ it since 2019.

ⓐ had   ⓑ had had   ⓒ has had   ⓓ will have

5 We _____ finished painting the wall by the time you get back home.

ⓐ will have   ⓑ have   ⓒ had   ⓓ have been

6 I cannot believe I _____ lived for so long without trying this food before.

ⓐ do   ⓑ have   ⓒ had   ⓓ will have

B Circle the inappropriate one between ⓐ and ⓑ. Then correct it.

1 She already saw the movie when I recommended it.   _____
             ⓐ   ⓑ

2 The professor was working at the university for a year before he left Korea.
                ⓐ   ⓑ

    _____

3 I am tired then because I had been working out hard.   _____
  ⓐ   ⓑ

4 I hope you will have changing your mind by tomorrow.   _____
   ⓐ   ⓑ

5 My grandparents are married for 50 years.   _____
               ⓐ   ⓑ

6 He had been sick since last Sunday, so he will see a doctor today._____
     ⓐ   ⓑ

2 Phrases to Sentences

A Complete the sentence by referring to the Korean translation.

1 엄마는 집에 안 계신다. 내 생각에 그녀는 쇼핑하러 간 것 같다. (go)

→ Mom is not at home. I think she _____ shopping.

2 우리는 한 시간 동안 버스를 기다리고 있는데 아직도 오지 않고 있다. (wait)

→ We _____ for the bus for an hour, but it has still not come.

3 초인종이 울렸을 때 그녀는 집을 청소하는 것을 막 끝마쳤다. (just, finish)

→ She _____ cleaning the house when the doorbell rang.

4 이 년 후면 우리는 새 사무실로 이사를 했을 것이다. (move)

→ Within the next two years, we _____ to a new office.

5 비가 막 그쳐서 나는 우산이 필요 없다. (just, stop)

→ It _____ raining, so I do not need my umbrella.

6 십 년 후에는 과학자들이 그 바이러스에 대한 백신을 발견했을 것이다. (find)

→ The scientists _____ a vaccine for the virus in 10 years.

B Underline the error and rewrite the sentence.

1 The author writes five novels so far.

→ _____

2 He has already left the house when his children get up tomorrow morning.

→ _____

3 Sue told her friends that she quit school.

→ _____

4 Mark have been digging a hole for an hour when I came into the garden.

→ _____

5 It will have been snowing hard for a few days.

→ _____

6 My sister studies Spanish since she entered the university.

→ _____

STEP 3 Sentence Practice

A Translate the Korean into English using the given words.

1 a. 나는 아직 숙제를 끝내지 못했다. (have, not)

→ I ＿＿＿＿＿＿＿＿＿＿＿＿＿ my homework yet.

b. 그는 아직 식사를 다 하지 못했다. (have, his meal)

→ ＿＿＿＿＿＿＿＿＿＿＿＿＿＿＿＿＿＿＿＿＿＿＿

2 a. 아빠가 돌아올 때쯤이면 우리는 자러 갔을 것이다. (go to bed)

→ We ＿＿＿＿＿＿＿＿＿＿＿＿＿ by the time our dad comes back.

b. 그 영화가 시작할 때쯤이면 우리는 저녁 식사를 다 끝냈을 것이다. (finish)

→ ＿＿＿＿＿＿＿＿＿＿＿＿＿＿＿＿＿＿＿＿＿＿＿

3 a. 삼촌은 지난주까지 우리와 함께 지내고 있었다. (stay with)

→ My uncle ＿＿＿＿＿＿＿＿＿＿＿ us until the previous week.

b. 그녀는 어제까지 그룹 프로젝트를 하고 있었다. (work on, the group project)

→ ＿＿＿＿＿＿＿＿＿＿＿＿＿＿＿＿＿＿＿＿＿＿＿

4 a. 나는 세 시간째 이 산을 오르고 있는 중이다. (climb up)

→ I ＿＿＿＿＿＿＿＿＿＿＿＿＿ this mountain for three hours.

b. 배관공은 두 시간째 싱크대를 수리하고 있는 중이다. (the plumber, fix, the sink)

→ ＿＿＿＿＿＿＿＿＿＿＿＿＿＿＿＿＿＿＿＿＿＿＿

B Unscramble the words to make a sentence.

1 나는 삼 개월째 학교 기숙사에 살고 있다.

(have, for, living, in, the, months, school dormitory, I, been, three)

→ ＿＿＿＿＿＿＿＿＿＿＿＿＿＿＿＿＿＿＿＿＿＿＿

2 내년이면 우리는 서로를 안 지 십 년이 될 것이다.

(we, ten years, have, each other, for, by, will, known, next year)

→ ＿＿＿＿＿＿＿＿＿＿＿＿＿＿＿＿＿＿＿＿＿＿＿

3 내가 방 청소를 끝내자마자, 나는 낮잠을 잤다.

(cleaned, took a nap, I, once, I, had, my room)

→ ＿＿＿＿＿＿＿＿＿＿＿＿＿＿＿＿＿＿＿＿＿＿＿

4 내가 집에 왔을 때, 내 여동생은 TV를 보고 있었다.

(I, TV, got, home, been, my sister, when, watching, had)

→ ＿＿＿＿＿＿＿＿＿＿＿＿＿＿＿＿＿＿＿＿＿＿＿

ACTUAL TEST

> Answers p. 6

[1-3] 빈칸에 들어갈 말로 알맞은 것을 고르시오.

1
> I _____ my phone. I can neither call nor text you today.

① lose
② am losing
③ am lost
④ will lose
⑤ have lost

2
> _____ your homework already?

① Are you finished
② Do you finish
③ Have you finished
④ Will you finish
⑤ Had you finished

3
> Penny _____ her dog for an hour when she met her neighbor in the park.

① will be walking
② has been walking
③ had been walked
④ had been walking
⑤ will have walked

[4-5] 밑줄 친 부분이 어법상 어색한 것을 고르시오.

4
① Her income has doubled this year.
② I have not seen her all day today.
③ Has he played the violin since he was a child?
④ The airplane has just left when I arrived at the airport.
⑤ We had been trying to open the door for an hour since the key broke.

5
① Earthquakes have happened several times already.
② We have been using this sofa for ten years.
③ I had known him since he was a baby.
④ I had just finished washing my car when it started raining.
⑤ The thief had left the building when the police arrived.

[6-7] 밑줄 친 부분이 어법상 알맞은 것을 고르시오.

6
① The ground is wet. It is raining for hours.
② They had moved into our building last week.
③ The archaeologists have just found some new historical evidence.
④ My father works for the company since he graduated from college.
⑤ When I opened the door, my cat has already escaped through it.

7
① He has been in bed when I came back.
② Nicky has taught physics in 2019.
③ By the end of this month, the project will have been finished.
④ The baby sleeps since last night.
⑤ I had not seen him at school until today.

8 빈칸에 들어갈 수 <u>없는</u> 것은?

> I have been to the zoo with my family
> _____.

① before ② once ③ twice
④ last month ⑤ many times

9 빈칸에 들어갈 수 있는 것을 <u>모두</u> 고르면?

> She has been the leader of our club
> _____.

① yesterday ② since 2018
③ last year ④ two weeks ago
⑤ for six months

[10-11] 두 문장의 의미가 같을 때 빈칸에 들어갈 말로 알맞은 것을 고르시오.

10
> She started traveling in Europe last June. She is still traveling there.
> = She _____ in Europe since last June.

① travel ② had been traveling
③ is traveling ④ has been traveling
⑤ will have traveled

11
> Jay's dad came home from work. Jay got home later than his dad.
> = When Jay got home, his dad _____ from work already.

① come ② had come
③ has come ④ is coming
⑤ will have come

12 밑줄 친 현재완료와 쓰임이 같은 것은?

> Joe <u>has been</u> to Canada three times.

① Kevin <u>has cooked</u> the pie for an hour.
② I <u>have left</u> my cell phone on the bus.
③ <u>Have</u> you <u>talked</u> to Jina lately?
④ Paul <u>has gone</u> to China for business.
⑤ The project <u>has</u> finally <u>been completed</u>.

[13-14] 대화의 빈칸에 들어갈 말을 고르시오.

13
> A: Are you a big fan of that soccer team?
> B: Yes. It _____ every game since last year.

① has won ② has been won
③ has winning ④ had won
⑤ had been won

14
> A: What was the suspect doing?
> B: When I saw her, she _____ with the cashier.

① has talked ② has been talking
③ had talked ④ had been talked
⑤ had been talking

[15-16] 빈칸에 들어갈 말로 알맞게 짝 지어진 것을 고르시오.

15
> • Sam recognized her since he ___(A)___ her before.
> • Julie ___(B)___ as a lawyer since last year.

　　　(A)　　　　　　　(B)
① has met – has worked
② has met – had worked
③ had met – has been working
④ had met – had been working
⑤ met – had worked

16

> • He told his friends that he ___(A)___ a new laptop.
> • My cat ___(B)___ above the table until I came back home.

	(A)	(B)
①	has bought	– had been sleeping
②	has bought	– has slept
③	had bought	– had been sleeping
④	had bought	– has slept
⑤	will buy	– had slept

[17-18] 우리말과 일치하도록 빈칸에 들어갈 알맞은 말을 고르시오.

17

> 비행기가 막 제주도로 가기 위해 떠났다.
> → The airplane _____ off to go to Jeju-do.

① has just taken   ② had just taken

③ had been taking   ④ will take

⑤ will have taken

18

> 네가 홀에 도착할 때쯤 콘서트는 이미 시작되었을 것이다.
> → The concert _____ by the time you arrive at the hall.

① had started   ② had been starting

③ has started   ④ has been starting

⑤ will have started

19 밑줄 친 ①~⑤ 중 어법상 어색한 것은?

> 나는 아직 내 안경을 찾지 못하고 있다.
> → I still had not found my glasses yet.
>   ①   ②   ③   ④   ⑤

20 우리말 해석이 알맞지 않은 것은?

① The baby has just fallen asleep.
   → 아기가 막 잠이 들었다.

② He had been waiting a while to get a taxi.
   → 그는 택시를 타기 위해 얼마간 기다리고 있었다.

③ Ron had been practicing the guitar until this afternoon.
   → Ron은 오늘 오후까지 기타 연습을 하고 있었다.

④ The professor has been giving a lecture for three hours.
   → 그 교수는 세 시간 동안 강의를 하고 있는 중이다.

⑤ Jenny has gone to Paris.
   → Jenny는 파리에서 돌아왔다.

21 어법상 알맞은 문장끼리 짝 지어진 것은?

> ⓐ I have been learning ballet for 10 years in 2030.
> ⓑ Eric told me his cat had been missing since last week.
> ⓒ Jay has bought a new car last week.
> ⓓ Emily has not had her lunch yet.
> ⓔ Have you ever been to London?
> ⓕ Harry has wait to buy a ticket for 30 minutes.

① ⓐ, ⓒ   ② ⓑ, ⓓ, ⓔ   ③ ⓑ, ⓓ

④ ⓔ, ⓕ   ⑤ ⓓ, ⓔ, ⓕ

[22-23] 다음 글을 읽고, 물음에 답하시오.

A trip to Paris was my longtime dream. I had saved money for years and finally bought a plane ticket last month. I had been looking forward to seeing the Eiffel Tower. While waiting in line at the tower, I realized that I (A) <u>lose</u> my wallet! Since then, (B) <u>나는 아직 그것을 찾지 못하고 있다.</u> (find, yet)

22 (A) lose를 알맞은 형태로 바꿔 쓰시오.

➡ _____

23 (B)의 우리말에 맞게 영작하시오.

➡ _____

24 두 문장이 같은 의미가 되도록 빈칸에 알맞은 말을 쓰시오.

I am writing my paper now. I will still be working on it at midnight.
= I will _____ on my paper for several hours by midnight.

25 다음 문장을 어법에 맞게 고쳐 쓰시오.

Vicky thought her parents first met in high school.

➡ _____

_____

[26-28] 우리말에 맞게 주어진 단어를 바르게 배열하여 문장을 완성하시오.

26 우리 오빠는 아침부터 지금까지 청소를 하고 있다.
(has, cleaning, been, morning, till now, from, my brother)

➡ _____

_____

27 비가 한 달 동안 오지 않았기 때문에 땅이 말라 있었다.
(the ground, for a month, dry, it, since, was, had not rained)

➡ _____

_____

28 한 번 더 그 영화를 보면 나는 그 영화를 다섯 번 보았을 것이다.
(have, will, the movie, see, watched, I, it, five times, if, one more time, I)

➡ _____

_____

🎯 CHALLENGE!

Write your own answer to the question.

01 Have you traveled outside of Korea?

_____

_____

02 How long will you have been studying English next year?

_____

_____

CHAPTER
03

Modals
조동사

UNIT
01
can, may, must, should
조동사의 종류와 용법

UNIT
02
Other Expressions with Modals
조동사의 관용적 표현

UNIT 01

can, may, must, should

조동사의 종류와 용법

A. can은 능력(~할 수 있다), 허가(~해도 좋다)를 나타낸다. could는 can의 과거형이지만, 허락이나 요청을 정중히 표현할 때도 쓴다.

- 능력을 나타내는 can은 be able to로 바꿔 쓸 수 있다.

B. may는 추측(~일지도 모른다), 허가(~해도 된다)를 나타낸다. 추측을 나타낼 때는 might, 허가를 나타낼 때는 can으로 바꿔 쓸 수 있다.

C. must는 의무(~해야 한다), 강한 추측(~임에 틀림없다)를 나타낸다.

- 의무를 나타내는 must는 have to로 바꿔 쓸 수 있다.

- 의무를 나타내는 must의 부정: must not (~해서는 안 된다)

cf. '~할 필요가 없다'는 don't have to로 나타내며 need not 또는 don't need to로도 쓸 수 있다.

D. should와 ought to는 약한 의무를 나타낼 때 쓴다.

A can/could

You **can** beat the other team. <ability>
You **can** (**could**) pay by credit card. <permission>
Can (**Could**) you hand me a stapler? <request>
The news **cannot** be true. <negative certainty>

B may/might

She **may** (**might**) be at the post office. <possibility>
You look exhausted. You **may** go home now. <permission>

C must

We **must** wear helmets when riding bicycles. <obligation>
You **must not** follow strangers. <prohibition>
Brandon is coughing hard. He **must** be sick. <certainty>

e.g. Students **must** (have to) pass an entrance examination to study at this school.

cf. The chef **had to** create an original recipe. <past tense>
She **will have to** stay at home tomorrow. <future tense>
You **don't have to** (**need not/don't need to**) worry about it.
(≠ You *must not* worry about it.)

D should/ought to

We **should** (**ought to**) offer our seats to elderly people.
<weak obligation>

Degrees of certainty: must > may > might
(확실 ← 불확실)

She **must** be wrong. > She **may** (**might**) be wrong.
그녀가 틀린 것이 틀림없다. 그녀가 틀릴 수도 있다.

EXERCISE

A Choose the correct one for each sentence.

1 Eric was so scared that he (can, could) not move around at all.

2 (May, Must) I use your cell phone? I left mine at home.

3 You (must, can) be careful with the glass. It is very fragile.

4 You (should not, cannot) touch other people's belongings without their permission.

B Fill in the blank so that the two sentences have the same meaning.

1 I don't have to buy an expensive watch.

= I _____ an expensive watch.

2 She must go now not to be late.

= She _____ now not to be late.

3 Jack could not complete the project on time.

= Jack was _____ the project on time.

C Complete the dialogue using the words in the box.

should	don't have to	be able to	could

1 A: Must I stay home?

B: No, you _____. You may go out now.

2 A: What time _____ I come home tonight?

B: Come home straight after school.

3 A: I'm afraid I may not _____ pass the exam.

B: I'm sure you will do fine.

4 A: Did he take his pills?

B: No, he didn't. He _____ not swallow the pills.

D Complete the sentence using the given words.

1 그는 은행에 있을지도 모른다. (bank)

→ He _____ .

2 Dan이 국제 변호사일 리가 없다. (international lawyer)

→ Dan _____ .

3 우리는 그 식당을 떠나기 전에 계산을 해야 했다. (have, pay the bill)

→ We _____ before we left the restaurant.

4 그 물건은 내일까지 배달되어야 한다. (ought to, deliver)

→ The goods _____ .

UNIT 02

Other Expressions with Modals 조동사의 관용적 표현

A used to

She **used to** do yoga three times a week. \<past habit\>

There **used to** be a convenience store around the corner.

<past state>

e.g. He **did not use to** watch horror movies when he was a teenager.

cf. **be used to + V-ing**: be familiar

I **am used to traveling** alone.

(→ I have experienced traveling alone, so it is no longer strange.)

A 과거의 습관(~하곤 했다) 또는 과거의 상태(~이었다)를 나타낸다.

B had better

You **had better** get rid of these photos. \<strong advice\>

e.g. We **had better not** eat too much junk food.

B '~하는 게 좋을 것이다'라는 경고의 뜻으로, 'd better로 줄여 쓸 수 있다.

C may as well

We **may as well** eat something before we depart. \<suggestion\>

e.g. You **may as well not** participate in the contest.

C '~하는 게 낫겠다'라는 뜻이다.
• I **may as well** start walking home **as** take a taxi.

D would rather

You **would rather** buy a book at the used bookstore.

<preference>

e.g. I **would rather not** say anything at this time.

D (차라리) ~하는 게 좋다, ~하겠다'라는 뜻으로, 'd rather로 줄여 쓸 수 있다.
• I **would rather** turn up the heater **than** put on thicker clothes.

E Modal verb + have p.p.

You **may have played** this game before. \<possibility about the past\>

He **must have remembered** what I said. \<certainty about the past\>

He **cannot have told** a lie. \<certainty about the past with a negative\>

She **should have finished** the work. \<weak obligation about the past\>
(Actually, she did not.)

E 「조동사 + have p.p.」는 과거의 일에 대한 추측, 후회, 유감 등을 나타낸다.
• may have p.p.: ~했을지도 모른다
• must have p.p.: ~했음에 틀림없다
• cannot have p.p.: ~이었을 리가 없다
• should have p.p.: ~했어야 했는데

EXERCISE

A Choose the correct one for each sentence.

1 You had better (leave, leaving) now to catch the train.

2 I (would rather, would better) have dinner later.

3 Tom (was not, did not) use to exercise at all.

4 She (had not better, had better not) drink so much soda.

5 We may as well (go, going) home. The show is so boring.

B Complete the sentence using the words in the box.

used to	had better	may as well	would rather

1 I _____ take a nap as go jogging.

2 I _____ stand up than sit on the bench.

3 My mom _____ read me a bedtime story every night when I was young.

4 You _____ eat more vegetables.

C Translate the English into Korean paying attention to the underlined part.

1 You had better put on warmer clothes in this weather.

→ _____

2 My teacher must have told my parents about my grades.

→ _____

3 The old building used to be a place for exhibitions.

→ _____

4 I would rather wash the dishes than do the laundry.

→ _____

D Complete the sentence using the given words.

1 Sarah는 월요일마다 학교에 지각하곤 했다. (late)

→ Sarah _____ for school on Mondays.

2 Henry는 영화의 결말을 알고 있다. 그는 영화를 봤을지도 모른다. (may, see)

→ Henry knows the ending of the movie. He _____ .

3 나는 내일 날씨를 알기 위해 인터넷을 검색하는 게 좋겠다. (rather, surf)

→ I _____ the Internet to find out tomorrow's weather.

4 그 비서는 일정을 확인했어야 했다. (check, schedule)

→ The secretary _____ .

WRITING CONNECTION

1 Grammar Check-up

A Choose the correct one.

1 That girl _____ be Laura. She looks much taller than Laura.

ⓐ used to ⓑ cannot ⓒ must not ⓓ had better

2 She _____ run 100 meters in 11 seconds when she was young.

ⓐ can ⓑ may ⓒ could ⓓ is able to

3 There _____ be a big tree here when I was a kid.

ⓐ have to ⓑ should ⓒ can ⓓ used to

4 All of the students _____ follow the school rules.

ⓐ cannot ⓑ ought to ⓒ may ⓓ must not

5 You still have a fever. You _____ take some strong medicine for that.

ⓐ had better ⓑ cannot ⓒ used to ⓓ should not

6 You _____ go back home. The game has been canceled because of the rain.

ⓐ used to ⓑ need not ⓒ cannot ⓓ may as well

B Circle the inappropriate one between ⓐ and ⓑ. Then correct it.

1 I may well as borrow the dress as buy it. _____
     ⓐ   ⓑ

2 You had not better eat that. You might be too full. _____
     ⓐ   ⓑ

3 I have to leave now. I must arriving at school by 7 a.m. _____
     ⓐ   ⓑ

4 She used to walking to school, but she takes the bus now. _____
     ⓐ   ⓑ

5 If I did not had to do my homework, I could go with you. _____
     ⓐ   ⓑ

6 You ought to not open this box until I come back. _____
     ⓐ   ⓑ

2 Phrases to Sentences

A Complete the sentence by referring to the Korean translation.

1 그는 너무 늦기 전에 숙제를 시작하는 것이 좋을 것이다. (better, start)

→ He _____ to do his homework before it is too late.

2 외교관이 되려면 외국어를 배워야 한다. (should, learn)

→ To become a diplomat, you _____ a foreign language.

3 나는 공포 영화보다는 차라리 코미디를 보겠어. (rather, watch)

→ I _____ a comedy than a horror movie.

4 빨간 불일 때는 도로를 건너서는 안 된다. (should, cross)

→ You _____ the road when there is a red light.

5 우리가 알지 못하는 이유가 있을지도 모른다. (may, reason)

→ There _____ that we do not know about.

6 Penny의 눈이 빨갛다. 그녀는 밤을 새웠을지도 모른다. (may, stay up)

→ Penny's eyes are red. She _____ last night.

B Underline the error and rewrite the sentence.

1 He must be lost his phone in the library yesterday.

→ _____

2 I may have leave my umbrella at school.

→ _____

3 You should come earlier. The bus has already left.

→ _____

4 Alice used to taking a walk during her lunch break every day.

→ _____

5 You should come to the party. Then you would have had a great time with us.

→ _____

6 I may like well finish cleaning my room before going out.

→ _____

3 Sentence Practice

A Translate the Korean into English using the given words.

1 a. 우리는 가난한 사람들을 도와줘야 한다. (should)

→ We _____ the poor.

b. 너는 그 화분에 자주 물을 줘야 한다. (should, the pot)

→ _____

2 a. 네가 본 것이 진짜이었을 리가 없다. (cannot, real)

→ What you saw _____.

b. 그 소문이 사실이었을 리가 없다. (the rumor, true)

→ _____

3 a. 너는 오늘 회의에 늦지 않는 게 좋을 거야. (had better)

→ You _____ late for the meeting today.

b. 너는 밤늦게까지 공부하지 않는 게 좋을 거야. (study, late at night)

→ _____

4 a. 나는 배가 아프다. 뭔가 잘못 먹은 것이 틀림없다. (must, eat)

→ My stomach hurts. I _____ something bad.

b. Joe는 학교에 결석했다. 그는 아팠던 것이 틀림없다. (absent, must, sick)

→ _____

B Unscramble the words to make a sentence.

1 네 가방은 거실에 있을 수도 있다. (in, might, your bag, be, the living room)

→ _____

2 너는 인터넷으로 설문 조사를 실시할 수 있다. (do, on the Internet, you, a survey, can)

→ _____

3 너는 선생님의 조언을 구하는 게 낫겠다. (may, well, ask for, your, as, teacher's advice, you)

→ _____

4 너는 거리에 쓰레기를 버려서는 안 된다. (the street, throw, not, you, the garbage, on, must)

→ _____

ACTUAL TEST

[1-2] 빈칸에 들어갈 알맞은 말을 고르시오.

1
> You _____ better go out now if you do not want to be late.

① would ② could
③ might ④ had
⑤ should

2
> He was absent from school for a week. Something _____ to him.

① must happen
② cannot happen
③ may have happened
④ should have happened
⑤ cannot have happened

[3-4] 두 문장이 같은 의미가 되도록 빈칸에 들어갈 알맞은 말을 고르시오.

3
> I did not write down his e-mail address. Now I regret it.
> = I _____ written down his e-mail address.

① will ② could
③ should have ④ may have
⑤ must have

4
> The party is too boring. I want to go home.
> = I _____ go home than stay at this party.

① had better ② would rather
③ may as well ④ used to
⑤ ought to

5 빈칸에 공통으로 들어갈 말로 알맞은 것은?
> • My brother _____ eat spinach when he was young.
> • There _____ be a castle by the lake in the past.

① use ② used to ③ is using
④ is used to ⑤ has used

[6-7] 우리말을 영어로 옮길 때 빈칸에 들어갈 말로 알맞은 것을 고르시오.

6
> 그 디자이너는 17살 때 옷을 만들 수 있었다.
> → The designer _____ make clothes when he was 17 years old.

① can ② will ③ should
④ could ⑤ might

7
> 그는 어제 아무것도 먹지 않았다. 그는 배가 고팠을 것이 틀림없다.
> → He did not eat anything yesterday. He _____ hungry.

① must have been ② may as well
③ would rather ④ cannot be
⑤ had better

8 대화의 빈칸에 들어갈 말로 알맞은 것은?
> A: What should we do now?
> B: We _____ something now. There is no food at home.

① used to eat
② may as well eat
③ may have eaten
④ must have eaten
⑤ cannot have eaten

[9-10] 어법상 어색한 문장을 고르시오.

9 ① You may as well act your age.

② She may not be at home.

③ You ought come back home by 5.

④ We could not accept their offer.

⑤ She did not have to do the dishes.

10 ① You should clean your desk.

② Dad used to go to work at 8.

③ I need not get any rest.

④ I had rather play soccer than watch TV.

⑤ Olivia used to go jogging every morning.

11 'not'이 들어갈 위치로 알맞은 것은?

> You ① should ② play ③ computer games ④ so ⑤ much.

12 우리말 해석이 잘못된 것은?

① The accident may have been caused by carelessness.

→ 그 사고는 부주의로 인해 일어났을지 모른다.

② We should have taken a different route to avoid the traffic jam.

→ 우리는 교통 체증을 피하기 위해 다른 길로 갔어야 했다.

③ She must have been scared of the dog.

→ 그녀는 그 개가 무서웠던 것이 틀림없다.

④ She cannot have known that I was preparing a surprise party.

→ 그녀는 내가 깜짝 파티를 준비하고 있었다는 사실을 알면 안 된다.

⑤ I may as well take a shower.

→ 나는 샤워를 하는 게 낫겠다.

[13-14] 밑줄 친 단어의 뜻이 나머지와 다른 것을 고르시오.

13 ① Jim may not be at home when you come.

② You may wear slippers in the room.

③ I may have a chance to meet Tom again.

④ There is a possibility that it may rain tomorrow.

⑤ The thief may have left evidence there.

14 ① You can drive when you turn 20.

② You can bring your friends to the party.

③ Animals cannot talk; only humans can.

④ They can borrow books from the library.

⑤ We can enter the store with the dog.

15 짝 지어진 문장의 의미가 같지 않은 것은?

① Sue might have had a cold.

= There is a possibility that Sue had a cold.

② Kevin should have told me the news.

= Kevin did not tell me the news. He had to do that.

③ You don't have to do it just for me.

= You must not do it just for me.

④ He used to write articles for the magazine.

= He wrote articles for the magazine, but he does not do that anymore.

⑤ Ron cannot be at school now. He is sick today.

= There is no possibility that Ron is at school today because he is sick.

16 밑줄 친 used to와 쓰임이 같은 것은?

> My mom used to clean the house every day.

① Mike is used to baking bread.
② Mario used to take a walk after dinner.
③ The mop is used to clean the floor.
④ Beef is used to make stew.
⑤ Plastic is used to make water bottles.

[17-18] 빈칸에 들어갈 말로 알맞게 짝 지어진 것을 고르시오.

17
> • You ____(A)____ keep your things in my cabinet.
> (너는 내 사물함에 네 물건을 보관해도 된다.)
> • You ____(B)____ eat less fast food.
> (너는 패스트푸드를 덜 먹는 것이 좋을 것이다.)

	(A)		(B)
①	can	–	might
②	may	–	had better
③	should	–	may as well
④	must	–	ought to
⑤	have to	–	can

18
> • Julie ____(A)____ tell the truth to her parents.
> (Julie는 부모님께 사실을 말해야 한다.)
> • My dog ____(B)____ the pie on the table.
> (나의 개가 테이블 위의 파이를 먹었음에 틀림없다.)

	(A)		(B)
①	must	–	must eat
②	would	–	should eat
③	may	–	must have eaten
④	ought to	–	should have eaten
⑤	should	–	must have eaten

[19-20] 주어진 단어를 바르게 배열한 것을 고르시오.

19
> It is almost time, so we _____.
> (the meeting, may, start, well, as)

① start as well may the meeting
② may the meeting start well as
③ may as well start the meeting
④ may start the meeting as well
⑤ start the meeting as may well

20
> The hamster has disappeared. You must _____.
> (open, have, left, the cage door)

① have the cage door open left
② have left the cage door open
③ open the cage door have left
④ have the cage door left open
⑤ have open the cage door left

21 어법상 알맞지 않은 것은?
① Jina used to walk her dog at the park every day.
② Suzy has plenty of common sense. She must have read many books.
③ Eric looks exhausted. He had better get some rest.
④ Kevin may have dropped by my home while I was at the gym.
⑤ Henry missed the train. He should leave home earlier.

22 빈칸에 알맞은 조동사를 쓰시오.

> I cannot understand people who steal others' stuff. I rode my bike to the subway station and locked it to the bike stand. When I came back, it was gone! I _____ not have left my bike there!

→ _____

23 우리말 뜻을 참고하여 어법에 맞게 문장을 다시 쓰시오.

> When you come to my home, you must not bring anything.
> (너는 우리 집에 올 때 아무것도 가져올 필요가 없다.)

→ _____

_____

[24-25] 두 문장이 같은 의미가 되도록 주어진 단어를 활용하여 빈칸에 알맞은 말을 쓰시오.

24

> I am not sure who called you, but maybe it was Tom. (may)

→ It _____ Tom who called you.

25

> I think that it was not possible that Kevin finished eating the pizza by himself. (can)

→ Kevin _____ the pizza by himself.

[26-28] 우리말에 맞게 주어진 단어를 바르게 배열하여 문장을 쓰시오.

26

> Kate는 머리카락이 길었는데 잘라버렸다.
> (have, she, had, but, used to, long, Kate, it, cut, hair, off)

→ _____

_____

27

> 너는 선생님에게 사과드리는 게 좋을 것이다.
> (you, apologize, had, to, better, your teacher)

→ _____

28

> 너는 계단을 뛰어 내려가서는 안 된다.
> (you, the stairs, not, ought, run down, to)

→ _____

🎯 CHALLENGE!

Write your own answer to the question.

01 What is something that you should have done last year?

_____

_____

02 What TV show did you use to watch the most when you were in elementary school?

_____

_____

CHAPTER

04

Passives
수동태

UNIT 01

Passive Voice
수동태의 형태와 시제

UNIT 02

Passives of S+V+I.O.+D.O. / S+V+O+O.C.
4형식·5형식 문장의 수동태

UNIT 03

Other Passive Forms
주의해야 할 수동태

Passive Voice 수동태의 형태와 시제

A Passive Voice

> The photos **were torn up** by Mary.
> The poem **was not read** by many people.
> **Was** the package **delivered** to you?
> The road **can be closed** if the rain turns to snow.

- **Object → Subject**

  The policeman catches the thief. <active voice>
  _____O_____

  The thief **is caught** by the policeman. <passive voice>
  __S__

cf. **Omit 「by + Agent」**

  Pineapples **are grown** in Hawaii (by people).

  The bank **was robbed** yesterday (by someone).

B Tense of Passive

> The weather forecasts **are being revised**. <present progressive>
> Her work **has** already **been finished**. <present perfect>
> The task **will be completed** by us tonight. <future>

- **Progressive: be being p.p.**

  My car **was being cleaned** then. <past progressive>

- **Perfect: have been p.p.**

  The cure **had been found**, but it was too late. <past perfect>

- **Future: will (be going to) be p.p.**

  The rescue team **is going to be sent** soon.

Verbs not used in the passive

1. happen, arrive, fall, rise, go, appear <목적어가 없는 자동사>

   They **arrived** at the airport on time. (○)

   They were arrived at the airport on time. (×)

2. have, fit, lack, resemble, belong to, consist of <상태나 소유를 나타내는 동사>

   Jack **resembles** his father. (○)

   His father is resembled by Jack. (×)

Sidebar notes

A 수동태

「be + p.p. (+ by 행위자)」형태로, 동작의 영향을 받는 대상에 중점을 두어 말할 때 쓴다.

cf. 행위자가 일반인이거나 또는 중요하지 않을 때는 「by + 행위자」를 생략한다.

B 수동태의 시제

수동태는 시제에 따라 여러 가지 형태로 쓰일 수 있다.

EXERCISE

A Choose the correct one for each sentence.

1 An accident (happened, was happened) last night.

2 The light bulb (changed, was changed) by Sue.

3 The song was (not sung, sung not) by a famous singer.

4 Was the new policy (announce, announced) by the president?

5 People (post, are posted) funny videos on this social networking site.

6 This blouse (be should washed, should be washed) in cold water.

B Unscramble the words to complete the sentence.

1 My wallet _____. (been, has, stolen)

2 The roads _____. (repaired, are, being)

3 The roof _____ the heavy rain. (by, damaged, was)

4 Instructions _____ to you tomorrow. (be, will, given)

C Rewrite each sentence in the passive form.

1 He was flying a kite at that time.

→ A kite _____ by him at that time.

2 The company is going to pay me weekly.

→ I _____ by the company.

3 The writer wrote a new science-fiction novel.

→ A new science-fiction novel _____.

4 I found that Dad had decorated the Christmas tree.

→ I found that _____.

D Complete the sentence using the given word.

1 그 일을 오후 다섯 시까지 끝낼 것이다. (finish)

→ The work _____ by 5 p.m.

2 승객들은 기차에서 내려달라는 요청을 받았다. (ask)

→ Passengers _____ to get off the train.

3 새로운 경기장이 시청 옆에 건설되고 있는 중이다. (build)

→ A new stadium _____ next to city hall.

4 오 월 이래로 약 백만 부의 소설이 팔렸다. (sell)

→ About a million copies of this novel _____ since May.

UNIT 02

Passives of S+V+I.O.+D.O./ S+V+O+O.C.

4형식·5형식 문장의 수동태

A 4형식 문장의 수동태

「주어 + 동사 + 간접목적어 + 직접목적어」에서 간접목적어와 직접목적어를 각각 주어로 하여 두 개의 수동태를 만들 수 있다.

A ▸ Passive of S + V + I.O. + D.O.

His grandfather gave <u>Bill</u> <u>a thousand dollars</u>.
　　　　　　　　　I.O.　　　D.O.

→ *Bill* **was given** a thousand dollars by his grandfather.

→ *A thousand dollars* **was given** to Bill by his grandfather.

◆ **Prepositions needed when D.O. used as a subject**

(1) **to**: give, send, teach, lend, show, bring, offer, tell, sell, promise

(2) **for**: make, buy, get, build, cook, find, bring

(3) **of**: ask, beg

　Nancy asks Professor Lyn some strange questions.

　　→ Professor Lyn **is asked** some strange questions by Nancy.

　　→ Some strange questions **are asked** of Professor Lyn by Nancy.

cf. **I.O. not be used as a subject:**

　buy, make, write, build, send, sell, bring

　We bought our son Christmas gifts at this mall.

　　→ Christmas gifts **were bought** *for* our son at this mall by us. (○)

　　→ Our son was bought Christmas gifts at this mall by us. (×)

B 5형식 문장의 수동태

「주어 + 동사 + 목적어 + 목적격 보어」에서 목적어를 주어로 하고 동사를 수동태로 바꾼 다음, 목적격 보어는 「be + p.p.」 뒤에 그대로 쓴다.

• 사역동사는 make만 수동태로 쓰이고, 이때 목적격 보어로 쓰인 동사원형은 to부정사로 바꿔 쓴다.

• 지각동사의 목적격 보어인 동사원형은 수동태 문장에서 to부정사나 현재분사로 바꿔 쓴다.

B ▸ Passive of S + V + O + O.C.

They considered <u>him</u> <u>one of the best soccer players</u>.
　　　　　　　　O　　　　O.C.

→ He **was considered** one of the best soccer players by them.

e.g. The doctor advised <u>me</u> <u>to eat balanced meals</u>.
　　　　　　　　　　　O　　　O.C.

　　→ I was advised to eat balanced meals by the doctor.

◆ **Causative verbs**

The teacher makes <u>some students</u> <u>take an extra class</u>.
　　　　　　　　　　O　　　　O.C.

　→ Some students **are made** *to take* an extra class by the teacher.

cf. **let, have: not used in the passive**

　We are never let to drink coke. (×)

　The boy was had to go to bed at nine. (×)

◆ **Sensory verbs**

I saw <u>you</u> <u>draw</u> some amazing pictures.
　　　 O　 O.C.

　→ You **were seen** *to draw (drawing)* some amazing pictures by me.

EXERCISE

A Choose the correct one for each sentence.

1 During the interview, a lot of questions were asked (to, of) me.

2 New bikes were bought (to, for) the kids.

3 The package will be sent (to, for) him by express mail.

4 The model airplane was made (of, for) my brother.

5 Hundreds of lunch boxes were given (to, for) the homeless.

B Rewrite each sentence in the passive form.

1 Tom gave me a bunch of flowers.

→ I _____ by Tom.

→ A bunch of flowers _____ by Tom.

2 The principal asked the girl her name.

→ The girl _____ by the principal.

→ Her name _____ by the principal.

3 My grandma made me thick gloves last winter.

→ Thick gloves _____ by my grandma last winter.

C Underline the error and correct it.

1 He was seen take the bus this afternoon. → _____

2 Were the boys told be helped Sue move? → _____

3 No one was allowed leaving the room without permission. → _____

4 The original song was made to popular by a TV program. → _____

5 The ancient palace is considered to one of the famous spots in Seoul.

→ _____

D Complete the sentence by referring Korean translation.

1 그는 딸의 미소로 행복해졌다. (make)

→ He _____ by his daughter's smile.

2 그 초콜릿은 Paul에 의해 우리에게 주어졌다. (give)

→ The chocolate _____ by Paul.

3 나는 엄마에 의해 설거지를 하도록 시켜졌다. (make, wash the dishes)

→ I _____ by Mom.

4 그녀는 많은 사람들에 의해 기타 치는 모습이 보여졌다. (see, play)

→ She _____ the guitar by many people.

Other Passive Forms
주의해야 할 수동태

A by 이외의 전치사를
쓰는 수동태

A Passive Without *by*

I **am interested in** jazz music.
Ann **was disappointed with** her grades.
He **was married to** an Italian.
I like animals, but I **am scared of** snakes.

be covered with	be satisfied with	be known to
be crowded with	be pleased with	be married to
be disappointed with	be composed of	be interested in
be filled with	be made of (from)	be worried about
be surrounded with (by)	be scared of	be surprised at (by)

B 동사구의 수동태

동사만 「be + p.p.」로 바꾸
고, 나머지 부분은 하나의 단
어처럼 취급하여 그대로 붙
여 쓴다.

B Passive of Verb Phrase

Someone *broke into* the pet shop.
→ The pet shop **was broken into** by someone.

e.g. They *called off* the event because of the heavy rain.
　　→ The event **was called off** because of the heavy rain.
　　Our neighbor will *take care of* our dogs.
　　→ Our dogs will **be taken care of** by our neighbor.

C that절이 목적어인 문
장의 수동태

가주어 it을 주어로 하여 「It
+ be + p.p. + that . . .」의 형
태로 쓴다. that절의 주어를
수동태 문장의 주어로 쓸 때
는 that절 동사를 to부정사
로 바꾼다.

C Passive with Clause Object

Everyone thought that she was clever.
→ *It* **was thought** that she was clever.
→ *She* **was thought** *to be* clever.

e.g. She strongly believes that he will come back home.
　　→ *It* **is** strongly **believed** that he will come back home.
　　→ *He* **is** strongly **believed** *to come* back home.

EXERCISE

A Choose the correct one for each sentence.

1 I was surprised (at, with) the news.

2 He is only interested (of, in) computer games.

3 Because of the cold weather, the road is covered (with, for) ice.

4 My parents were disappointed (to, with) my behavior.

5 Ben was worried (with, about) his mom's health.

6 They were satisfied (of, with) the results of the election.

B Fill in the blank to complete the passive voice.

1 I looked after Nicky's cat yesterday.

= Nicky's cat was _____ me yesterday.

2 Someone turned off all the lights.

= All the lights were _____ someone.

3 My dad will not be able to pick us up tomorrow.

= We will not be able to _____ by my dad tomorrow.

4 People know that the scientist made a great discovery.

= It _____ the scientist made a great discovery.

C Correct the underlined part.

1 The room <u>is filled of</u> hundreds of boxes. → _____

2 They <u>are worried at</u> completing the project by tomorrow.

→ _____

3 The information <u>looked was up</u> on the website by Rachel.

→ _____

4 Sally <u>is said be</u> one of the tallest girls at the school. → _____

D Complete the sentence by referring the Korean translation.

1 선수들은 그들의 라이벌을 상대로 우승해서 기뻤다. (please)

→ The players _____ their victory against their rival.

2 거짓말을 하는 것은 나의 부모님에게는 용납이 되지 않는다. (put up with)

→ Telling lies _____ by my parents.

3 인간의 몸의 약 70퍼센트는 물로 구성되어 있다. (compose)

→ About 70 percent of the human body _____ water.

4 공룡은 6천 5백만 년 전에 멸종되었다고 믿어진다. (believe)

→ _____ the dinosaurs went extinct 65 million years ago.

WRITING CONNECTION

1 Grammar Check-up

A Choose the correct one.

1 It _____ that he was a brave soldier.

ⓐ thinks　　　　ⓑ to think　　　　ⓒ thought　　　　ⓓ was thought

2 Dinner is _____ for us by the waiter.

ⓐ serve　　　　ⓑ served　　　　ⓒ serving　　　　ⓓ serves

3 These issues should _____ lightly.

ⓐ not take　　　　ⓑ not be taken　　　　ⓒ be not taken　　　　ⓓ not be taking

4 _____ the backpack sold on the Internet?

ⓐ Is　　　　ⓑ Does　　　　ⓒ Has　　　　ⓓ Did

5 The pie is _____ cream, chocolate, and fruit.

ⓐ fills　　　　ⓑ filled by　　　　ⓒ filled with　　　　ⓓ will fill

6 My ticket was shown _____ the staff by me.

ⓐ for　　　　ⓑ of　　　　ⓒ to　　　　ⓓ with

B Circle the inappropriate one between ⓐ and ⓑ. Then correct it.

1 Sue <u>was had</u> many pants, but only her jeans <u>were worn</u> by her.　　_____
　　　　ⓐ　　　　　　　　　　　　　　　　　　　ⓑ

2 I did not <u>win</u> a prize. First prize <u>won</u> by Tom.　　_____
　　　　　　　ⓐ　　　　　　　　　　　ⓑ

3 They <u>were seen</u> <u>by take</u> a walk in the park.　　_____
　　　　　ⓐ　　　　ⓑ

4 The movie is well <u>known by</u> the public <u>for</u> its exciting story.　　_____
　　　　　　　　　　ⓐ　　　　　　　　ⓑ

5 A toy was <u>bought</u> to the baby <u>by</u> her uncle.　　_____
　　　　　　　ⓐ　　　　　　　　ⓑ

Phrases to Sentences

A Complete the sentence by referring to the Korean translation.

1 너의 차는 Jim에 의해 수리되고 있는 중이다. (fix)

→ Your car _____ Jim.

2 이 사진들은 내 친구에 의해 찍혔다. (take)

→ These pictures _____ my friend.

3 피자는 배달원에 의해 20분 만에 배달될 것이다. (deliver)

→ A pizza _____ by a delivery guy in 20 minutes.

4 그 남자는 과거에 그 은행에서 일을 했었다고 믿어진다. (believe)

→ The man _____ have worked at the bank.

5 그 도로는 차 사고 때문에 막히고 있니? (block)

→ Is the road _____ because of the car accident?

6 몇 가지 조언이 상담사에 의해 너에게 주어질 것이다. (give)

→ Some advice _____ by the counselor.

B Rewrite each sentence in the passive form.

1 Finally, Andrew created a new invention.

→ Finally, _____.

2 The doctor looked at the patient.

→ The patient _____.

3 The parents make their son solve the problem alone.

→ Their son _____.

4 I showed Wendy my puppy's photos.

→ My puppy's photos _____.

5 Michael cooked his family some pasta.

→ Some pasta _____.

6 All of the students consider Ben the smartest student at school.

→ _____.

3 Sentence Practice

A Translate the Korean into English using the given words.

1 a. 워싱턴은 연간 1,900만 명의 사람들에 의해 방문된다. (visit)

→ Washington, D.C. _____ 19 million people a year.

b. 그 산은 연간 100만 명의 관광객들에 의해 등반된다. (climb, tourist)

→ _____

2 a. 식물들이 그녀에 의해 물이 주어지고 있는 중이니? (water)

→ _____ the plants _____ by her?

b. 강아지들이 그녀에 의해 돌봄을 받고 있는 중이니? (puppy, take care of)

→ _____

3 a. Chris는 테니스를 치는 데 관심이 있다. (interest)

→ Chris _____ playing tennis.

b. 그 학생들은 사진을 찍는 데 관심이 있다. (take pictures)

→ _____

4 a. 몇 가지 질문이 기자들에 의해 그 배우에게 질문되었다. (ask)

→ Some questions _____ the actor by reporters.

b. 편지는 Ron에 의해 내게 보내졌다. (send)

→ _____

B Unscramble the words to make a sentence.

1 Jenny는 팀 리더로 선출될 것이다. (will, Jenny, elected, be, team leader)

→ _____

2 내 자전거는 지금 수리되고 있는 중이다. (now, being, is, my bike, repaired)

→ _____

3 Alex는 몇 달 전에 그 나라를 떠났다고 한다. (ago, left, the country, is, it, that, months, Alex, said)

→ _____

4 그 행사는 나쁜 날씨 때문에 취소되어야 한다. (be, because of, the event, the bad weather, canceled, should)

→ _____

ACTUAL TEST

> Answers p. 10

[1-3] 빈칸에 들어갈 알맞은 말을 고르시오.

1

> A pair of new shoes _____ for Patrick yesterday.

① bought   ② is bought
③ are bought ④ are buying
⑤ were bought

2

> The way to the subway station was asked _____ us by a tourist.

① for ② to ③ of
④ with ⑤ at

3

> A prescription was given _____ the patient by the doctor.

① to ② for ③ of
④ from ⑤ with

4 빈칸에 들어갈 수 <u>없는</u> 것은?

> All of the rooms at the hotel _____ .

① are booked ② have booked
③ were booked ④ will be booked
⑤ have been booked

5 두 문장이 같은 의미가 되도록 빈칸에 들어갈 알맞은 말은?

> He made this popular cartoon.
> = This popular cartoon _____ by him.

① was made ② made
③ are made ④ will be made
⑤ have been made

6 어법상 <u>어색한</u> 문장은?
① The river is filled in very much garbage.
② I am worried about my father's health.
③ The children are interested in music.
④ He was thought to be a diligent student at school.
⑤ The game was put off because of the rain.

7 빈칸에 들어갈 말이 바르게 짝 지어진 것은?

> • Mona was married _____ Ted.
> • People are worried _____ environmental pollution.

① with – as ② with – for
③ to – by ④ to – about
⑤ by – about

8
가장 높은 성적을 받은 학생에게 장학금이 제공될 것이다.
= A scholarship _____ the student who gets the highest grade.

① will offer to   ② is offered for
③ offer to   ④ will be offered for
⑤ will be offered to

9
그녀는 가장 뛰어난 운동선수 중 하나로 여겨졌다.
= She was considered _____ the most outstanding athletes.

① one of   ② for   ③ be
④ to   ⑤ to be

10 두 문장이 같은 의미가 되도록 빈칸에 들어갈 알맞은 말은?

People think that he is a good swimmer.
= He _____ be a good swimmer.

① is thought   ② thought
③ thought to   ④ is thought to
⑤ was thought

11 주어진 우리말을 바르게 영작한 것은?

테니스는 두 명 또는 네 명에 의해 경기될 수 있다.

① Tennis can play by two or four people.
② Tennis can played by two or four people.
③ Tennis can be play by two or four people.
④ Tennis can be played by two or four people.
⑤ Tennis can is played by two or four people.

[12-13] 문장을 수동태로 바꾼 것이 옳지 않은 것을 고르시오.

12
① She told me a lie again.
→ A lie was told to me by her again.
② I said that Tom was in the hospital.
→ Tom was said to be in the hospital by me.
③ The boy asked his mom the meaning of the word.
→ The meaning of the word was asked of his mom by the boy.
④ James sent me a card.
→ A card was sent to me by James.
⑤ My dad bought me a shirt.
→ I was bought a shirt by my dad.

13
① We completed the project well.
→ The project was completed by us well.
② The boss called off the morning meeting.
→ The morning meeting was called off by the boss.
③ I wrote down everything Dr. Smith said.
→ Everything Dr. Smith said was written me down.
④ The nanny took good care of the baby.
→ The baby was taken good care of by the nanny.
⑤ My family cleans the house on Sundays.
→ The house is cleaned by my family on Sundays.

14 빈칸에 being이 들어갈 수 없는 것은?
① The group project is _____ done by us.
② All the pictures are _____ put up on the wall by the staff.
③ The turkey will _____ roasted perfectly in two hours.
④ The fallen leaves in the garden are _____ cleared by my dad.
⑤ The new machines are _____ tested by engineers.

[15-16] 빈칸에 들어갈 전치사가 나머지 넷과 <u>다른</u> 것을 고르시오.

15　① My teacher was pleased _____ our surprise party.

② They were disappointed _____ the results of the game.

③ The hall was filled _____ beautiful flowers.

④ The audience was satisfied _____ the concert.

⑤ Parents are always worried _____ their children.

16　① Pottery is made _____ clay.

② The committee was composed _____ ten members.

③ He was surprised _____ my unexpected visit.

④ He is scared _____ enclosed spaces.

⑤ A dollar was asked _____ me by a begger.

[17-18] 밑줄 친 (A), (B)의 형태를 고친 것으로 알맞게 짝 지어진 것을 고르시오.

17
- This sweater (A) <u>made</u> for me by my mom last winter.
- The neon sign (B) <u>can see</u> in the dark.

　　　(A)　　　　　(B)

① was made　–　can seen

② was made　–　can see

③ was made　–　can be seen

④ has made　–　can see

⑤ has made　–　can be seen

18
- Dolphins (A) <u>consider</u> smart by many people.
- The offer (B) <u>not was accept</u> by my classmates.

　　　(A)　　　　　　(B)

① considered　–　not be accepted

② are considered　–　was not be accepted

③ are considered　–　was not accepted

④ are considered　–　not was accepted

⑤ are considering　–　was not be accepted

19　어법상 올바른 문장은?

① Coal is consisted mostly of carbon.

② The bus was arrived on time.

③ The sun was fallen below the horizon.

④ My brother is resembled by my dad a lot.

⑤ The brochure lacked important information for sightseeing.

20　어법상 올바른 문장끼리 짝 지어진 것은?

ⓐ The show was watched by them.

ⓑ The kitten was looked after by Mary.

ⓒ A book was bought for me by my mom.

ⓓ The wall is being painting by me.

ⓔ This plant should being watered often.

① ⓐ, ⓑ　　② ⓐ, ⓑ, ⓒ　　③ ⓑ, ⓒ, ⓓ

④ ⓑ, ⓒ, ⓔ　　⑤ ⓒ, ⓓ, ⓔ

21　수동태로 바꿔 쓸 수 있는 문장은?

① Eric became the founder of a computer company.

② Jenny belongs to a soccer club.

③ Our teacher seems to know everything.

④ Sandra loves to play board games.

⑤ Mr. Smith has a big family.

[22-23] 다음 글을 읽고, 물음에 답하시오.

Dolmens are ancient tombs. They (A) (build) about 6,000 years ago. Ancient people put up big stones to make tombs. The walls were formed with the standing stones. Another huge stone (B) (place) on top of the other stones. Nowadays, dolmens can see in Ireland, Wales, and Scotland.

22 (A), (B)에 주어진 단어를 각각 알맞은 형태로 쓰시오.

(A) _____ (B) _____

23 윗글의 밑줄 친 문장을 어법에 맞게 고쳐 쓰시오.

→ _____

_____

[24-25] 밑줄 친 단어를 주어로 하는 수동태 문장을 쓰시오.

24 The reporter has asked me tricky questions.

→ _____

_____

25 We will hang a huge poster outside the building.

→ _____

_____

26 두 문장이 같은 의미가 되도록 빈칸에 알맞은 말을 쓰시오.

People think that he is a good swimmer.
= He _____ be a good swimmer.

[27-28] 우리말에 맞게 주어진 단어를 바르게 배열하여 문장을 쓰시오.

27 그는 자신의 친구들에 의해 학교에서 나가는 것이 목격되었다.
(the school, was, he, by, come out of, seen, his friends, to)

→ _____

_____

28 그녀는 부모님에게 모든 것을 말하도록 시켜졌다.
(to, was, she, made, tell, her parents, everything)

→ _____

_____

◎ CHALLENGE!

Write your own answer to the question.

01 By whom were you taught English last year? (Use the passive voice.)

_____

_____

02 What gift were you given last Christmas? (Use the passive voice.)

_____

_____

CHAPTER

05

To-infinitives

to부정사

UNIT
01
Substantive To-infinitives
to부정사의 명사적 용법

UNIT
02
Adjective & Adverbial To-infinitives
to부정사의 형용사적·부사적 용법

UNIT
03
Subject, Tense, and Voices of To-infinitives
to부정사의 의미상의 주어, 시제, 태

UNIT
04
Infinitives as Object Complements
목적격 보어로 쓰이는 부정사

UNIT
05
Common Structures of Infinitives
to부정사의 주요 구문

Substantive To-infinitives

to부정사의 명사적 용법

A to부정사의 명사적 용법
to부정사는 명사처럼 문장에서 주어, 보어, 목적어로 쓰인다.

A To-infinitive as a Noun

To do your best is important. <subject>
My job is **to send** the invitation cards. <complement>
I plan **to visit** my aunt in the Netherlands. <object>

* **want, wish, hope, expect, offer, plan, promise, refuse, agree, decide** + **To-infinitive**

B 가주어와 가목적어 it
주어나 목적어로 쓰인 to부정사가 길 때, 가주어 또는 가목적어 it을 쓰고 to부정사는 뒤로 보낸다.

B Preparatory Subject/Object *it*

It is dangerous **to go out** at night in this area.
preparatory subject   real subject
GPS makes *it* easy **to find** places.
  preparatory object   real object

* **Preparatory subject *it***
  It was a great honor **to be invited** to the party.
  (← **To be invited** to the party was a great honor.)

* **Preparatory object *it***
  I found *it* difficult **to concentrate** on the class after lunch.

C 의문사 + to부정사
「의문사(what/when/where/who/which/how) + to부정사」는 '무엇을/언제/어디서/누구를(에게)/어느것을/어떻게 ~할지'라는 뜻을 나타낸다.
「의문사 + 주어 + should/could + 동사원형」으로 바꿔 쓸 수 있다.

C Wh-word + To-infinitive

Nobody told me **what to do**.
                   = what I should do

e.g. Can you suggest **where to go** for dinner?
                      = where I could go
They are talking about **when to start** a campaign.
I am not sure **who(m) to ask** for help.

cf. 「why + to부정사」는 쓰지 않는다.

Negative infinitives
to부정사의 부정: not이나 never를 to부정사 앞에 쓴다.
I want you *not* **to make** any noise here.
He asked me *never* **to be** late again.

EXERCISE **A** **Choose the correct one for each sentence.**

1 (Meet, To meet) new people is always fun.

2 Kelly wants (going, to go) to Italy someday.

3 (It, That) is important to get a good night's sleep.

4 My plan is (to read, reads) three books a month.

5 It is not wise (to make, making) your parents upset.

B **Complete the sentence using the given words.**

1 It is not _____. (easy, become, a vegetarian)

2 It is _____. (good, for your throat, drink, lots of warm water)

3 You will find _____. (difficult, live in, a new country)

4 I consider _____. (unhealthy, eat, late at night)

C **Fill in the blank so that the two sentences have the same meaning.**

1 Our teacher told us what we should do first.

= Our teacher told us _____ first.

2 I cannot decide where I should go for vacation.

= I cannot decide _____ for vacation.

3 The old lady asked me how she could send text messages on her cell phone.

= The old lady asked me _____ text messages on her cell phone.

4 He wanted to talk to someone, but he did not know whom he should call.

= He wanted to talk to someone, but he did not know _____.

D **Complete the sentence using the given words.**

1 매일 아침 조깅을 하는 것은 쉽지 않다. (go jogging)

→ It is not easy _____ every morning.

2 이 기계를 어떻게 사용하는지 설명해 줄 수 있어요? (use)

→ Can you explain _____ this machine?

3 나는 영어로 일기를 쓰는 것이 도움이 된다는 것을 알았다. (find, useful)

→ _____ keep a journal in English.

4 그녀의 조언은 그에게 먼저 사과 편지를 쓰라는 것이었다. (advice, write)

→ _____ an apology letter to him first.

UNIT 02

Adjective & Adverbial To-infinitives to부정사의 형용사적·부사적 용법

A To-infinitive as an Adjective

I do not have *enough money* **to buy** the bike.
Students *are* **to wear** uniforms at this school.

- **Noun + To-infinitive**
  Can you suggest *a good movie* **to watch** tonight?

cf. **Noun + To-infinitive + Preposition**
  She needed *someone* **to talk to** at that moment.
  The children have *a lot of toys* **to play with**.

- **be + To-infinitive**
  1. Adam *is* **to leave** Korea next week. <plan and arrangement>
  2. A lot of stars *are* **to be** seen tonight. <possibility>
  3. You *are* **to stay** here until I come back. <obligation>
  4. They *were* **to meet** again. <fate>
  5. If you *are* **to succeed**, you should be honest. <pre-condition>

B To-infinitive as an Adverb

You have to study hard **to get** the scholarship. <purpose>
　　　　　　　　　　　　　　= in order to, so as to
People were relieved **to hear** the news. <cause>
Steve grew up **to become** a famous movie director. <result>
He must be warm-hearted **to do** such a thing.
　　　　　　　　　　　　　　　　<ground for judgement>
This sofa is comfortable **to sit on**. <adjective + to-infinitive>

To-infinitives (purpose) → so that + S + V
He ran (in order) **to catch** the thief.
= He ran *so that he could catch* the thief.
I practiced hard not **to fall behind**.
= I practiced hard *so that I would not fall behind*.

EXERCISE

A Choose the correct one for each sentence.

1 I lost the key (opened, to open) the drawer.

2 She has lots of homework (do, to do) today.

3 They need a house (to live, to live in).

4 We are looking for someone (to work, to work with).

5 The kid just moved to this town, so he wanted to find a friend to play (with, about).

B Correct the underlined part.

1 Sally and Tim <u>be to marry</u> next month.   → _____

2 Tim got up early <u>catch</u> the first train.   → _____

3 I am very happy <u>win</u> a prize.   → _____

4 This medicine <u>is be to taken</u> three times a day after meals. → _____

5 If you <u>to are succeed</u>, you should put a lot of effort in it. → _____

C Translate the English into Korean paying attention to the underlined part.

1 You <u>are to follow</u> the traffic rules.

→ _____

2 Nothing <u>is to be seen</u> in the darkness.

→ _____

3 Andy must be a genius <u>to solve</u> this question.

→ _____

4 I go to the gym three times a week <u>to stay</u> healthy.

→ _____

5 Not everyone grows up <u>to become</u> a famous musician.

→ _____

D Complete the sentence using the given words.

1 너 같은 친구를 두다니 John은 운이 좋다. (lucky, have)

→ John is _____ like you.

2 우리는 다음 달에 여행을 시작할 예정이다. (begin, our trip)

→ We _____ next month.

3 그 사건 후에 Sam은 말할 누군가가 필요했다. (talk)

→ Sam needed _____ after the incident.

4 나의 형은 스페인어를 공부하기 위해 아르헨티나에 가고 싶어 한다. (study, Spanish)

→ My brother wants to go to Argentina _____.

UNIT 03

Subject, Tense, and Voices of To-infinitives

to부정사의 의미상의 주어, 시제, 태

A Subject of To-infinitive

> It is easy *for young children* **to learn** a new language.
> It was careless *of me* **to break** the cup.

- **for + Object**
  It is difficult *for me* **to finish** the homework by tomorrow.

- **of + Object**
  Adjectives describing personalities + of + Object
  (polite, sweet, rude, careless, cruel, foolish,
  thoughtful, generous, considerate)
  It was impolite *of you* **to talk back** to her.

Without subject of to-infinitive 의미상의 주어를 쓰지 않는 경우

1. 일반인이 주어: It is wrong **to tell** lies.
   (← It is wrong *for people* to tell lies.)
2. 문장의 주어와 일치: I expect **to see** you there.
   (← I expect that *I* will see you there.)
3. 문장의 목적어와 일치: I expect *him* **to call** you.
   (← I expect that *he* will call you.)

B Tense of To-infinitive

> He seems **to understand** the situation.
> You appear **to have lost** a lot of weight.

- **Simple infinitive: to V**
  The kid appears **to be** lost. (= It *appears* that the kid is lost.)
  They seemed **to like** his song. (= It *seemed* that they *liked* his song.)

- **Perfect infinitive: to have p.p.**
  The boy is believed **to have witnessed** the accident.
  (= It *is* believed that the boy *witnessed* the accident.)
  Susan seemed **to have been** ill.
  (= It *seemed* that Susan *had been* ill.)

C To-infinitive in Passive Voice

> The cell phone needs **to be repaired** today.
> It is fortunate for him **to have been found** by the passers-by.

A to부정사의 의미상의 주어

문장의 주어와 to부정사의 주어가 다른 경우 to부정사 앞에 「for + 목적격」 또는 「of + 목적격」을 써서 의미상의 주어를 나타낸다.

B to부정사의 시제

주절의 시제와 to부정사의 시제가 같을 때 단순부정사 「to V」를 쓰고, 주절의 시제보다 to부정사의 시제가 앞설 때 완료부정사 「to have p.p.」를 쓴다.

C 수동형 to부정사

to부정사가 수동의 의미일 경우 「to be p.p.」의 형태로 쓴다.

EXERCISE

A Choose the correct one for each sentence.

1 It is foolish (for you, of you) to believe his lie.

2 It is necessary (for us, of us) to follow the school rules.

3 It is so sweet (for him, of him) to comfort her when she is sad.

4 It is smart (for you, of you) to take advantage of the opportunity.

5 It is difficult (for me, of me) to memorize the poem.

B Fill in the blank so that the two sentences have the same meaning.

1 It was thought that the Sun traveled around the Earth.

= The Sun was thought _____ around the Earth.

2 It seems that James caught a cold.

= James seems _____ a cold.

3 It is said that he had three cats and two dogs.

= He is said _____ three cats and two dogs.

4 It seemed that Sally and Mary did not like each other at first.

= Sally and Mary did not _____ each other at first.

C Correct the underlined part and rewrite the sentence.

1 It was rude <u>him to say</u> that to his parents.

→ _____

2 Sam is believed <u>speaking</u> five different languages.

→ _____

3 These shirts are <u>to wash</u> by tomorrow.

→ _____

D Complete the sentence using the given words.

1 그는 그 사실을 아는 것 같다. (know, fact)

→ He seems _____ .

2 나에게 조언해 주다니 너는 사려 깊구나. (advise)

→ It is considerate _____ .

3 Tom이 수학 시험에 합격하는 것은 쉬운 일이 아니다. (pass)

→ It is not easy _____ the math test.

4 그 작가는 감옥에서 그의 소설의 대부분을 썼다고 한다. (write)

→ The writer is said _____ most of his novels in prison.

Infinitives as Object Complements
목적격 보어로 쓰이는 부정사

A To-infinitive as an Object Complement

I want you **to take** this matter more seriously.
　　O　　　　　　O.C.

e.g. My parents do not *allow* me **to use** bad words.
They *asked* all the passengers **to show** their ID cards.

 A to부정사가 목적격 보어
want, tell, order, force, allow, ask, expect, cause 등의 동사는 목적격 보어로 to부정사를 쓴다.

B Bare Infinitive as an Object Complement

I *saw* a strange man **go** into the bank.
　　　　　O　　　　O.C.
Our school does not *let* us **keep** our cell phones during class.
　　　　　　　　O　　　　O.C.

- **see, hear, smell, feel (Perception verbs) + O + Bare infinitive**
  I could *smell* the food **burn** on the stove.

- **let, make, have (Causative verbs) + O + Bare infinitive**
  My mom *made* me **clean** up the living room.

  cf. 1 **help + O + To-infinitive / Bare infinitive**
  Could you *help* me **(to) carry** this box?

  cf. 2 **get + O + To-infinitive**
  The animal trainer *got* the dog **to jump** over a fence.

B 원형부정사가 목적격 보어
지각동사와 사역동사는 목적격 보어로 원형부정사를 쓴다.

cf. 1 help는 목적격 보어로 to부정사와 원형부정사 둘 다 쓸 수 있다.

cf. 2 get이 사역동사처럼 쓰일 때 목적격 보어로 to부정사를 쓴다.

ONE MORE +

1. Perception verbs + O + v-ing
지각동사는 목적어가 진행 중인 동작을 강조할 때 현재분사를 목적격 보어로 쓴다.
The professor *saw* him **playing** the drum.
I can *feel* something **crawling** on my back.

2. Idiomatic expressions using bare infinitives

cannot but + V ~하지 않을 수 없다	do nothing but + V 단지 ~하기만 하다
had better + V ~하는 것이 좋을 것이다	Why not + V? ~하지 그래?
would rather + V (+ than V) (~하느니) 차라리 …하고 싶다	

The new plan *did nothing but* **confuse** everyone at work.

EXERCISE **A** Choose the correct one for each sentence.

1 My parents expect me (come, to come) home early today.

2 No one can force you (leaving, to leave) this place.

3 I asked him (to turn, turning) down the volume.

4 Dr. Brown advised me (exercise, to exercise) regularly.

5 Making flashcards will help you (remember, remembering) new words.

B Fill in the blank using the given word.

1 I heard the bus _____ up the street. (come)

2 I got my brother _____ my computer. (fix)

3 My parents will not let me _____ camping with my friends. (go)

4 The teacher had the students _____ their books. (close)

5 I felt the ground _____ during the earthquake. (tremble)

C Correct the underlined part.

1 I felt something to touch my back. → _____

2 Mr. Smith does not let his son to go out after 9 p.m. → _____

3 I saw him to carry the old woman's groceries. → _____

4 My parents made me studied for six hours last night. → _____

5 I watched the astronauts are walked toward the space shuttle.

→ _____

D Complete the sentence using the given words.

1 나는 네가 다시는 내 옷을 입도록 허락하지 않을 것이다. (allow, wear)

→ I will never _____ my clothes again.

2 우리는 헬리콥터 한 대가 경찰서 근처에 착륙하고 있는 것을 보았다. (see, land)

→ We _____ near the police station.

3 모두가 운동장에서 누군가 소리지르는 것을 들었다. (hear, shout)

→ Everyone _____ on the playground.

4 엄마는 내가 패스트푸드를 그만 먹기를 원하신다. (want, stop)

→ My mom _____ eating fast food.

Common Structures of Infinitives
to부정사의 주요 구문

Ⓐ too . . . to-infinitive

I am **too** *tired* **to get up** early.
= I am **so** *tired* **that** I **cannot get up** early.

e.g. The movie was **too** *complicated* for him **to understand**.
= The movie was **so** *complicated* **that** he **could not understand** it.

Ⓑ . . . enough to-infinitive

John is *tall* **enough to reach** the shelf.
= John is **so** *tall* **that** he **can reach** the shelf.

e.g. She was *old* **enough to take** a trip by herself.
= She was **so** *old* **that** she **could take** a trip by herself.

cf. 「**enough + Noun + to V**」
I do not have **enough** *money* **to buy** the dress.

Ⓒ Absolute Infinitive

To begin with, this is beyond our ability.
To make matters worse, we are running out of money.
To be frank with you, you are not qualified for this job.

to be sure 확실히	strange to say 이상하게 들리겠지만	so to speak 말하자면, 소위
to tell the truth 사실대로 말하면	to begin with 우선, 먼저	to be honest with you 솔직히 말하면
to make matters worse 설상가상으로	to be frank with you 솔직히 말하면	to do someone justice 공정하게 판단하면

too . . . to V → not + 반의어 + enough to V
You are **too** *young* **to see** this movie.
= You are **not** <u>old</u> **enough to see** this movie.

Ⓐ too + 형용사/부사 + to부정사

'너무 ~해서 …할 수 없는' 이라는 뜻으로 「so + 형용사/부사 + that + 주어 + cannot (could not)」으로 바꿔 쓸 수 있다.

Ⓑ 형용사/부사 + enough + to부정사

'~할 만큼 충분히 …하다' 라는 뜻으로 「so + 형용사/부사 + that + 주어 + can (could)」으로 바꿔 쓸 수 있다.

cf. enough가 형용사로 명사를 수식하는 경우, 「enough + 명사 + to부정사」 순서로 쓴다.

Ⓒ 독립부정사

to부정사가 포함된 부사구가 독립적으로 쓰여 문장 전체를 꾸미는 것으로, 문장의 시제나 인칭에 영향을 받지 않는다.

EXERCISE

A Choose the correct one for each sentence.

1 The situation is too complicated (to explain, explaining).

2 The stew is too spicy (to eat for me, for me to eat).

3 This coat is (enough warm, warm enough) to wear on snowy days.

4 He does not have (enough time, time enough) to meet you.

B Fill in the blank so that the two sentences have the same meaning.

1 He is too stubborn to change his mind.

= He is _____.

2 This story is so short that I can read it in a day.

= This story is _____.

3 This suitcase is so big that it cannot fit under the seat.

= This suitcase is _____.

4 Julian was so smart that he could overcome his difficulties.

= Julian was _____.

C Translate the English into Korean paying attention to the underlined part.

1 To be frank with you, the food was terrible.

→ _____

2 To tell the truth, the math class is boring.

→ _____

3 Strange to say, the bed was very comfortable, but I could not sleep well.

→ _____

4 They were lost in the woods. To make matters worse, it started to rain.

→ _____

D Complete the sentence using the given words.

1 그 가방은 들기에 충분히 가볍다. (light, carry)

→ The bag is _____.

2 그녀는 너무 피곤해서 숙제를 끝낼 수가 없다. (too, tired)

→ She is _____ her homework.

3 그는 집에 혼자 있을 만큼 나이가 들지 않았다. (old, stay)

→ He is not _____ at home alone.

4 솔직히 말하면, 나는 그의 말을 믿을 수가 없다. (honest)

→ _____, I cannot trust his words.

WRITING CONNECTION

 1 Grammar Check-up

A Choose the correct one.

1 I have to visit the embassy in order _____ renew my visa.
ⓐ to   ⓑ for   ⓒ of   ⓓ at

2 Could you teach me _____ start this machine?
ⓐ of   ⓑ how   ⓒ how to   ⓓ what to

3 As spring is coming, a lot of flowers _____ seen soon.
ⓐ are   ⓑ are to   ⓒ are to be   ⓓ are to have

4 It was impolite _____ to use other people's belongings without asking.
ⓐ him   ⓑ of him   ⓒ for him   ⓓ his

5 The teacher had the students _____ their books to page 43.
ⓐ open   ⓑ opened   ⓒ to open   ⓓ opening

6 Ben was too happy _____ that everybody was watching him cry.
ⓐ for realizing   ⓑ realizing   ⓒ realize   ⓓ to realize

B Circle the inappropriate one between ⓐ and ⓑ. Then correct it.

1 Will you bring him a chair to sit with?   _____
ⓐ   ⓑ

2 My parents will not let me to stay out late.   _____
ⓐ   ⓑ

3 We saw her sang in the practice room.   _____
ⓐ ⓑ

4 She did not want me read her diary.   _____
ⓐ ⓑ

5 It was not my intention to hurting you, but I am sincerely sorry.   _____
ⓐ   ⓑ

6 The whole village was silent until I heard a window broken.   _____
ⓐ   ⓑ

2 Phrases to Sentences

A Complete the sentence by referring to the Korean translation.

1 그런 일을 할 수 있을 정도로 너는 충분히 똑똑하다. (smart)

→ You are _____ do such a thing.

2 우선, 응급 상황에 대한 지침서를 만들 필요가 있다. (begin)

→ _____ , we need to make a manual for emergencies.

3 이 문제는 너무 어려워서 내가 답을 찾을 수 없다. (difficult, for)

→ This question is _____ find the answer.

4 모든 사람들이 Cathy가 팀의 지도자가 되기를 원했다. (leader)

→ Everyone wanted Cathy _____ of the team.

5 그 프로젝트를 마치는 것이 Chris에게 중요한 것처럼 보였다. (finish)

→ It seemed important _____ .

6 심사 위원에게 좋은 인상을 남기는 법을 알려줄 수 있겠니? (make, impression)

→ Can you tell me _____ on the judges?

B Underline the error and rewrite the sentence.

1 He found difficult it to drive on the left side of the road.

→ _____

2 The inside of the tunnel is too dark seeing anything.

→ _____

3 It is important of you to make the right decision.

→ _____

4 Thank you so much for helping me fixing my bike.

→ _____

5 The police are known to capture the suspect last year.

→ _____

6 It was very nice for him to apologize to me first.

→ _____

3 Sentence Practice

A Translate the Korean into English using the given words.

1 a. 그는 너무 바빠서 나와 시간을 보낼 수가 없다. (too, spend)

→ He is _____ time with me.

b. 나는 너무 피곤해서 저녁을 만들 수 없다. (tired, cook)

→ _____

2 a. 불쌍한 아이들을 지원하다니 그는 좋은 사람이다. (support)

→ He is a good person _____ the poor children.

b. 길을 묻는 여자를 무시하다니 그는 불친절한 사람이다. (unkind, ignore, lady, for directions)

→ _____

3 a. 음악을 듣는 것이 긴장을 푸는 데 도움이 된다. (relax)

→ Listening to music helps me _____ .

b. 따뜻한 차를 한 잔 마시는 것이 잠을 잘 자는 데 도움이 된다. (a cup of, tea)

→ _____

4 a. 나는 일주일에 세 번 운동하는 것을 규칙으로 삼고 있다. (exercise)

→ I make _____ a rule _____ three times a week.

b. 나는 하루에 물을 여덟 잔 마시는 것을 규칙으로 삼고 있다. (eight glasses of water)

→ _____

B Unscramble the words to make a sentence.

1 우리는 등산하는 동안 마실 물을 좀 가져가야 한다. (take, we, while, some, hiking, water, should, to, drink)

→ _____

2 어머니는 내 행동에 실망하신 것 같았다. (be, my mother, seemed, to, with, disappointed, my behavior)

→ _____

3 할머니에게 자리를 양보하다니 너는 참 친절하다. (to, give, your seat, it, the old lady, so, of, kind, you, is, to)

→ _____

4 Mr. Parker는 시장으로 선출되기를 바라고 있었다. (the mayor, was, elected, as, Mr. Parker, to, be, hoping)

→ _____

> Answers **p. 13**

[1-3] 빈칸에 들어갈 수 <u>없는</u> 것을 고르시오.

1

> I _____ to see her again.

① want ② hope
③ wish ④ expect
⑤ suggest

2

> My teacher _____ us clean the classroom.

① had ② let ③ got
④ made ⑤ helped

3

> It is _____ for him to communicate in English.

① easy ② polite ③ difficult
④ impossible ⑤ important

[4-5] 어법상 <u>어색한</u> 문장을 고르시오.

4　① I found it difficult to talk to him.
　② The computer has enough memory to save this data.
　③ I do not know how to use this bread maker.
　④ The guard forces me step back from the safety line.
　⑤ The boss wants the employee to take part in the meeting.

5　① We saw the cook to make our meals.
　② Jack seems to live in England.
　③ You are to go home after 4:30.
　④ The book was too complicated for me to understand.
　⑤ It is so nice of you to help me with the dishes.

[6-7] 밑줄 친 부분과 쓰임이 같은 것을 고르시오.

6

> They felt happy <u>to help</u> the poor.

① The letters are too small to read.
② I am so relieved to hear that.
③ My goal is to win a gold medal at the Olympics.
④ She went to Canada to learn figure skating.
⑤ They moved to the countryside to work on an apple farm.

7

> She <u>was to arrive</u> in Seoul this morning.

① Nothing was to be heard.
② He was to be a musician from birth.
③ The medicine is to be taken after meals.
④ They are to visit here soon.
⑤ If you are to pass the exam, study harder.

8 주어진 문장과 의미가 같은 것은?

> He was not strong enough to do that job.

① He was too weak to do that job.
② He was so strong that he could do that job.
③ He was not weak enough to do that job.
④ He was so weak that he could do that job.
⑤ He was not too weak that he could not do that job.

9 빈칸에 공통으로 들어갈 말로 알맞은 것은?

> • _____ can be dangerous to cross the street at a red light.
> • She found _____ annoying to hear noise from the house next door.

① That [that]
② It [it]
③ This [this]
④ What [what]
⑤ These [these]

10 두 문장의 의미가 <u>다른</u> 것은?

① To learn something new is exciting.
 = It is exciting to learn something new.
② It seemed that he knew the answer.
 = He seemed to have known the answer.
③ I dropped by my friend's house to borrow a book.
 = I dropped by my friend's house in order to borrow a book.
④ My wallet was too big to fit in my pocket.
 = My wallet was so big that it could not fit in my pocket.
⑤ I do not know what to do after graduation.
 = I do not know what I should do after graduation.

11 빈칸에 들어갈 수 있는 것을 <u>모두</u> 고르면?

> I told her _____ to meet her.

① why
② where
③ when
④ that
⑤ whose

[12-14] 빈칸에 들어갈 알맞은 말을 고르시오.

12

> The lecture was _____.

① for everyone to boring listen to
② to listen to everyone for boring
③ boring to listen for everyone to
④ boring for everyone to listen to
⑤ to boring for everyone to listen

13

> I missed the bus, and _____, I left my homework at home.

① so to speak
② to begin with
③ to do him justice
④ strange to say
⑤ to make matters worse

14

> Tom wants to get a driver's license, but he is _____.

① to drive enough young
② too young to drive
③ young enough to drive
④ so that young to drive
⑤ so young that he could drive

15 우리말 해석이 바르지 <u>않은</u> 것은?

① I am sure that you are glad to go on a field trip.

→ 네가 소풍을 가서 기쁠 거라고 나는 확신한다.

② It was exciting to get my cousin's letter.

→ 내 사촌의 편지를 받는 것은 신나는 일이었다.

③ My mom promised to take me to the movies.

→ 엄마는 나를 영화관에 데려가기로 약속했다.

④ The ladder was long enough to reach the roof.

→ 사다리는 지붕에 닿을 만큼 충분히 길었다.

⑤ It was nice of you to take him home.

→ 너를 집에 데려다주다니 그는 참 친절하다.

[16-17] 빈칸에 들어갈 말이 바르게 짝 지어진 것을 고르시오.

16

- It is important ____(A)____ children to have balanced meals.
- It was careless ____(B)____ you to leave the door open.

	(A)	(B)		(A)	(B)
①	that	–	for	② for	– at
③	that	–	of	④ of	– for
⑤	for	–	of		

17

- My teacher's feedback made me ____(A)____ about my attitude.
- The man's achievement needs ____(B)____ for a long time.

	(A)		(B)
①	thinking	–	to remember
②	think	–	to be remembered
③	to think	–	to be remembered
④	thinking	–	to remembering
⑤	think	–	to remembering

18 가주어 it이 포함된 문장이 <u>아닌</u> 것은?

① It was important for me to get the job.

② It was rainy, so we canceled our picnic.

③ It was comfortable to sit on the sofa.

④ It was great to have you as our guest.

⑤ It was not necessary to answer the call.

19 빈칸에 to가 들어갈 수 <u>없는</u> 것은?

① He needs someone _____ talk to now.

② They are looking for a house _____ live in.

③ I want a strong chair _____ sit on.

④ She thinks that there is no one _____ depend on.

⑤ They saw me _____ fall on the ground.

[20-21] 밑줄 친 부분이 어법상 <u>어색한</u> 것을 고르시오.

20 ① He seemed <u>to have heard</u> the news already.

② Peter <u>is to write</u> his essay by tonight.

③ I was glad <u>to know</u> Jake was doing well.

④ It is not safe <u>riding</u> a bike without wearing a helmet.

⑤ It was brave <u>of her</u> to help the boy who was stuck on the railroad tracks.

21 ① The pants <u>to wash</u> are in the basket.

② The documentary was <u>too boring for us to watch</u> until the end.

③ The criminal <u>is to appear</u> in court tomorrow.

④ <u>To tell the truth</u>, I broke the vase.

⑤ She practiced hard <u>enough to win</u> the basketball game.

[22-23] 두 문장이 같은 의미가 되도록 빈칸에 알맞은 말을 쓰시오.

22

> It seemed that he had recovered from his illness.
> = He seemed _____ from his illness.

23

> My brother is so strong that he can carry the box.
> = My brother is _____ the box.

24 주어진 문장을 It으로 시작하는 문장으로 다시 쓰시오.

> To live with many family members is not easy.

→ _____

_____

25 밑줄 친 부분을 어법에 맞게 고쳐 문장을 다시 쓰시오.

> It was polite for they write a thank-you letter to my grandma.

→ _____

_____

[26-27] 우리말에 맞게 주어진 단어를 바르게 배열하여 문장을 쓰시오.

26

> 그 그림은 너무 무거워서 내가 벽에 걸 수가 없다. (the picture, for, heavy, too, is, me, to, on the wall, hang)

→ _____

_____

27

> 그 곰은 사람을 무서워하지 않는 것 같다.
> (not, humans, of, the bear, be, does, to, seem, afraid)

→ _____

_____

28 주어진 문장을 so . . . that을 이용하여 다시 쓰시오.

> They were too poor to buy Christmas presents for each other.

→ _____

_____

🎯 CHALLENGE!

Write your own answer to the question.

01 What do you do to stay healthy?

_____

_____

02 What is difficult for you to do in your school life?

_____

_____

CHAPTER

06

Gerunds

동명사

UNIT 01

Functions & Usage of Gerunds
동명사의 역할과 쓰임

UNIT 02

Gerunds vs. To-infinitives
동명사와 to부정사

UNIT 01

Functions & Usage of Gerunds 동명사의 역할과 쓰임

A Function of Gerund

A 동명사의 역할

동명사는 문장에서 주어, 보어, 목적어로 쓰일 수 있다.

Drinking too much coffee is not good. <subject>
One of my hobbies is **singing** songs.   <complement>
He *postponed* **returning** to Korea because of his illness.
<object of a verb>
I am not interested *in* **interfering** in your business.
<object of a preposition>

◆ **enjoy, stop, finish, mind, keep, avoid, consider, suggest + v-ing**
I *considered* not **responding** to his message.

B Subject of Gerund

B 동명사의 의미상의 주어

동명사의 주어가 문장의 주어와 다를 때 동명사 앞에 소유격 또는 목적격을 써서 나타낸다.

Your mother mentioned *your* (*you*) **coming** to class late.
I dislike *my brother's* (*my brother*) **making** excuses.

C Tense of Gerund

C 동명사의 시제

동명사의 시제가 문장 동사의 시제와 같을 때는 단순동명사(v-ing)를, 문장 동사의 시제보다 앞설 때는 완료동명사(having p.p.)를 쓴다.

She is satisfied with **using** the traditional methods.
I am ashamed of **having made** such a stupid mistake.

◆ **Simple gerund: v-ing**
She was proud of **having** such a kind son.
(= She was proud that she had such a kind son.)

◆ **Perfect gerund: having p.p.**
He denied **having seen** her.
(= He denied that he had seen her.)

D Passive Gerund

D 수동형 동명사

수동의 의미를 나타내는 동명사의 시제가 문장 동사의 시제와 같으면 단순형 수동태(being p.p.), 문장 동사의 시제보다 앞설 때는 완료형 수동태(having been p.p.)를 쓴다.

She was happy about **being involved** in the project.
I remember **having been given** the offer before.

◆ **Passive gerund: being p.p.**
The movie star is afraid of **being judged** by the public.
(= The movie star is afraid that he **is judged** by the public.)

◆ **Passive perfect gerund: having been p.p.**
Justin disliked **having been told** what to do.
(= Justin disliked that he **had been told** what to do.)

EXERCISE

A Choose the correct one for each sentence.

1 I suggest (drink, drinking) a glass of water regularly.

2 He does not mind (I, my) helping him.

3 Would you mind (closing, to close) the window?

4 (Studying, Study) a foreign language takes a lot of time.

5 His job is (teach, teaching) students at a university.

B Rewrite the sentence using a gerund.

1 She regrets that she did not study harder.

= She regrets _____ harder.

2 He admitted that he was invited to the party.

= He admitted _____ to the party.

3 Nick is proud that he overcame his difficulties.

= Nick is proud of _____ his difficulties.

4 I am upset that my brother uses my computer without my permission.

= I am upset about _____ my computer without my permission.

C Correct the underlined part.

1 I am afraid of <u>be traveled</u> alone.   → _____

2 My dog dislikes <u>touching</u> by strangers.   → _____

3 I do not mind <u>to be called</u> by my nickname.

→ _____

4 Please stop <u>being bothered</u> me while I am reading a book.

→ _____

D Complete the sentence using the given words.

1 우리 부모님은 도시로 이사하는 것을 고려하셨다. (consider, move)

→ My parents _____ to the city.

2 선수들은 팬들에게 격려를 받아 기뻤다. (encourage)

→ The players were pleased about _____ by the fans.

3 나는 그들이 소파 위에서 먹는 것을 정말 싫어한다. (hate, eat)

→ I really _____ on the sofa.

4 곤경에 처했을 때 내가 그녀를 도와줬던 것에 대해 그녀는 고마워했다. (help)

→ She thanked me for _____ her when she was in trouble.

Gerunds vs. To-infinitives
동명사와 to부정사

A 동명사만을 목적어로
취하는 동사

A **Verbs Followed by Gerund**

I I sometimes *avoid* **answering** his phone calls.

- admit, avoid, enjoy, stop, finish, quit, give up,
  mind, keep, consider, suggest, deny, delay,   + V-ing
  postpone, imagine, recommend, dislike

B to부정사만을 목적어
로 취하는 동사

B **Verbs Followed by To-infinitive**

I We *decided* **to participate** in the music festival this year.

- want, wish, decide, hope, expect, agree,
  choose, learn, plan, promise, refuse, seek   + To-infinitive

C 동명사와 to부정사를
모두 목적어로 취하는
동사

C **Verbs Followed by Gerund & To-infinitive**

I The volunteers *started* **picking up** (**to pick up**) the trash.
I She *forgot* **turning off** the gas valve. (→ She turned it off.)
I She *forgot* **to turn off** the gas valve. (→ She did not turn it off.)

- with the same meaning: like, love, hate, begin, start, continue
  He *loves* **climbing** (**to climb**) a mountain on the weekend.

- with different meanings: remember, forget, try, regret

remember + to v ~할 것을 기억하다 (미래)	remember + v-ing ~했던 것을 기억하다 (과거)
forget + to v ~할 것을 잊다 (미래)	forget + v-ing ~했던 것을 잊다 (과거)
try + to v ~하려고 노력하다	try + v-ing 시험 삼아 ~해 보다
regret + to v ~하게 되어 유감이다	regret + v-ing ~한 것을 후회하다

D 동명사의 관용적 표현

D **Idiomatic Usage of Gerunds**

I **It is no use crying** over spilled milk.
I She **was used to staying** up all night.

be busy v-ing	be worth v-ing	be used to v-ing
feel like v-ing	look forward to v-ing	spend time (money) v-ing
cannot help v-ing	it is no use v-ing	there is no v-ing
on v-ing	go (keep) on v-ing	How (What) about v-ing?
have difficulty v-ing	keep (prevent) . . . from v-ing	

EXERCISE

A Complete the sentence using the given word.

1 He delayed _____ his homework. (do)

2 Brad promised not _____ late again. (be)

3 Tom suggested _____ a movie with him. (watch)

4 She agreed _____ a speech to the class. (give)

B Translate the English into Korean paying attention to the underlined part.

1 I <u>forgot to pay</u> the money back to my friend.

→ _____

2 Minho <u>regrets missing</u> the opportunity to win.

→ _____

3 I <u>tried to catch</u> the bus, but I could not run fast enough.

→ _____

4 She <u>remembered bringing</u> the book to school, but she could not find it.

→ _____

C Rewrite the sentence using a gerund.

1 It is worthwhile to watch this documentary.

→ This documentary _____ .

2 It is useless to turn on the air conditioner with the window open.

→ _____ the air conditioner with the window open.

3 I do not want to have lunch today.

→ I do not feel _____ today.

4 Fixing the machine keeps my uncle busy.

→ My uncle _____ the machine.

D Complete the sentence using the given words.

1 그녀는 선반에서 물건을 내리는 데 어려움이 있었다. (take down)

→ She had _____ the stuff from the shelf.

2 외출하기 전에 문을 잠그는 것을 잊지 마. (forget, lock the door)

→ Do not _____ before going out.

3 그는 식사 중에 휴대폰을 사용하는 것을 그만두었다. (stop, use)

→ He _____ his cellphone while eating.

4 제가 음악을 꺼도 될까요? (turn off)

→ Do you mind _____ the music?

WRITING CONNECTION

1 Grammar Check-up

A Choose the correct one.

1 His hobby is _____ kites with his friends.

ⓐ flies ⓑ flied ⓒ flying ⓓ to flying

2 She decided _____ the problem on her own.

ⓐ solve ⓑ solving ⓒ to solve ⓓ to solving

3 They do not mind _____ at this table.

ⓐ his sitting ⓑ him to sit ⓒ his sat ⓓ him to be sat

4 He tried to avoid _____ his math teacher.

ⓐ meet ⓑ meeting ⓒ to meet ⓓ be met

5 He did not want to spend time _____ about the small things.

ⓐ worry ⓑ to worrying ⓒ worrying ⓓ to worry

6 The teacher told her students to stop _____ noise in the classroom.

ⓐ make ⓑ made ⓒ making ⓓ to make

B Circle the inappropriate one between ⓐ and ⓑ. Then correct it.

1 She is busy to preparing for the exam.
　　　　　　ⓐ　　　ⓑ　　　　　　　　　　_____

2 He promised to fix it, but he keeps on to postpone it.
　　　　　　　ⓐ　　　　　　　　　　ⓑ　　　_____

3 He tried to avoid to making eye contact with me.
　　　　　ⓐ　　　ⓑ　　　　　　　　　　　_____

4 Before the test, do not forget turning off your phone.
　　　ⓐ　　　　　　　　　　ⓑ　　　　　　_____

5 Since I got cold, I felt like to get some a rest.
　　　　　ⓐ　　　　　　　　ⓑ　　　　　　_____

6 Mary was embarrassed of being fallen down in front of her friends. _____
　　　　　　ⓐ　　　　　　ⓑ

STEP 2 Phrases to Sentences

A Complete the sentence by referring to the Korean translation.

1 TV를 켜는 것을 꺼리시나요? (mind, turn on)

→ Would you _____ the TV?

2 내가 네 생일 파티에 갈 수 없다고 말하게 되어 유감이다. (regret, say)

→ I _____ that I cannot attend your birthday party.

3 냄새가 너무 좋아서 그는 그 케이크를 먹지 않을 수 없었다. (help, eat)

→ Because the smell was so good, he _____ the cake.

4 나는 내가 가장 좋아하는 배우를 만났던 것을 결코 잊지 못할 것이다. (forget, meet)

→ I will never _____ my favorite actor.

5 짙은 연기는 그가 건물 안으로 들어가는 것을 막았다. (prevent, enter)

→ The heavy smoke _____ the building.

6 우리는 그 콘서트에 가는 것을 고대하고 있다. (look, forward)

→ We are _____ to the concert.

B Underline the error and rewrite the sentence.

1 Can you imagine to climb the highest mountain in the world?

→ _____

2 I am really sorry for having losing your umbrella.

→ _____

3 On heard the news of the accident, he burst into tears.

→ _____

4 I remember to be taught how to ride a bicycle by my father when I was 6.

→ _____

5 Dan forgot bringing his wallet when he left his house.

→ _____

6 My father decided working in a different industry.

→ _____

3 Sentence Practice

A Translate the Korean into English using the given words.

1 a. 나는 그 책을 더 일찍 읽지 않은 것이 후회스럽다. (regret, read)

→ I _____ the book earlier.

b. 나는 더 일찍 너에게 사과를 하지 않은 것이 후회스럽다. (apologize to)

→ _____

2 a. 내일 무슨 일이 일어날지 걱정해도 소용없다. (use, worry about)

→ It is _____ what will happen tomorrow.

b. 과거에 네가 한 일에 대해 후회해도 소용없다. (regret, in the past)

→ _____

3 a. 나는 인도 요리를 먹는 것을 시도했지만, 그것을 좋아하지 않았다. (try, Indian food)

→ _____ , but I did not like it.

b. Sam은 그의 컴퓨터를 고치려고 시도했지만, 그는 실패했다. (fix, fail)

→ _____

4 a. 집에 가는 길에 할머니를 방문하는 것을 잊지 마라. (forget, Grandma)

→ Do not _____ on your way home.

b. 학교 가는 길에 펜을 사는 것을 잊지 마라. (buy)

→ _____

B Unscramble the words to make a sentence.

1 마라톤을 뛰는 것은 시도해 볼 만한 가치가 있다. (trying, running, is, worth, a marathon)

→ _____

2 나는 안경을 잃어버려서, 책을 읽는 데 어려움이 있었다.

(so, lost, a book, I, I, my glasses, difficulty, reading, had)

→ _____

3 나는 올해 너와 함께 여행할 것을 고대하고 있다.

(I, you, am, traveling, looking, to, forward, with, this year)

→ _____

4 우리는 George가 이긴 것을 축하하기 위해 파티를 열 것이다.

(to celebrate, will, winning, hold, George's, we, a party)

→ _____

ACTUAL TEST

> Answers **p. 15**

[1-3] 빈칸에 들어갈 알맞은 말을 고르시오.

1

> Would you mind me _____ you a piece of advice?

① give ② to give
③ given ④ to be given
⑤ giving

2

> Didn't you promise _____ him my secret?

① telling ② not telling
③ to tell not ④ not to tell
⑤ telling not

3

> This book is worth _____ many times.

① read ② reading
③ to read ④ to reading
⑤ be reading

4 빈칸에 들어갈 수 없는 것은?

> Tim _____ visiting the Great Wall of China.

① enjoyed ② suggested
③ decided ④ imagined
⑤ considered

[5-6] 밑줄 친 부분이 어법상 어색한 것을 고르시오.

5 ① I feel like eating sweets.
② You may begin to take the test.
③ My father stopped smoking last year.
④ Did you have difficulty to find this place?
⑤ Buying vegetables at this market is a good idea.

6 ① She considered moving to New York.
② I did not mind waiting until he came.
③ Everything depends on John's come in time.
④ It is no use trying to persuade her.
⑤ The kids are excited about going to the zoo.

7 짝 지어진 두 문장의 의미가 다른 것은?
① We all felt like celebrating.
  = We all wanted to celebrate.
② There is no telling about the weather.
  = It is impossible to tell about the weather.
③ It is no use worrying about her.
  = It is useless to worry about her.
④ On seeing me, he ran away.
  = As soon as he saw me, he ran away.
⑤ I kept him from making any noise.
  = I had him make some noise.

8 어법상 어색한 것은?

> Nick regrets ① not ② having ③ take ④ care ⑤ of his sick dog.

[9-10] 어법상 올바른 문장을 고르시오.

9
① Tom agreed going with me.
② I tried to staying awake, but I could not.
③ He delayed to finish the project.
④ We suggested going on a trip together.
⑤ Would you mind to helping me?

10
① They are learning painting.
② I am worried about yours risking your life.
③ Mom recommended us to eat spinach.
④ They consider to hold a concert.
⑤ She admitted breaking the vase.

[11-12] 우리말과 일치하도록 빈칸에 들어갈 알맞은 말을 고르시오.

11
> 나는 어젯밤 더 일찍 자지 않았던 것을 후회한다.
> → I regret _____ to bed earlier last night.

① not went
② not to go
③ not having gone
④ having not gone
⑤ having been gone

12
> 강한 바람 때문에 우산을 써 봐야 소용없다.
> → It is no _____ because of the strong wind.

① use putting up an umbrella
② use to put up an umbrella
③ put up to use an umbrella
④ use put up an umbrella
⑤ use to putting up an umbrella

13 빈칸에 들어갈 주어진 단어의 형태가 다른 것은?
① We postponed _____ the mountain due to the bad weather. (climb)
② My parents enjoy _____ tennis. (play)
③ She imagined _____ in Africa. (live)
④ I promised _____ Henry tomorrow morning. (visit)
⑤ Sue did not stop _____ the scary movie. (watch)

[14-15] 우리말을 영어로 바르게 옮긴 것을 고르시오.

14
> 나는 Ben과 함께 공원에 갔던 것을 기억한다.

① I remember to go to the park with Ben.
② I remember not to go to the park with Ben.
③ I remember going to the park with Ben.
④ I remember going not to the park with Ben.
⑤ I remember to going to the park with Ben.

15
> 아침을 먹지 않는 것은 너의 건강에 해롭다.

① Not eat breakfast is bad for your health.
② Eat not breakfast is bad for your health.
③ Eating breakfast is not bad for your health.
④ Eating not breakfast is bad for your health.
⑤ Not eating breakfast is bad for your health.

16 어법상 어색한 문장을 모두 고른 것은?

> ⓐ I often go surfing with my brothers.
> ⓑ Tom is interested in learn calligraphy.
> ⓒ I tried ringing a bell to get someone's attention.
> ⓓ Traveling to other countries are always full of surprises.

① ⓒ   ② ⓐ, ⓑ   ③ ⓑ, ⓒ
④ ⓑ, ⓓ   ⑤ ⓒ, ⓓ

17 우리말과 의미가 다른 문장은?

① 나의 학교 근처에 있는 그 공원은 방문할 가치가 있다.
   → The park near my school is worth visiting.
② 아기는 요람에서 잠드는 것에 익숙하다.
   → The baby used to sleep in the cradle.
③ 그 남자는 계속해서 축구 이야기를 했다.
   → The man kept talking about soccer.
④ 나는 이번 주말에는 집에 있고 싶어.
   → I feel like staying at home this weekend.
⑤ 비행기가 이미 떠났다고 말씀드리게 되어 유감입니다.
   → I regret to tell you that the flight has already left.

[18-19] 빈칸에 들어갈 말이 알맞게 짝 지어진 것을 고르시오

18
> • The doctor recommended ____(A)____ TV in the dark.
> • The teacher wants ____(B)____ you after school.

	(A)		(B)
①	not to watch	–	to see
②	not watching	–	to seeing
③	to not watch	–	to seeing
④	not watching	–	to see
⑤	not to watch	–	seeing

19
> • I expect ____(A)____ a panda at the zoo.
> • Peter wishes ____(B)____ a famous singer when he grows up.

	(A)		(B)
①	to seeing	–	to become
②	to see	–	becoming
③	seeing	–	to have become
④	to see	–	to become
⑤	seeing	–	becoming

20 어법상 올바른 문장의 개수는?

> • Swimming in the river is our plan for the weekend.
> • Tina is sure of she passing the exam.
> • I apologized for not keeping my promise to him.
> • Andy is proud of never being late for school.
> • We decided holding a surprise party for our new teacher.

① 1개   ② 2개   ③ 3개   ④ 4개   ⑤ 5개

21 어법상 어색한 문장은?

① He avoided giving the presentation.
② Chris is looking forward to see the musical.
③ Jina was angry at Paul trying to lie to her.
④ Everyone was surprised at his being absent.
⑤ My mom does not mind shopping online.

[22-23] 다음을 읽고, 물음에 답하시오.

> Sometimes my mom is forgetful. The other day, she forgot (A) (turn off) the gas stove. She left the house with the stove flame on. Hours later, she came home and smelled gas. She was terrified. Now, even though she turns off the gas, she always comes home to check the stove because she does not remember (B) (turn off) the gas. I decided hanging a reminder note on the front door: "Check the gas stove!"

22 (A)와 (B)를 각각 알맞은 형태로 고쳐 쓰시오.

(A) _____   (B) _____

23 밑줄 친 부분에서 어법상 어색한 부분을 찾아 알맞게 고쳐 쓰시오.

_____ → _____

[24-25] 두 문장이 같은 의미가 되도록 빈칸에 알맞은 말을 쓰시오.

24
> Fred has trouble dealing with his dogs.
> = Fred _____ his dogs.

25
> I do not want to work out today.
> = I do not feel _____ today.

[26-27] 우리말에 맞게 주어진 단어를 바르게 배열하여 문장을 쓰시오.

26
> 그는 어른들에게 아이 취급을 받는 것을 불평했다.
> (being, about, by, treated, he, complained, a child, like, adults)

→ _____

_____

27
> 그는 혼자 저녁을 먹는 것에 익숙했다.
> (used, dinner, he, was, alone, to, eating)

→ _____

28 다음 문장을 어법에 맞게 고쳐 쓰시오.

> There are different ways of protect the environment.

→ _____

🎯 CHALLENGE!

Write your own answer to the question.

01 What do you regret the most in your life so far?

_____

_____

02 What is your wish for the future?
(Use "I wish to . . . ")

_____

_____

Participles
분사

UNIT

01

Functions of Participles
분사의 기능

UNIT

02

Participle Clauses
분사구문

UNIT

03

Various Participle Clauses
다양한 분사구문들

UNIT 01

Functions of Participles

분사의 기능

A 분사의 종류

분사에는 현재분사(동사원형 -ing)와 과거분사(동사원형 -ed)가 있다. 현재분사는 능동(~하는)과 진행(~하고 있는)의 의미를, 과거분사는 수동(~된)과 완료(~한)의 의미를 나타낸다.

B 명사를 수식하는 분사

분사는 형용사처럼 앞이나 뒤에서 명사를 수식한다.

C 보어로서의 분사

분사는 주어나 목적어의 상태나 동작을 설명하는 보어로 쓰인다. 주어나 목적어가 동작의 주체이면 현재분사를, 동작의 대상이 되면 과거분사를 쓴다.

• 지각동사의 목적격 보어:
 see, hear, feel, watch +
 목적어 + 목적격 보어
  (동사원형/현재분사/과거분사)

• 사역동사의 목적격 보어:
 - have + 목적어 +
 목적격 보어
  (동사원형/현재분사/과거분사)

 - make + 목적어 +
 목적격 보어
  (동사원형/과거분사)

 - get(준사역동사) +
 목적어 + 목적격 보어
  (to부정사/현재분사/과거분사)

• keep, leave, find +
 목적어 + 목적격 보어
  (현재분사/과거분사)

A Kinds of Participles

| a **dancing** boy | **melting** snow | **falling** leaves |
| a **broken** branch | a **locked** door | **fallen** leaves |

B Participles Modifying Nouns

A **barking** dog usually does not bite. <present participle>
I know the boy **standing** by the window.
This is a **broken** arrow. <past participle>
All the photos **taken** at the amusement park were lost.

e.g. It is an **interesting** book. You should read it.
　　　The **excited** fans screamed when they saw the singer.

C Participles as Complements

The performance was very **disappointing**.
I saw him **dancing** on the stage.

* **Participles as subject complements**
 He looks **worried** about something today.

* **Participles as object complements**
 She *heard* her name **called**.
 This song *makes* me **depressed**.
 They *kept* me **waiting** until the doctor came in.

ONE MORE +

interesting vs. interested

interest**ing**, excit**ing**, bor**ing**: '~한 감정을 일으키는' 능동의 의미
interest**ed**, excit**ed**, bor**ed**: '~한 감정을 느끼는' 수동의 의미

It was **exciting** news.　　　　I was **excited** about the news.
The movie was **boring**.　　　　I was **bored** in math class.

EXERCISE

A Choose the correct one for each sentence.

1 The people (waiting, waited) for the bus for over an hour became angry.

2 The (crying, cried) baby drew everybody's attention to her.

3 The detective found the (stealing, stolen) money inside the wall.

4 This warm weather is quite (pleased, pleasing) to us.

5 John seems (depressing, depressed) after his summer vacation.

6 Amy stepped on the (breaking, broken) glass on the floor.

B Correct the underlined part.

1 After a long meeting, everybody became <u>exhausting</u>. ➝ _____

2 Once you meet him, you will find him so <u>bored</u>. ➝ _____

3 I was <u>disappointing</u> to see the final episode of the drama. ➝ _____

4 We were quite <u>satisfying</u> with the results. ➝ _____

5 I did not mean to keep you <u>waited</u> for so long. ➝ _____

6 The view from the window of our room was <u>amazed</u>. ➝ _____

C Fill in the blank using the given word.

1 Sonia could hear Jane _____ in the bathroom. (cry)

2 My family watched my father _____ the marathon. (finish)

3 We had better get the heater _____ before winter comes. (repair)

4 We could hear the band _____ from five blocks away. (play)

5 I would like to have this gift _____ nicely. (wrap)

6 I have to get this work _____ today. (do)

D Complete the sentence using the given words.

1 술 취한 남자가 벤치에 누워 있었다. (drink)

  ➝ A _____ was lying on the bench.

2 바람이 깨진 창문을 통해 안으로 불어오고 있었다. (break)

  ➝ The wind was blowing inside through the _____.

3 나는 오늘 아침 일찍 그가 집을 떠나는 소리를 들었다. (hear, leave)

  ➝ I _____ the house early this morning.

4 이 바지를 내일까지 다림질 해 주길 바랍니다. (have, iron)

  ➝ I would like to _____ these pants _____ by tomorrow.

Participle Clauses 분사구문

Ⓐ 분사구문

「접속사 + 주어 + 동사」의 부
사절에서 ① 접속사를 생략
② 부사절과 주절의 주어가
같으면 생략 ③ 동사를 현재
분사 '동사원형-ing'로 바꾸
어 분사구로 쓸 수 있다.

Ⓐ Participle Clauses

When[①] she[②] watches[③] TV, she forgets everything around her.
→ **Watching** TV, she forgets everything around her.

e.g. As soon as the man saw the fire in the house, he called 911.
→ **Seeing** the fire in the house, the man called 911.

Ⓑ Meanings of Participle Clauses

Putting down the magazine, he went out.
(= After he put down the magazine, he went out.)

- **Time** (after, when, while, as, since)
  Finishing her homework, Mary had dinner. (= After she finished . . .)
- **Cause** (because, since, as)
  Not getting a reply, I emailed her again. (= Because I did not get . . .)
- **Condition** (if)
  Turning to the right, you will see the building. (= If you turn . . .)
- **Concession** (though, although)
  Being rich, he is very thrifty. (= Though he is . . .)
- **Accompanying actions** (and, as, with, while)
  Using a laptop, he ate dinner. (= While he was using . . .)

Ⓒ 완료형 분사구문

「having + p.p.」형태로, 부
사절의 내용이 주절의 내용
보다 이전에 일어난 일을 나
타낼 때 쓴다.

Ⓒ Perfect Participle Clauses

Having heard the news, I still cannot believe it.
(= Although I heard the news, I still cannot believe it.)

e.g. **Not having seen** snow before, they were very excited.
(= As they had not seen snow before, . . .)

Ⓓ 수동 분사구문

「(Being +) p.p. / (Having
been +) p.p.」형태로, Being
이나 Having been은 생략할
수 있다.

Ⓓ Participle Clauses in the Passive Voice

(Being) Cleaned every week, the house looks great.
(= As it is cleaned every week, the house looks great.)
(Having been) Born in Canada, she speaks English fluently.
(= Because she was born in Canada, she speaks English fluently.)

EXERCISE

A Correct the underlined part.

1 <u>Sent</u> text messages, she was talking on the phone. → _____

2 <u>Cut</u> the dead flowers, she was working in the garden. → _____

3 <u>Have</u> felt a tremor, we escaped from the building. → _____

4 <u>Has</u> seen a horrible scene, the girl ran out of the movie theater.

→ _____

B Rewrite the sentence with the proper conjunction.

1 Not having an umbrella, I got soaked by the rain.

→ _____ , I got soaked by the rain.

2 Intending to do a certain thing, he tries to do it perfectly.

→ _____ , he tries to do it perfectly.

3 Being invited to his birthday party, she did not go.

→ _____ , she did not go.

4 Walking slowly, we will not arrive on time.

→ _____ , we will not arrive on time.

C Circle the words that can be omitted and translate the underlined part.

1 <u>Being exhausted by a lack of sleep</u>, he dozed off in class.

→ _____

2 <u>Being given an opportunity</u>, he will show how talented he is.

→ _____

3 <u>Having been fired by his company</u>, he got a job offer by a rival company.

→ _____

4 <u>Having been written many decades ago</u>, the book is still popular.

→ _____

D Complete the sentence using the given words.

1 사람들 앞에서 말할 때 그는 전혀 긴장하지 않았다. (speak, in front of)

→ _____ , he was not nervous at all.

2 한 달 동안 공부를 했기 때문에 그는 시험을 쉽게 통과했다. (study)

→ _____ for a month, he passed the test easily.

3 그녀의 전화번호를 알고는 있지만 내가 먼저 그녀에게 전화하지는 않겠다. (know)

→ _____ her phone number, I will not call her first.

Various Participle Clauses 다양한 분사구문들

A Absolute Participle Clauses

Ⓐ 독립분사구문
부사절의 주어와 주절의 주
어가 다를 때는 분사 앞에 주
어를 써 준다.

| *It* **being** nice and warm, we went for a walk.
| (= As it was nice and warm, we went for a walk.)

e.g. *Our work* **(being) finished**, we said goodbye and left.
　　　 (= When our work was finished, . . .)
　　　 The sun **having** set, they made a fire.
　　　 (= After the sun had set, . . .)

cf. 비인칭 독립분사구문:
부사절의 주어가 we,
you, they, people(일반
인)일 경우, 주절의 주어
와 다를지라도 주어를 생
략하고 관용어처럼 쓴다.

cf. **Impersonal Absolute Participle Clauses**
Generally speaking, women live longer than men.
Judging from the title, the movie will be quite funny.
Considering her age, she is very open-minded.

Generally speaking 일반적으로 말해서	Compared with ~와 비교하면
Considering ~을 고려하면	Speaking of ~에 대해 말하자면
Judging from ~로 판단하건대	Talking of ~ 말인데
Strictly speaking 엄격히 말하면	Frankly speaking 솔직히 말해서

B Participle Clauses with Conjunctions

Ⓑ 접속사가 있는 분사구문
분사구문의 뜻을 명확하게
하기 위해 접속사를 분사 앞
에 남겨두기도 한다.

| *Since* **having learned** baking, I can bake a cheesecake.
| (= Since I learned baking, I can bake a cheesecake.)

e.g. *Though* **having** many things to do, he fell asleep.
　　　 (= Though he had many things to do, . . .)

Ⓒ with + 명사 + 분사
'~한 채로, ~하고서'라는 뜻
으로, 보통 부대상황을 나타
내는 경우가 많다. 명사와 분
사가 능동의 관계이면 현재
분사를, 수동의 관계이면 과
거분사를 쓴다.

C with + Noun + Participle

| He walked in the park *with his dog* **following** him.

e.g. She listened to his story quietly *with her eyes* **closed**.
　　　 The boy could not see anything *with his glasses* **broken**.

EXERCISE

A Rewrite the sentence with the adverb clause.

1 It being cold, the children stayed at home.

→ _____, the children stayed at home.

2 You doing me a favor, I will buy you lunch.

→ _____, I will buy you lunch.

3 When playing the piano, she hummed.

→ _____, she hummed.

4 Taeho having lived in America for years, English is still not easy for him.

→ _____, English is still not easy for him.

B Translate the underlined part into Korean.

1 Talking of travel, Max has a lot of information about it. → _____

2 Judging from his skin tone, he does not look healthy. → _____

3 Frankly speaking, I do not believe she is telling the truth.

→ _____

4 Considering that he is young, he can play the piano exceptionally well.

→ _____

C Correct the underlined part.

1 It was a Sunday morning with a cool breeze blown. → _____

2 The kids got shots with their eyes closing tight. → _____

3 With night fallen, the temperature suddenly dropped. → _____

4 He kept talking to me with his mouth stuffing with pizza.

→ _____

D Complete the sentence using the given words.

1 날씨가 허락한다면 우리는 내일 발야구를 할 것이다. (permit)

→ _____, we will play kickball tomorrow.

2 엄격히 말하면 이 책은 네 것이 아니라 내 것이다. 내가 이것을 샀다. (strict, speak)

→ _____, this book is mine, not yours. I bought it.

3 그녀의 여동생과 비교하면 Jenny는 더 활동적이다. (compare)

→ _____, Jenny is more active.

4 그녀는 손가락으로 탁자를 두드리면서 그녀의 차례를 기다리고 있었다. (her fingers, drum)

→ She was waiting for her turn _____ on the table.

WRITING CONNECTION

1 Grammar Check-up

A Choose the correct one.

1 I still remember the _____ moment that I tripped on a stone and fell down.
ⓐ embarrass   ⓑ embarrassing   ⓒ embarrassed   ⓓ to embarrass

2 Students should bring a _____ lunch with a drink on the tour.
ⓐ pack   ⓑ packing   ⓒ packed   ⓓ to pack

3 The _____ artwork from the students will be exhibited soon.
ⓐ collect   ⓑ collecting   ⓒ collected   ⓓ to collect

4 They found the _____ treasure.
ⓐ steal   ⓑ stolen   ⓒ stealing   ⓓ was stolen

5 The _____ news made everybody happy.
ⓐ exciting   ⓑ excited   ⓒ excite   ⓓ being excited

6 It looks dangerous to leave the _____ glass on the floor like that.
ⓐ breaking   ⓑ broken   ⓒ break   ⓓ being broken

B Circle the inappropriate one between ⓐ and ⓑ. Then correct it.

1 Her best friend <u>being</u> away, she felt <u>boring</u>.   _____
              ⓐ   ⓑ

2 <u>Cleaning</u> the floor, <u>exhausting</u> Cinderella fell asleep.   _____
   ⓐ   ⓑ

3 <u>Considered</u> that he is only 8 years old, he can be <u>regarded</u> as a genius.
   ⓐ   ⓑ   _____

4 <u>Put</u> his new suit on, he left for work <u>early</u> in the morning.   _____
   ⓐ   ⓑ

5 <u>Broadcasting</u> throughout the nation, the news made the politician
     ⓐ
<u>frustrated</u>.   _____
 ⓑ

2 Phrases to Sentences

A Complete the sentence by referring to the Korean translation.

1 떨어진 팝콘은 바닥을 지저분하게 만들었다. (fall)

→ The _____ made the floor messy.

2 약 5백만의 사람들이 그 경기를 보면서 TV 앞에 붙어 있었다. (watch, match)

→ About 5 million people were glued to the TV, _____.

3 비가 오기 시작해서 우리는 행사를 종료해야만 했다. (rain, start)

→ _____ to fall, we had to end the event.

4 그 일을 완료한 후에 우리는 식사를 하러 나갔다. (complete)

→ _____, we went out to eat.

5 자신의 머리가 울타리에 끼여서 그는 도움을 기다려야만 했다. (head, stick)

→ _____ in the fence, he had to wait for help.

6 해변을 걸어 내려가면서 나는 훨씬 더 편안해졌다. (walk, beach)

→ _____, I felt much more relaxed.

B Underline the error and rewrite the sentence.

1 Finished cleaning the bathroom, she sat on the sofa to rest.

→ _____

2 Judged from the dark circles on his face, he must be under lots of stress.

→ _____

3 Her mom being arrived, she looked happy and cheerful.

→ _____

4 Having nominated for the award, the actor did not show up.

→ _____

5 I could not focus on the test with the teacher watch over my shoulder.

→ _____

6 Having held the flashlight steadily, Jennifer slowly entered the building.

→ _____

3 Sentence Practice

A Translate the Korean into English using the given words.

1 a. 그 지루한 연설은 청중들을 졸리게 만들었다. (bore, speech)

→ _____ made the audience sleepy.

b. 그 힘든 야간 근무는 간호사들을 지치게 만들었다. (tire, night shift, exhaust)

→ _____

2 a. 솔직히 말해서 그 영화는 그다지 인상적이지 않았다. (frank, speak)

→ _____, the movie was not that impressive.

b. 엄격히 말하면 그의 보고서는 그다지 훌륭하지 않았다. (report, great)

→ _____

3 a. 구조된 후에, 그 부상당한 남자는 병원으로 보내졌다. (rescue, wound)

→ _____ was taken to the hospital.

b. 치료를 받은 후에, 그 소년은 그의 부모에게 보내졌다. (treat, take)

→ _____

4 a. 낮은 급여에 낙담하여 나는 마침내 일을 그만두기로 결정했다. (discourage, the low pay)

→ _____, I finally decided to quit my job.

b. 응원에 용기를 받아 그 팀은 결승에서 최선을 다했다. (encourage, cheers, the finals)

→ _____

B Unscramble the words to make a sentence.

1 Paul은 자신의 권투 글러브를 좋아해서 그것을 침대에서조차 끼었다.

(even, them, his, Paul, boxing gloves, in bed, loving, wore)

→ _____

2 한국에서 서기 751년에 출판되었으므로, 그 문서는 엄청나게 가치가 있다. (having been, in Korea, in 751 A.D., the document, valuable, is, published, extremely)

→ _____

3 경기장의 거의 모든 사람이 선수들을 응원하며 일어섰다.

(in the stadium, stood, the players, almost, cheering for, everyone)

→ _____

4 생각에 빠져서 Daniel은 Kelly가 자신을 부르는 것을 듣지 못했다.

(Daniel, him, thought, lost, hear, Kelly, did not, in, calling)

→ _____

ACTUAL TEST

[1-3] 빈칸에 들어갈 말로 알맞은 것을 고르시오.

1

> Most goods _____ in China are exported to countries around the world.

① make   ② makes

③ made   ④ having making

⑤ are made

2

> The _____ baby is drawing everybody's attention on the plane.

① cry   ② crying

③ cried   ④ being cried

⑤ being crying

3

> Suji went to school with her homework _____ at home.

① leaving   ② leaves   ③ be left

④ leave   ⑤ left

[4-5] 어법상 어색한 것을 고르시오.

4

> Not having saw the weather report, I did
> ①   ②   ③
> not know it would be raining hard today.
>   ④   ⑤

5

> He stopping the car, the police officer
> ①   ②
> wanted to see the man's driver's license.
> ③   ④   ⑤

[6-7] 분사구문으로 알맞게 바꾼 것을 고르시오.

6

> Though I understand why you are upset, I still cannot allow you to break the rules.

① I understood why you are upset

② Having understood why you are upset

③ Understanding why you are upset

④ Understood why you are upset

⑤ Being understood why you are upset

7

> As it was written in a hurry, the essay has a lot of typos.

① Being writing in a hurry

② Having been written in a hurry

③ As being written in a hurry

④ The essay having written in a hurry

⑤ As having written in a hurry

8 괄호 안에 알맞은 것끼리 짝 지어진 것은?

> • The child fell and got a (broking / broken) arm.
> • Do not give your child (uncooking / uncooked) food.
> • He has a (winning / winned) mindset.

① broking – uncooking – winning

② broking – uncooking – winned

③ broken – uncooking – winning

④ broken – uncooked – winning

⑤ broken – uncooked – winned

9

- The police _____(A)_____ the case are looking for the suspect.
- My uncle decided to buy a _____(B)_____ car to save money.

(A)	(B)
① investigated	– used
② investigating	– used
③ investigated	– using
④ investigating	– using
⑤ investigating	– use

10

- All things _____(A)_____ , she is a pretty talented musician.
- _____(B)_____ no idea, I just remained silent.

(A)	(B)
① considering	– Had
② considering	– Having
③ considered	– Had
④ considered	– Having
⑤ considered	– Have

[11-12] 밑줄 친 부분이 어법상 어색한 것을 고르시오.

11
① When I tried *baduk*, I found it <u>interesting</u>.
② This rainy weather is really <u>depressing</u>.
③ Everybody was <u>thrilling</u> to hear her singing.
④ Due to the noisy people, I was <u>annoyed</u>.
⑤ Doing the same work over and over is really <u>tiring</u>.

12
① <u>Judging</u> from his looks, he was in a bad mood.
② With my eyes <u>closing</u>, I could only hear their footsteps.
③ Strictly <u>speaking</u>, this article is not worth reading.
④ <u>Considering</u> everything, it was not a bad trip.
⑤ <u>Speaking</u> of food, what would you like to order?

13 의미상 빈칸에 들어갈 수 있는 말을 모두 고르면?

_____ his way of speaking, I assume he is from abroad.

① Judging from
② Considering
③ Compared with
④ Strictly speaking
⑤ Generally speaking

14 분사의 쓰임이 다른 것은?
① Sue said hello to me with a <u>smiling</u> face.
② Minhee left the front door <u>unlocked</u>.
③ I heard him <u>singing</u> loudly.
④ That rumor made me <u>surprised</u>.
⑤ Tom will get the work <u>done</u> by tomorrow.

15 빈칸에 들어갈 단어 write의 형태가 다른 하나는?
① These phrases are mainly used in _____ texts.
② _____ his first diary entry, Brian felt proud of himself.
③ Marie instantly noticed the sign _____ in red letters.
④ _____ in a hurry, these articles contain spelling errors.
⑤ _____ in plain English, all the students could understand it.

16 밑줄 친 부분과 바꿔 쓸 수 있는 것을 <u>모두</u> 고르면?

> <u>Though they were printed</u> a long time ago, the books do not look that old.

① Printed ② Had printed
③ Being printed ④ Having printed
⑤ Having been printed

17 우리말을 영어로 옮긴 것 중 알맞지 <u>않은</u> 것은?

> He proudly walked down the aisle (자신의 트로피를 손에 든 채로).

① his trophy being in his hand
② his trophy was in his hand
③ with his trophy in his hand
④ holding his trophy in his hand
⑤ as he held his trophy in his hand

18 밑줄 친 부분을 바꿔 쓴 것 중 알맞지 <u>않은</u> 것은?
① <u>Worried about her son's condition</u>, she made a call to school.
 (= Because she was worried about her son's condition,)
② <u>Having finished her training</u>, she packed her bag.
 (= After she had finished her training,)
③ <u>Having read the manual twice</u>, he still could not turn the light on.
 (= Although he had read the manual twice,)
④ <u>Coming back from his business trip</u>, he fell asleep on the couch.
 (= As soon as he came back from his business trip,)
⑤ <u>Packing her things</u>, she listened to the radio.
 (= Though she packed her things,)

[19-20] 어법상 어색한 문장을 고르시오.

19 ① What makes you excited?
② The clerk left him unattending.
③ I am sorry to have kept you waiting.
④ I would like to have it delivered to my place.
⑤ Please keep me updated if anything new comes up.

20 ① Having finished my dinner, I went into the study.
② Having worked all day, Leslie decided to stay home.
③ Having confused by the assignment, I emailed my teacher.
④ Having met the neighbors, she liked the new neighborhood.
⑤ Having spoken to the professor, he finally decided on his career.

21 우리말을 영어로 알맞게 옮기지 <u>못한</u> 것은?
① 선생님이 결근하셔서 오늘 우리 수업은 취소되었다.
 → The teacher being absent, our class was canceled today.
② 흐린 밤이어서 우리는 달을 볼 수 없었다.
 → Being a cloudy night, we could not see the moon.
③ 반대가 없어서 논의는 결론에 도달했다.
 → There being no objections, the discussion came to a conclusion.
④ 파티가 끝나서 손님들은 떠나기 시작했다.
 → The party being over, the guests began to leave.
⑤ 의사가 도착하자 환자들은 그를 맞이했다.
 → The doctor arriving, the patients greeted him.

[22-23] 다음을 읽고, 물음에 답하시오.

A dog's tail position serves as a social signal. In other words, it can be considered a sort of emotional meter. A vertical tail is a warning, which means, "I'm the boss around here. Back off!" A middle height suggests the dog is relaxed. <u>If the tail is held horizontally, the dog is alert.</u> As the tail position drops lower, it is a sign the dog is becoming worried. The tail (A) (tuck) under the body is a sign of fear, meaning, "Please don't hurt me." Remember that a dog (B) (wag) its tail is not always happy and friendly.   * tuck: 끼워 넣다, 접다

22 밑줄 친 문장을 분사구문으로 고쳐 쓰시오.

→ _____

_____

23 (A), (B)에 주어진 단어를 알맞은 형태로 쓰시오.
(A) _____ (B) _____

[24-25] 다음 문장을 분사구문을 이용하여 다시 쓰시오.

24
As he had been interrupted several times, he was annoyed.

→ _____

_____

25
As Cathy has lived in Korea for 10 years, her Korean is very natural.

→ _____

_____

[26-28] 우리말에 맞게 주어진 단어를 바르게 배열하여 문장을 쓰시오.

26
우리는 귀신이 나오는 집에 겁을 먹었다.
(the, were, terrified, by, house, we, haunted)

→ _____

27
이틀 동안 잠을 못 자서 그녀는 집중할 수가 없었다.
(for, she, not, slept, concentrate, was not, to, able, two days, having)

→ _____

_____

28
엄격히 말하면 토마토는 과일이 아니라 채소이다.
(not, but, fruits, strictly, are, speaking, vegetables, tomatoes)

→ _____

_____

🎯 CHALLENGE!

Write your own answer to the question.

01 Which class is exciting or boring to you?

_____

_____

02 While studying, do you usually do something else at the same time?

_____

_____

CHAPTER

08

Comparisons
비교

UNIT 01

Comparisons Using the Positive Degree
원급을 이용한 비교

UNIT 02

Comparisons Using Comparatives
비교급을 이용한 비교

UNIT 03

Comparisons Using Superlatives
최상급을 이용한 비교

UNIT 01

Comparisons Using the Positive Degree 원급을 이용한 비교

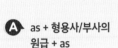

A as + 형용사/부사의 원급 + as
…만큼 ~한

A as . . . as

| The brown sofa is **as comfortable as** the gray one.
| I play the guitar **as well as** my friend John.

◆ **as much/many . . . as**
Jessica has **as many friends as** I do.
My little brother saves **as much money as** I do.

B not as + 원급 + as
…만큼 ~하지 않은

B not as . . . as

| This test is **not as difficult as** the last one.

e.g. The living room is **not as messy as** my bedroom.
(= My bedroom is messier than the living room.)
The movie is **not as good as** the book.
(= The book is better than the movie.)

C 배수사 + as + 원급 + as
…보다 몇 배 더 ~한
(= 배수사 + 비교급 + than)

C Multiplicative + as . . . as

| This box is **three times as heavy as** that one.

e.g. The water in the middle is **twice as deep as** the water on the edges.
(= The water in the middle is two times deeper than the water on the edges.)
This backpack is **three times as expensive as** that one.
(= This backpack is three times more expensive than that one.)

D as + 원급 + as possible
가능한 한 ~하게
(= as + 원급 + as + 주어 + can (could))

D as . . . as possible

| To prevent the flu, wash your hands **as often as possible**.

◆ **as . . . as possible (= as . . . as + S + can (could))**
I will give you a call **as soon as possible**.
= as soon as I can
They are working <u>**as hard as possible**</u> to meet the deadline.
= as hard as they can

EXERCISE

A Choose the correct one for each sentence.

1 This book is as (thick, thickly) as the Bible.

2 He donated as much money (as, so) his parents did.

3 I studied for the exam as (hard, hardly) as you did.

4 The weather this year is not (as, than) bad as last year.

5 *Toy Story 2* was (as not, not as) funny as the first one.

B Correct the underlined part.

1 Karen is <u>twice as older as</u> your mother.　　　　→ _____

2 The plane is <u>three times so fast as</u> the train.　　→ _____

3 My uncle eats <u>three times as more as</u> I do.　　　→ _____

4 As the thief saw the police, he ran <u>as faster as possible</u>. → _____

5 Please let me know whether you can come or not <u>as possible as soon</u>.

　　　　　　　　　　　　　　　　　　　　　　　　→ _____

C Fill in the blank so that the two sentences have the same meaning.

1 Please call me as soon as you can.

= Please call me _____ .

2 Peter is fifteen years old. Brian is fifteen years old.

= Peter is _____ Brian.

3 This snake is 120 cm long. That snake is 40 cm long.

= This snake is _____ as that one.

4 His headphones are more expensive than mine.

= My headphones are not _____ his.

D Complete the sentence using the given words.

1 어머니는 아버지만큼 바쁘시다. (busy)

→ My mother is _____ my father.

2 Michael은 지난번만큼 경기를 잘하지 못했다. (play, well)

→ Michael _____ he did last time.

3 가능한 한 자주 따뜻한 물을 마시려고 노력하세요. (warm water, often, possible)

→ Try to drink _____ .

4 국립 도서관은 그 도서관보다 세 배 많은 책을 보유하고 있다. (have)

→ The national library _____ as the library.

UNIT 02

Comparisons Using Comparatives 비교급을 이용한 비교

A 비교급 + than
…보다 더 ~한

A Comparative + than

Josh is **taller than** his father.
The roller coaster is **more exciting than** the Ferris wheel.

+ **Comparative forms**
  • adjective/adverb -er
    The weather today is **colder than** it was yesterday.
  • more + adjective/adverb
    I am **more interested** in music **than** sports.

cf. 비교급을 강조할 때 very 는 쓰지 않는다.

cf. **even, much, far, still, a lot + Comparative**
    I think history is *much* **more difficult than** math.

+ **less . . . than (= not as . . . as)**
  The singer is **less popular than** she was two years ago.
  = The singer **is not as popular as** she was two years ago.

B the + 비교급,
the + 비교급
…하면 할수록 더 ~한

B The + Comparative, the + Comparative

I **The more** I know about you, **the more** I like you.

e.g. **The sooner** you begin, **the sooner** you will finish.
    The harder you exercise, **the healthier** you become.

C 비교급 and 비교급
「become/get/grow + 비교급 and 비교급」 형태로 많이 쓰이며, '점점 더 ~하게 되다' 라는 뜻이다.

C Comparative and Comparative

It was getting **darker and darker** outside.
As time went on, he grew **more and more tired**.

e.g. The snowball became **bigger and bigger**.
    Mina's English became **more and more fluent**.

Comparatives using *to*
• superior to ~보다 나은   • inferior to ~보다 못한
• senior to ~보다 나이가 많은   • junior to ~보다 나이가 적은
Mike is **superior to** his classmates in many ways.
This computer is much **inferior to** the latest computer.

EXERCISE   A   Choose the correct one for each sentence.

1   This box is (heavier, more heavy) than that one.

2   David understands the material in the course more easily (to, than) her.

3   The test is (less difficult, less more difficult) than I expected.

4   I am (much, very) taller than my sister.

5   The new version of this game is superior (to, than) the old one.

6   James is (popularer, more popular) in the class than Tommy.

B   Translate the English into Korean.

1   The busier you are, the faster time goes by.

→ _____

2   The kinder you are, the happier people are.

→ _____

3   The colder the weather gets, the fewer children there are on the playground.

→ _____

C   Correct the underlined part.

1   After midnight, the pain got worse and worst.   → _____

2   If you keep doing yoga, you will become more flexible and flexible.

→ _____

3   I cannot stand that noise. It is growing more loud and more loud.

→ _____

4   As the contest approached, he grew more and most nervous.

→ _____

D   Complete the sentence using the given words.

1   시험이 지난번 시험보다 더 쉬웠다. (easy)

→ The exam _____ the last one.

2   중학교에 들어간 후, 그녀는 점점 더 활동적이 되었다. (active)

→ After she entered middle school, she became _____.

3   더 많이 연습하면 할수록 너는 더 잘하게 될 것이다. (much, good)

→ _____ you practice, _____ you will be.

4   이 식당의 종업원들이 저 식당의 종업원들보다 훨씬 더 친절하다. (much, friendly)

→ The waiters in this restaurant are _____ those in that restaurant.

Comparisons   **109**

Comparisons Using Superlatives 최상급을 이용한 비교

Ⓐ the + Superlative

She is **the smartest** (one) *of* all the students.
The city hall is **the most modern** building *in* the city.

Ⓐ the + 최상급
(+ in (of) . . .)
(… 중에서) 가장 ~한

◆ **Superlative forms**
  • adjective/adverb -est
    Russia is **the biggest** country in the world.
  • most + adjective/adverb
    Billy is **the most earnest** student *of* all my classmates.
    What is **the least expensive** way to travel in Japan?

cf. 1 **much, by far + the + Superlative**
    Waikiki is *by far* **the most beautiful** beach.

cf. 2 **the + Comparative** (+ of the two)
    This salad is **the cheaper** of the two. (○)
    This salad is the cheapest of the two. (×)

◆ **the + Superlative + Singular noun + (that) + S + have ever p.p.**
    The Exorcist is **the scariest film** (that) I have ever seen.

Ⓑ one of the + Superlative + Plural Noun

Ⓑ one of the + 최상급
+ 복수명사
가장 ~한 … 중의 하나

l That was **one of the happiest moments** in my life.

e.g. **One of the most generous people** in my family is my uncle.

Ⓒ Additional Superlatives

Ⓒ 원급과 비교급을 이용한
최상급 표현

The soup was **the most delicious of all the food.**
= The soup was **more delicious than any other food.**
= **No (other) food was more delicious than** the soup.
= **No (other) food was as delicious as** the soup.

Drop *the* in Superlatives

1. Tom is **happiest** when he is with his puppy. <동일인(동일물)을 다른
                                                      상황에서 비교할 경우>
2. Do *your* **best**. <최상급 앞에 소유격이 있는 경우>
3. He practices (the) **hardest** on his team. <부사의 최상급>

EXERCISE

A Choose the correct one for each sentence.

1 This phone is the (late, latest) model.

2 Jessica is the (prettier, prettiest) of the two.

3 I think physics is the (difficultest, most difficult) subject.

4 Mr. Kim offered the (better, best) swimming class I have ever taken.

5 James is (by far, more) the smartest boy at my school.

B Correct the underlined part.

1 Richard is one of the richest man in the world. → _____

2 Sally is one of most beautiful women in this town.

→ _____

3 That was one of the most impressive documentary film.

→ _____

4 One of the better ways to manage stress is to exercise regularly.

→ _____

C Fill in the blanks so that all the sentences have the same meaning.

1 | This is the best pizza I have ever had. |

= This is better than _____ I have ever had.

= _____ other pizza is _____ than this.

= _____ other pizza is as _____ as this.

2 | I am the luckiest student at the school. |

= I am _____ at the school.

= _____ other student is _____ I am at the school.

= _____ other student is _____ lucky _____ I am at the school.

D Complete the sentence using the given words.

1 Cory가 세계에서 가장 못생긴 개 중의 하나로 선발되었다. (ugly)

→ Cory was selected as _____ in the world.

2 우리 반에서 아무도 Jerry만큼 수학 문제를 빨리 풀 수 있는 학생은 없다. (fast)

→ _____ in my class can solve math problems _____

Jerry.

3 이것은 내가 본 것 중 가장 기억에 남는 장면이다. (memorable, scene)

→ This is _____.

WRITING CONNECTION

 1 Grammar Check-up

A Choose the correct one.

1 Babies are not as _____ as adults.
ⓐ patient   ⓑ patienter   ⓒ more patient   ⓓ most patient

2 I think Tina's sister is _____ than her.
ⓐ friendly   ⓑ friendlier   ⓒ more friendly   ⓓ the friendliest

3 That is the _____ supermarket in this town.
ⓐ bigger   ⓑ biggest   ⓒ even big   ⓓ as big as

4 The chocolate ice cream is _____ than the vanilla ice cream.
ⓐ good   ⓑ more good   ⓒ better   ⓓ best

5 The purple onions taste _____ sweeter than the white ones.
ⓐ much   ⓑ very   ⓒ so   ⓓ quite

6 Ethan is the most talkative person I _____.
ⓐ meet ever   ⓑ met ever   ⓒ have ever met   ⓓ had ever met

B Circle the inappropriate one between ⓐ and ⓑ. Then correct it.

1 Please return my call as soon than possible.   _____
                                              ⓐ   ⓑ

2 He is one of the funniest comedian in England.   _____
               ⓐ   ⓑ

3 The richer she gets, the generous she becomes.   _____
          ⓐ   ⓑ

4 He is stronger than you, but he is not as fastest as you.   _____
         ⓐ   ⓑ

5 The stadium is three times older as the school gym.   _____
            ⓐ   ⓑ

6 After the teacher's comment, the students grew quietly than ever.   _____
                                             ⓐ   ⓑ

2 Phrases to Sentences

A Complete the sentence by referring to the Korean translation.

1 그는 그의 친구들 중에서 다른 어떤 사람보다 더 부지런하다.

→ He is more diligent _____ among his friends.

2 새로운 시스템은 예전 시스템만큼 효율적이지 않다. (efficient)

→ The new system is not _____ the old one.

3 다른 어떤 아기도 이 마을에서 Bobby보다 더 귀엽지 않다. (cute)

→ _____ Bobby in this village.

4 Scott은 예전보다 훨씬 더 느긋해 보였다. (much, relaxed)

→ Scott looked _____ than before.

5 Ms. Camper는 내가 만났던 가장 예의 바른 사람 중 하나이다. (polite)

→ Ms. Camper is _____ I have ever met.

6 연설이 길어질수록 청중들은 더 지루해진다. (bored)

→ The _____ the speech takes, _____ the audience gets.

B Underline the error and rewrite the sentence.

1 Today is the most happy day of my life.

→ _____

2 The least you spend, the more you save.

→ _____

3 My brother is superior than me in many ways.

→ _____

4 The climate of this region is hotter than those of the southern region.

→ _____

5 Andy worked twice as hardly as others.

→ _____

6 Online learning is getting more or more popular around the world.

→ _____

3 Sentence Practice

A Translate the Korean into English using the given words.

1 a. 뉴욕은 보스턴보다 훨씬 더 크다. (much, big)

→ New York is _____ Boston.

b. 토론토는 서울보다 훨씬 더 춥다. (Toronto, much, cold)

→ _____

2 a. 시애틀로의 여행은 예전만큼 오래 걸리지 않았다. (long, as)

→ The journey to Seattle did not take _____ before.

b. 파리로의 여행은 예전만큼 지루하지 않았다. (boring)

→ _____

3 a. 그들이 더 높이 올라갈수록 더 추워졌다. (high, cold)

→ _____ they climbed, _____ it got.

b. 더 열심히 공부할수록 너는 더 많이 배우게 될 것이다. (hard, learn)

→ _____

4 a. 이것은 가게에서 가장 비싼 물건들 중 하나이다. (expensive)

→ This is one of _____ items in the store.

b. 이것은 가게에서 가장 최신형 휴대 전화 중 하나이다. (new, cell phone)

→ _____

B Unscramble the words to make a sentence.

1 내 표는 네 것만큼 돈이 많이 들지 않았다. (as, as, yours, did not, my ticket, cost, much)

→ _____

2 그 경기는 점점 더 흥미로워졌다. (the game, more, exciting, more, became, and)

→ _____

3 그 행성은 태양보다 세 배 더 크다. (big, three times, the sun, as, is, as, the planet)

→ _____

4 이것은 지금까지 내가 본 최고의 영화 중 하나이다. (movies, have, best, the, ever, of, is, this, one, seen, I)

→ _____

ACTUAL TEST

> Answers **p. 20**

[1-3] 빈칸에 들어갈 수 <u>없는</u> 말을 고르시오.

1
> This model is _____ than that one.

① newer   ② better
③ nicer   ④ as cheap as
⑤ more expensive

2
> Justin runs _____ faster than Tommy.

① even   ② a lot   ③ far
④ much   ⑤ very

3
> Sam is the _____ boy in the class.

① smartest   ② tallest
③ most diligent   ④ most bravest
⑤ most popular

4 나머지 넷과 의미가 <u>다른</u> 하나는?
① The elephant is the heaviest animal.
② Other animals are as heavy as the elephant.
③ No other animal is as heavy as the elephant.
④ The elephant is heavier than any other animal.
⑤ No other animal is heavier than the elephant.

[5-6] 빈칸에 들어갈 알맞은 말을 고르시오.

5
> This puppy is the youngest _____ all.

① to   ② in   ③ of
④ on   ⑤ from

6
> No subject is _____ for me than math.

① difficult   ② difficulter
③ difficultest   ④ more difficult
⑤ most difficult

[7-8] 어법상 <u>어색한</u> 문장을 고르시오.

7
① Bill collected as many coins as I did.
② She is the oldest person in her family.
③ Your computer is a lot faster than mine.
④ Liverpool F.C. did not play as well than Manchester United F.C.
⑤ This cake is ten times as delicious as that one.

8
① She is two years junior than me.
② The speed gets slower and slower.
③ It is the most expensive gift I have ever gotten.
④ Mt. Everest is the highest mountain in the world.
⑤ Traveling by plane is much quicker than traveling by car.

9 주어진 문장과 의미가 같은 것은?

> Korea is not as big as Russia.

① Russia is as big as Korea.
② Korea is less big than Russia.
③ Korea is bigger than Russia.
④ No other country is as big as Russia.
⑤ No other country is bigger than Korea.

[10-11] 밑줄 친 부분이 어법상 어색한 것을 고르시오.

10 ① Ann is <u>the youngest</u> child in her family.
② I think golf is <u>more boring than</u> football.
③ I am <u>the worst</u> soccer player on the team.
④ Their new apartment is <u>much smaller than</u> their old one.
⑤ Every time he goes to a buffet, he eats <u>as more as</u> possible.

11 ① The garden is not <u>as big as</u> I thought.
② The balloon got <u>bigger and bigger</u>.
③ <u>The deeper</u> you go, the colder it becomes.
④ Times Square is <u>one of the most popular place</u> in New York.
⑤ The movie is <u>much more interesting</u> than the book.

12 표의 내용과 일치하지 <u>않는</u> 것은?

	Anna	Jina	Patty
age	16	14	8

① Anna is the oldest of all.
② Patty is the youngest of all.
③ Jina is not as old as Patty.
④ Anna is twice as old as Patty.
⑤ Anna is two years older than Jina.

[13-15] 빈칸에 들어갈 말이 <u>다른</u> 하나를 고르시오.

13 ① My boss is senior _____ me by four years.
② A culture cannot be inferior _____ another culture.
③ The article was so difficult _____ me to understand.
④ This table is too similar _____ the one we are using now.
⑤ It is wrong to consider humans to be superior _____ animals.

14 ① My mom has brighter skin _____ I do.
② The animals looked as nervous _____ can be.
③ We did not enjoy the pasta as much _____ the salad.
④ Call me as soon _____ you find out anything about the test results.
⑤ My son can play the piano as elegantly _____ a professional pianist.

15 ① This is _____ worst musical I have seen this year.
② The less you eat, _____ lighter you will feel.
③ I am more interested in music _____ in sports.
④ One of _____ best features of this book is the vibrant colors.
⑤ My room is almost two times _____ size of yours.

16 두 문장의 의미가 같을 때 빈칸에 알맞은 것은?

> I want you to come as soon as you can.
> = I want you to come _____.

① as soon as possible
② as sooner as possible
③ not as soon as possible
④ sooner and sooner
⑤ sooner than you can

17 어법상 어색한 것은?

> Daniel is <u>more</u> <u>diligent</u> <u>than</u> <u>any</u> <u>other</u>
>   ①   ②   ③   ④
> <u>students</u>.
>   ⑤

18 우리말 해석이 알맞지 <u>않은</u> 것은?

① Which is the shortest way to the department store?
→ 백화점으로 가는 가장 짧은 길은 어느 것입니까?

② The actress is not as inexperienced as before.
→ 그 여배우는 예전만큼 미숙하지 않다.

③ Tom became more and more confident as he spoke.
→ Tom은 말을 하면서 자신감이 점점 떨어졌다.

④ My right leg is a bit longer than my left leg.
→ 나의 오른쪽 다리는 나의 왼쪽 다리보다 약간 더 길다.

⑤ The sooner you start the project, the sooner you can finish it.
→ 네가 그 프로젝트를 빨리 시작할수록 더 빨리 그것을 끝낼 수 있다.

[19-20] 빈칸에 들어갈 말이 알맞게 짝 지어진 것을 고르시오.

19
> · The movie was not ____(A)____ enjoyable as the book.
> · The math test was ____(B)____ easy as I had expected.

	(A)	(B)		(A)	(B)
①	such	as	②	so	such
③	than	as	④	as	as
⑤	as	to			

20
> · Our new house is larger ____(A)____ our previous house.
> · Laugh ____(B)____ much as possible.

	(A)	(B)		(A)	(B)
①	than	to	②	as	than
③	than	so	④	as	as
⑤	than	as			

21 두 문장의 의미가 같지 <u>않은</u> 것은?

① This work requires more than I can offer.
= I cannot offer all that this work requires.

② The zoo is twice as crowded as before.
= The zoo is two times less crowded than before.

③ This is the longest bridge in the country.
= No other bridge in the country is longer than this.

④ This dog is the fastest runner of all dogs.
= This dog runs faster than any other dog.

⑤ The more you stay up late, the more tired you will feel.
= If you stay up late more, you will feel more tired.

[22-23] 다음을 읽고, 물음에 답하시오.

I think (Ron은 가장 운이 좋은 소년들 중의 하나이다) in the world. Although his family is not rich, he has wonderful parents, loving grandparents, a cute little sister, and a supportive big brother. His dad is the (A) (good) cook I have ever known, and his brother plays the guitar (B) (well) than any other musician in town.

22 밑줄 친 우리말을 주어진 단어를 이용하여 영어로 쓰시오.

→ ______________________ (lucky)

23 (A), (B)에 주어진 단어를 알맞은 형태로 쓰시오.

(A) ____________ (B) ____________

[24-25] 우리말에 맞게 주어진 단어를 바르게 배열하여 문장을 쓰시오.

24 영어가 점점 더 중요해질 것이다.
(English, become, will, more, important, and, more)

→ ______________________

____

25 이 청바지가 저 청바지보다 두 배 더 비싸다.
(twice, are, as, as, those ones, expensive, these jeans)

→ ______________________

____

[26-27] 우리말 뜻을 참고하여 어법에 맞게 문장을 다시 쓰시오.

26 The dish that the chef recommended is not as more delicious as the other dishes.
(주방장이 추천한 요리는 다른 요리들만큼 맛있지 않다.)

→ ______________________

____

27 The dark it got, the cold it got.
(날이 어두워질수록 더 추워졌다.)

→ ______________________

28 두 문장이 같은 의미가 되도록 빈칸에 알맞은 말을 쓰시오.

Health is the most important thing in life.
= Nothing is ______________ in life than health.

CHALLENGE!

Write your own answer to the question.

01 What was the most exciting school event last semester?

____

____

02 What do you do better than anyone in your class?

____

____

Conjunctions
접속사

UNIT

01

Subordinating Conjunctions
종속접속사

UNIT

02

**Correlative Conjunctions /
Indirect Questions**
상관접속사 / 간접의문문

Subordinating Conjunctions 종속접속사

A 시간의 접속사

when, as, while, before, after, until (till), since, as soon as
• ~ 동안에
  - while + 주어 + 동사
  - during + 명사(구)
    전치사

A Time

When she becomes healthy again, she will come to school.
I was holding the baby **while** Mom was cooking.
As we got closer to Seoul, the traffic started getting bad.
I have not seen him **since** he transferred to another school.

B 이유의 접속사

because, as, since

B Reason

She was taken to the hospital **because** she had a high fever.
Since (As) it is hot and humid here, I cannot do anything.

C 조건의 접속사

if, unless, in case, once

C Condition

If it is sunny tomorrow, I will go to the botanical garden.
You will regret it **unless** you wear a coat.
(= You will regret it *if* you do *not* wear a coat.)

D 양보의 접속사

though, although, even though

- though + 주어 + 동사
- despite + 명사(구)
  전치사

D Concession

Though (Although) he was hungry, he gave his sandwich to the boy.
Even though the food was not delicious, we had a good time at the restaurant.

E 목적의 접속사

so that, in order that

E Purpose

She has three cats **so that (in order that)** she does not feel lonely.

Chapter 09

EXERCISE

A **Choose the correct one for each sentence.**

1 (As soon as, In case) he saw the police, he ran away.

2 (Even though, Since) he is not rich, he regularly donates money to charity.

3 I had difficulties with English grammar (when, if) I was a student.

4 The children read some stories (unless, before) they went to bed.

5 We enjoyed our vacation (although, as) the weather was terrible.

B **Choose the correct word in the box and fill in the blank.**

in case	since	so that	if

1 _____ you have any questions, please contact me.

2 Would you open the windows _____ some fresh air can come in?

3 Do your homework now _____ you do not have enough time later.

4 _____ he did not have to get up early, he stayed up until late at night.

C **Fill in the blank so that the two sentences have the same meaning.**

1 The salary was high, but Kate did not accept the job.

= Kate did not accept the job _____ the salary was high.

2 Unless we make a reservation, we will wait very long.

= _____ we _____ make a reservation, we will wait very long.

3 The bakery opens so late that I have to wait to get fresh bread.

= _____ the bakery opens very late, I have to wait to get fresh bread.

D **Complete the sentence using the given words.**

1 나는 오늘 아침 일어난 후부터 아무것도 먹지 않았다. (wake up)

→ I have not eaten anything _____ this morning.

2 우리가 좋은 결정을 내릴 수 있도록 너의 의견을 공유해라. (make a decision)

→ Share your opinion _____.

3 일단 네가 모든 사람을 알게 되면 너는 여기서 행복해질 것이다. (get to know)

→ You will be happy here _____ everyone else.

4 삼촌은 내 근처에 살지만 나는 그를 자주 만나지 않는다. (even, near)

→ _____, I do not often meet him.

Conjunctions **121**

UNIT 02

Correlative Conjunctions / Indirect Questions

상관접속사 / 간접의문문

A 상관접속사

두 개 이상의 단어가 짝을 이루어 접속사 역할을 하며, 접속사로 연결되는 문장 요소는 문법적으로 대등한 형태와 문장 성분이어야 한다.

A Correlative Conjunctions

He is **both** educated **and** humble.
Either take it **or** leave it.
Justin is **neither** energetic **nor** ambitious.
He visited **not only** Europe **but (also)** Asia.

both A and B A와 B 둘 다	either A or B A와 B 둘 중 하나
neither A nor B A도 B도 아닌	not only A but (also) B A뿐만 아니라 B도

cf. **not only A but (also) B (= B as well as A)**
Not only Alice **but (also)** Emily had food poisoning.
= Emily **as well as** Alice had food poisoning.

B 간접의문문

의문사가 이끄는 절이 문장의 주어, 보어, 목적어로 쓰이는 경우 간접의문문이라고 한다. 이때 의문사가 접속사 역할을 하며 명사절을 이끈다.
cf. 1 의문사가 간접의문문의 주어로 쓰일 때 「의문사 + 동사」의 형태가 된다.

B Indirect Questions

He asked **where Tom was**.
I don't know **if he is British**.

◆ **Wh-questions** (의문사가 있는 의문문) → 「Wh-words + S + V」
I don't know **why she left** so early.
(← I don't know. + Why did she leave so early?)
cf. 1 「Wh-words + V」
          S
The problem is **who will play** as the goalkeeper.
cf. 2 「Wh-words + do you think/believe/guess/suppose + S + V」
What do you *think* **she is** going to say?

cf. 2 주절의 동사가 think, believe, guess, suppose 등인 경우 의문사를 문장의 맨 앞에 둔다.

◆ **Yes/no-questions** (의문사가 없는 의문문) → 「whether 〔if〕 + S + V」
I wonder **whether 〔if〕 she has** a sibling (or not).
(← I wonder. + Does she have a sibling?)

Singular and Plural 상관접속사의 수일치
1. both A and B → 항상 복수 취급
   Both Ashley **and** I *collect* souvenirs from other countries.
2. either A or B, neither A nor B → B에 동사의 수일치
   Either you **or** he *has* to run an errand.
3. not only A but also B, B as well as A → B에 동사의 수일치
   Not only my parents **but also** my sister *prepares* the meal.
   = My sister **as well as** my parents *prepares* the meal.

EXERCISE

A Choose the correct one for each sentence.

1 I will (either, neither) go hiking or stay home.

2 Either you or your sister (have, has) to take care of the pets.

3 Both John (or, and) Peter participated in the project.

4 The musician's album was neither well known (or, nor) best selling.

5 The talk show was not only informative (and, but) also interesting.

B Correct the underlined part.

1 The boy told me why was he crying. → _____

2 Do you know what time does the bank open?

→ _____

3 Could you tell me your parents are joining us for dinner?

→ _____

4 If you have a dream or not is important.

→ _____

C Fill in the blank to combine the two sentences into one.

1 I was wondering. What did you buy for me?

→ I was wondering _____ for me.

2 Did you hear? How did he get in shape so quickly?

→ Did you hear _____ so quickly?

3 The receptionist asked Jake. Have you been here before?

→ The receptionist asked Jake _____.

4 The woman asked me. Do you have your passport with you?

→ The woman asked me _____.

D Complete the sentence using the given words.

1 나는 누가 차기 대통령이 될지 상상할 수가 없다. (become, next president)

→ I cannot imagine _____.

2 Sam도 Tom도 식당 음식에 대해서 불평하지 않았다. (nor, complain about)

→ _____ the cafeteria food.

3 오늘밤 객실 하나를 쓸 수 있는지 알고 싶다. (room, available)

→ I'd like to know _____ for tonight.

4 여름 캠프는 수영뿐 아니라 캠핑 강의도 제공한다. (not, swimming, camping instruction)

→ Summer camp offers _____.

WRITING CONNECTION

 Grammar Check-up

A Choose the correct one.

1 I recommend this camera _____ it is heavy.
  ⓐ before   ⓑ even though   ⓒ so that   ⓓ until

2 They had already started the party _____ I arrived.
  ⓐ if   ⓑ although   ⓒ since   ⓓ when

3 Do you know where _____ yesterday afternoon?
  ⓐ did Julie   ⓑ Julie did   ⓒ was Julie   ⓓ Julie was

4 You will not pass the exam _____ you study harder.
  ⓐ if   ⓑ as   ⓒ unless   ⓓ while

5 _____ Tom nor Jerry could figure out the problem.
  ⓐ Neither   ⓑ Either   ⓒ Both   ⓓ Not

6 Both Sally _____ Jake know what happened to James last Friday.
  ⓐ nor   ⓑ or   ⓒ but   ⓓ and

B Circle the inappropriate one between ⓐ and ⓑ. Then correct it.

1 I want <u>to live</u> in this town <u>such</u> that I can walk to school.   _____
      ⓐ   ⓑ

2 <u>Because</u> she was <u>so</u> dizzy, she stood up.   _____
      ⓐ   ⓑ

3 Amy was <u>only not</u> smart <u>but</u> also humorous.   _____
           ⓐ   ⓑ

4 He got up late <u>so</u> the alarm clock did not <u>go off</u>.   _____
               ⓐ   ⓑ

5 I am <u>not</u> sure <u>though</u> she will apply for the position or not.   _____
         ⓐ   ⓑ

6 <u>If</u> Jamie will attend the meeting <u>is</u> important to us.   _____
     ⓐ   ⓑ

Phrases to Sentences

A Complete the sentence by referring to the Korean translation.

1 나는 그녀가 어린 시절을 기억하는지 궁금하다. (remember, childhood)

→ I wonder _____.

2 그는 수학뿐 아니라 미술도 가르친다. (mathematics, art)

→ He teaches _____.

3 등이 아파서 나는 의사를 만나 봐야 한다. (back, hurt)

→ I need to see a doctor _____.

4 그녀는 일단 학교를 졸업하면 프랑스로 갈 것이다. (graduate from)

→ _____, she will go to France.

5 우리는 저녁 식사를 공연 전이나 후에 할 수 있다. (dinner, show)

→ We can _____.

6 그는 얼마나 많은 사람들이 그 회의에 참석할지 몰랐다. (would, attend)

→ He did not know _____.

B Underline the error and rewrite the sentence.

1 It began to rain during they were playing soccer.

→ _____

2 My mom was only sixteen if she met my father.

→ _____

3 She practiced hard such that she could perform well in the competition.

→ _____

4 The librarian asked the students that they could be quiet or not.

→ _____

5 Despite my best friend moved to a different city, we still keep in touch.

→ _____

6 Neither you nor I were responsible for the matter.

→ _____

3 Sentence Practice

A Translate the Korean into English using the given words.

1 a. 비록 그는 높은 곳을 무서워하지만 절벽에서 다이빙했다. (heights)

→ _____ he is afraid of _____, he dived off the cliff.

b. 비록 나는 어둠을 무서워하지만 밤에 집에 혼자 갔다. (the dark, alone)

→ _____

2 a. 나는 등산을 하러 가거나 TV를 볼 것이다. (watch)

→ I will _____ go for a hike _____ TV.

b. 그녀는 연극부에 들어가거나 새로운 동아리를 만들 것이다. (join, drama club)

→ _____

3 a. 그녀의 집은 30년 이상 되었기 때문에 좋은 상태가 아니다. (since)

→ _____ her house is more than 30 years old, it is not in

_____ condition.

b. 아버지의 자동차는 15년 이상 되었기 때문에 좋은 상태가 아니다. (since, my father's car)

→ _____

4 a. 너는 그들이 왜 그렇게 늦게 도착했는지 아니? (arrive)

→ Do you know _____ they _____ so late?

b. 너는 그녀가 왜 최근에 직장을 바꿨는지 아니? (change, recently)

→ _____

B Unscramble the words to make a sentence.

1 나는 너무 피곤했기 때문에 숙제를 할 수 없었다. (could, I, do, my homework, because, I, too, not, tired, was)

→ _____

2 그가 병원에 있는 동안 선생님과 반 친구들 모두 그를 방문했다. (was, in the hospital, both, his classmates, and, the teacher, visited, while, he, him)

→ _____

3 그곳에 도착하려면 버스나 지하철을 타라. (or, get, to, either, take, the bus, there, the subway)

→ _____

4 그녀는 내가 어떻게 케이크를 만들었는지 알고 싶어 한다. (the cake, made, she, know, to, wants, how, I)

→ _____

ACTUAL TEST

> Answers p. 22

[1-2] 빈칸에 들어갈 말이 알맞게 짝 지어진 것을 고르시오.

1

_____ my parents are very strict, they will allow me to go camping _____ you go with me.

① When – unless
② Although – if
③ As – though
④ Since – when
⑤ If – when

2

_____ she was going in the wrong direction, she could not find _____ the bank was.

① Before – how
② If – how
③ Because – where
④ Though – where
⑤ While – whether

[3-4] 밑줄 친 부분과 바꿔 쓸 수 있는 것을 고르시오.

3

As I have been to Jejudo, I would rather go somewhere else.

① When
② If
③ Whether
④ Since
⑤ That

4

I want to know if you have any special plans for tomorrow.

① until
② unless
③ in case
④ even if
⑤ whether

[5-7] 어법상 어색한 문장을 고르시오.

5

① As soon as the baby is born, James will have to make some changes.
② Please call the police in case I do not make it home by 11 p.m.
③ If Rebecca apologizes to me, I will not talk to her.
④ I lived close to my parents so that we could all get together often.
⑤ The teacher put up the class rules on the wall in order that the students do not forget them.

6

① I need both a table and a microwave oven.
② Not only I but also Blair has many friends.
③ Jisub as well as I like dancing.
④ Either you or your sister has to wash the dishes.
⑤ Neither she nor I need a blanket.

7

① I would like to know who your favorite actor is.
② I wonder where you bought the jeans.
③ I do not know whether Kelly has a kid.
④ Do you know when is Olivia's birthday?
⑤ Jay asked if I ate fruits and vegetables for dinner.

[8-11] 두 문장이 같은 의미가 되도록 빈칸에 들어갈 알맞은 말을 고르시오.

8

The lecture was not either short or interesting.

= The lecture was _____ short _____ interesting.

① so – that
② not – but
③ not only – but
④ neither – nor
⑤ both – and

9

Nick wore his raincoat not to get wet from the rain.

= Nick wore his raincoat _____ that he did not get wet from the rain.

① as
② soon
③ so
④ order
⑤ if

10

Changes in blood pressure might occur with age.

= Changes in blood pressure might occur _____ we get older.

① as
② unless
③ though
④ in case
⑤ so that

11

I do not know what happened between them while I was absent.

= I do not know what happened between them _____ my absence.

① before
② since
③ because of
④ despite
⑤ during

[12-13] 빈칸에 공통으로 들어갈 알맞은 말을 고르시오.

12

• Jim cannot go to university in Canada _____ he does not speak English.

• The phone rang _____ I walked in the door.

① when
② while
③ if
④ as
⑤ because

13

• _____ I was standing in line, someone stole my bag.

• _____ my mom wants to eat at home, my dad prefers to eat out.

① As
② While
③ Although
④ Until
⑤ Before

14 밑줄 친 부분이 어법상 어색한 것은?

① Before I came to Korea, I learned Korean.

② The family was excited as they bought a new house.

③ Try your best such that you will not have any regrets later.

④ Even though I dislike Nick, I agree that he is highly talented.

⑤ While Anne was talking on the phone, her kids were making a mess in the kitchen.

15 주어진 문장과 같은 의미의 문장은?

I will go out unless it is too cold.

① I will go out if it is too cold.

② I will go out if it is not too cold.

③ I will go out once it is too cold.

④ I will go out until it is not too cold.

⑤ I will go out in case it is too cold.

[16-17] 밑줄 친 단어의 의미가 <u>다른</u> 하나를 고르시오.

16
① We entered the shop <u>as</u> it was closing.
② <u>As</u> the sun started to rise, Paul felt his heart beat faster.
③ I saw a stray dog <u>as</u> I was walking down the street.
④ I did exactly <u>as</u> the doctor told me to do.
⑤ People stopped whispering <u>as</u> the movie started.

17
① I have not seen Julie <u>since</u> she moved to Hawaii in 2018.
② Jeff has had several jobs <u>since</u> he graduated from high school.
③ Everything has changed <u>since</u> yesterday when you left me.
④ I have been waiting for his reply <u>since</u> 3 p.m.
⑤ I am heading home <u>since</u> there is no more work left.

18 밑줄 친 if의 쓰임이 <u>다른</u> 하나는?
① Jenny asked Paul <u>if</u> it was raining outside.
② Eric does not know <u>if</u> he has math class today.
③ I wonder <u>if</u> there are any vegetarians among the guests.
④ Mr. Smith is not sure <u>if</u> he has ever visited the restaurant.
⑤ James will not know you are angry <u>if</u> you do not tell him.

[19-20] 주어진 말을 바르게 배열한 것을 고르시오.

19
Can you tell me (<u>submitted, report, she, if, has, her</u>)?

① she submitted her report if has
② her report if she has submitted
③ has her report if she submitted
④ if she has submitted her report
⑤ if her report has she submitted

20
I am not sure (<u>job, his, why, previous, quit, he</u>).

① why quit he his previous job
② why he quit his previous job
③ why he his previous job quit
④ his previous job why he quit
⑤ he quit why his previous job

21 우리말 해석이 알맞지 <u>않은</u> 것은?
① As this town has a small population, everybody knows each other.
→ 이 도시는 인구가 적어서 모두가 서로를 안다.
② Not only Tony but also I am planning to enter the competition.
→ Tony뿐만 아니라 나도 대회에 나갈 계획이야.
③ The auditioner could neither sing nor dance.
→ 오디션 참가자는 노래를 하거나 춤을 출 수 있었다.
④ Eric did not know if he should return the shirt.
→ Eric은 자신이 셔츠를 반품해야 할지 알지 못했다.
⑤ Whether you carry on or give up is up to you.
→ 네가 계속할지 아니면 포기할지는 너에게 달렸다.

[22-23] 두 문장이 같은 의미가 되도록 빈칸에 알맞은 말을 쓰시오.

22
Selina left the door open in order that her puppy could come in.

= Selina left the door open _____ _____ her puppy could come in.

23
The movie was shown in Korea as well as in 50 other countries at the same time.

= The movie was shown _____ in 50 other countries _____ in Korea at the same time.

[24-25] 다음 문장을 어법에 맞게 고쳐 쓰시오.

24
I would like to know that each room has a separate bathroom.

→ _____

_____

25
Do you think what the importance of learning languages is?

→ _____

_____

[26-28] 우리말에 맞게 주어진 단어를 바르게 배열하여 문장을 쓰시오.

26
비록 가격이 적당하긴 하지만 나는 그 제품을 사지 않을 것이다.
(I, reasonable, will, not, though, buy, the goods, is, the price)

→ _____

_____

27
Helen은 나에게 Michael이 어디 갔는지 말했다.
(gone, me, where, Helen, told, had, Michael)

→ _____

28
너는 누가 내 신발을 가져갔는지 아니?
(know, do, took, shoes, my, who, you)

→ _____

🎯 CHALLENGE!

Write your own answer using the given words.

01 How would you describe your personality? (both . . . and)

_____

_____

02 What are you good at?
(not only . . . but also)

_____

_____

Relatives

관계사

UNIT

01
Relative Pronouns
관계대명사

UNIT

02
Relative Adverbs
관계부사

UNIT

03
Nonrestrictive Relative Clauses
관계사절의 계속적 용법

UNIT

04
Compound Relatives
복합관계사

UNIT 01

Relative Pronouns 관계대명사

A 관계대명사
「접속사 + 대명사」의 역할을 하며, 관계대명사가 이끄는 절은 선행사를 수식한다.

A Relative Pronouns

Chris likes *stories* **which** have happy endings.
      Antecedent
(← Chris likes stories. + They have happy endings.)

Antecedent	Relative Pronoun		
	Subject	Object	Possessive
people	who	who(m)	whose
things	which	which	whose, of which
people, things	that	that	-
–	what	what	-

- **Subject: who, which, that**
  She has many friends **who** [**that**] are willing to help her.
  The temple **which** [**that**] was destroyed in the fire has been rebuilt.
  cf. Daniel likes the books (**which** [**that**] **were**) written by J. K. Rowling.

- **Object: who(m), which, that**
  He is the teacher **who(m)** [**that**] every student respects.
  Jamie picked out the vegetables **which** [**that**] he disliked.
  cf. He often throws out the clothes (**which** [**that**]) he is tired of.

- *cf.* **Quantifier (-thing, all, no, little, few, much, only), the -est + that**
  Happiness is not *something* **that** someone else can give to you. (○)
  Happiness is not something **which** someone else can give to you. (×)

- **Possessive: whose, of which**
  A woman **whose** name is Paula is on the phone.
  Mr. Lee has the house **whose** [**of which**] garden is full of roses.

- **what (= the thing which [that])**
  This is **what** [**the thing that**] I have been looking for.

cf. 「주격관계대명사 + be동사」와 목적격 관계대명사는 생략 가능하다.

• 관계대명사 what은 선행사를 포함한다.

Preposition + Relative pronoun (관계대명사가 전치사의 목적어일 때)
He often throws out the clothes **of which** he is tired. (○)
He often throws out the clothes **which** [**that**] he is tired **of**. (○)
cf. 전치사 + that (×)
    He often throws out the clothes of that he is tired. (×)

EXERCISE

A Choose the correct one for each sentence.

1 All the tickets had been sold to the fans (who, whom) arrived before noon.

2 Never go to a doctor (who, whose) office plants have died.

3 I enjoyed talking with the woman (whose, whom) I sat next to on the train.

4 I am looking for someone (that, which) can give me a ride to the airport.

5 We have shipped everything (which, that) you ordered.

B Cross out the relative pronoun that cannot go in the brackets.

1 Carl's brother (who, that, which) lives in Detroit is a banker.

2 Tim is dating a girl (who, whose) family does not seem to like him.

3 Do you understand (that, what) I am saying?

4 The people with (that, whom) Jenny works are nice and polite.

5 The characters (whom, what, that) the novelist wrote about were based on his friends and family members.

6 Kate has written a cookbook (which, that, whose) has traditional recipes of her region.

C Correct the underlined part.

1 Dan is going to visit his aunt <u>whom</u> is a nurse in Shanghai. → _____

2 The thing <u>what</u> really surprised me was his attitude. → _____

3 What is the name of the girl <u>who</u> umbrella you borrowed? → _____

4 This is the famous rock from <u>that</u> the village took its name. → _____

5 The lady to <u>who</u> Tony was going to get married canceled the wedding.

→ _____

D Complete the sentence using the given words.

1 안전벨트를 착용하고 있었던 소년은 부상을 입지 않았다. (be wearing)

→ The boy _____ his seatbelt was not injured.

2 어머니가 내게 사 주신 그 바지는 나에게 완벽하게 맞는다. (pants, which)

→ _____ for me fit me perfectly.

3 내가 이야기를 나눈 사람들이 매우 도움이 되었다. (that, talk to)

→ _____ were very helpful.

4 체육은 그가 유일하게 관심이 있는 과목이다. (that, be interested in)

→ P.E. is the only _____ .

UNIT 02

Relative Adverbs 관계부사

A Relative Adverbs

This is *the house* **where** Shakespeare lived.
(← This is the house. + Shakespeare lived in the house.)
→ This is *the house* **in which** Shakespeare lived.
→ This is *the house* **which** Shakespeare lived **in**.

Antecedent	Relative Adverb (→ Prep. + Relative Pronoun)
place (town, city)	where (→in/at/on/from which)
time (day, year)	when (→at/on/in which)
the reason	why (→for which)
the way	how (→in which)

e.g. I remember *the day* **when** (**on which**) I first met her.
Stanley did not know *the reason* **why** (**for which**) people behind him were laughing.

cf. That is **how** she has overcome her stage fright.
(← That is the way. + She has overcome her stage fright in that way.)
→ That is *the way* she has overcome her stage fright.
That is the way how she has overcome her stage fright. (×)

B Omission of Relative Adverbs

Home is *the place* **where** you are always welcome.
→ Home is **where** you are always welcome.
→ Home is *the place* you are always welcome.

cf. Central Park is (the place) **where** I often take a walk. (○)
That is (Central Park) **where** I often take a walk. (×)

e.g. I should check *the time* **when** the meeting starts.
→ I should check **when** the meeting starts.
→ I should check *the time* the meeting starts.
Do you know *the reason* **why** he came here?
→ Do you know **why** he came here?
→ Do you know *the reason* he came here?

Sidebar

A 관계부사
「접속사 + 부사(구)」의 역할을 하며, 관계부사가 이끄는 절은 선행사를 수식한다. 「전치사 + 관계대명사」로 바꿔 쓸 수 있다.

cf. 다른 관계부사와 달리 how는 선행사 the way와 함께 쓰일 수 없고, 둘 중 하나가 생략되어야 한다.

B 선행사 혹은 관계부사의 생략
선행사가 place, time, reason과 같이 일반적일 때 선행사나 관계부사 중 하나를 생략할 수 있다.
cf. 구체적인 장소를 나타내는 선행사는 생략할 수 없다.

EXERCISE

A Choose the correct one for each sentence.

1 This is the station (when, where) Steve met Amy.

2 July and August are the months (where, when) most people go on vacation.

3 A famine was the reason (why, how) many Irish people emigrated to the USA.

4 I want to know (the way, the way how) he lost weight and developed his muscles.

B Combine the two sentences using a relative adverb.

1 There must be some reasons. They ran away from their homes for some reasons.

→ There must be _____ they ran away from their homes.

2 Can you teach me the way? You made these cookies in that way.

→ Can you teach me _____ you made these cookies?

3 The day was the best day of my life. I met you on the day.

→ _____ I met you was the best day of my life.

4 Look at this house. Chopin used to live in this house.

→ Look at _____ Chopin used to live.

C Correct the underlined part.

1 Do you know a shop <u>which</u> I can buy used laptops?   → _____

2 Do you know the <u>place</u> why she dropped out of school?   → _____

3 That was the moment <u>which</u> I knew I would marry her.   → _____

4 This is the church <u>where</u> my parents got married at.   → _____

5 The farmers' market is the place <u>at that</u> you can buy fresh vegetables.

→ _____

D Complete the sentence using the given words.

1 우리가 하와이에 도착한 날은 날씨가 흐렸다. (day, when, arrive)

→ _____ in Hawaii was cloudy.

2 에든버러는 Conan Doyle이 태어난 도시이다. (city, in)

→ Edinburgh is _____ Conan Doyle was born.

3 그것이 내가 너와 이야기를 하고 싶지 않은 이유이다. (reason, why)

→ That is _____ want to talk to you.

4 이 문제를 네가 어떻게 풀었는지 나에게 말해 줄래? (solve)

→ Would you tell me _____ this problem?

Nonrestrictive Relative Clauses 관계사절의 계속적 용법

A Nonrestrictive Relative Pronouns

관계대명사의 계속적 용법

관계대명사 앞에 콤마(,)를 쓰고 선행사에 대한 추가 정보를 제공한다. 계속적 용법의 관계대명사는 생략할 수 없다.

① 한정적(제한적) 용법: 관계사절이 선행사를 수식하여 선행사의 의미를 한정한다.

• which로 시작하는 계속적 용법의 관계사절은 주절의 내용 전체 또는 일부분을 받을 수 있다.

cf. 관계대명사 that은 계속적 용법으로 쓸 수 없다.

I like this picture, **which** shows some beautiful scenery.
  = and it   <nonrestrictive>
It is the picture *which* my friend took. <restrictive> ①

◆ **Nonrestrictive relative pronoun → 「and/but/because+Pronoun」**
We will have a new teacher, **who** graduated from this school.
  = and he
I had no chance to say goodbye to Brian, **which** was a pity.
  = and it
It is Sean's house, **whose** balcony looks out over a beach.
  = and its
cf. There was an earthquake in Greece, that is bad news. (×)

◆ **some/all/many/most + of + whom/which/whose**
I met my kindergarten classmates, **many of whom** I did not recognize.
He made 30 sculptures, **most of which** were sold at high prices.

B Nonrestrictive Relative Adverbs

관계부사의 계속적 용법

관계부사 when과 where 앞에 콤마(,)를 쓴다. 계속적 용법의 관계부사는 생략할 수 없다.

That happened in 2010, **when** I still was a baby. <nonrestrictive>
  = and at that time
It is the season *when* the leaves fall from the trees. <restrictive>

◆ **Nonrestrictive relative adverb → 「and/but/because + Adverbial」**
We spent our vacation in Jejudo, **where** my uncle lives.
  = and there
I went to the shop on Sunday morning, **when** it was not open yet.
  = and at that time

Pseudo-relative pronoun (유사관계대명사): but, than, as
There is *no* rule **but** has exceptions.
Do not use *more* words **than** are necessary.
These are *the same* shoes **as** I bought in New York.
He has *such* bags **as** I want to have.
He is *as* wise a man **as** I ever met.

EXERCISE

A Choose the correct one for each sentence.

1 My mother, (that, who) was born overseas, can speak five languages.

2 He stays up late, (that, which) is why he cannot wake up early.

3 There was more money (than, where) was needed.

4 I go to the same school (as, with) he does.

B Fill in the blank with the correct relative pronoun or adverb.

1 The theater, _____ the musical was performed, could seat 500 people.

2 She was a little nervous before the test, _____ was common.

3 Yesterday, I met a girl named Alice, _____ father works in Seoul.

4 Three years ago, Jimmy first met Chanho, _____ is his best friend now.

5 Chris, _____ Steve admired the most, died last month.

C Fill in the blank so that the two sentences have the same meaning.

1 Please come to my office in the afternoon because I will be free then.

= Please come to my office in the afternoon, _____ I will be free.

2 He had spent his youth in the city, but the city was totally destroyed.

= The city, _____ he had spent his youth, was totally destroyed.

3 He has no time to prepare for the meeting, but the meeting is this afternoon.

= He has no time to prepare for the meeting, _____ is this afternoon.

4 There were lots of people at the party, and I had known many of them for years.

= There were lots of people at the party, many of _____ I had known for years.

D Complete the sentence using the given words.

1 나의 할아버지는 70세이신데, 막 은퇴하셨다. (grandfather)

→ My _____, _____, has just retired.

2 나는 그 문을 부숴서 열어 보려 했지만, 불가능하다는 것을 알았다. (which, find)

→ I tried to break the door open, _____.

3 그는 수백 권의 책을 가지고 있는데, 그는 그 책의 대부분을 읽었다. (most of)

→ He had hundreds of books, _____ he had read.

4 그는 1989년에 태어났는데, 그때는 체코와 슬로바키아가 하나의 국가였다. (be born, when)

→ _____, _____ Czech and Slovakia were a single country.

UNIT 04

Compound Relatives
복합관계사

A 복합관계대명사
관계대명사 who, which, what에 -ever를 붙인 형태이고, 명사절이나 양보의 부사절을 이끈다.

A Compound Relative Pronouns

Compound relative pronoun	Noun clause	Adverbial clause
whoever	(= anyone who)	(= no matter who)
whichever	(= anything that)	(= no matter which)
whatever	(= anything that)	(= no matter what)

- ◆ **whoever**
  We will give this prize to **whoever** arrives first. (= anyone who)
  Whoever may say that, I will not give up. (= No matter who)

- ◆ **whichever**
  You can order **whichever** you want to eat. (= anything that)
  Whichever you choose, you will not regret it. (= No matter which)

- ◆ **whatever**
  I will do **whatever** makes you happy. (= anything that)
  Whatever happens, we will trust you. (= No matter what)

cf. **whichever/whatever + Noun**
  Whichever *decision* you make, I will support you.

cf. whichever와 whatever는 명사 앞에서 명사를 수식하는 형용사 역할을 하기도 한다.

B 복합관계부사
관계부사 when, where, how에 -ever를 붙인 형태이고, 시간, 장소, 양보의 부사절을 이끈다.

• 「however + (형용사/부사) + 주어 + 동사」 어순에 주의한다.

B Compound Relative Adverbs

Compound relative adverb	Time/place adverbial clause	Concession adverbial clause
whenever	(= at any time when	(= No matter when)
wherever	(= at any place where	(= No matter where)
however	-	(= No matter how)

- ◆ **whenever**
  Whenever I call you, you are busy. (= At any time when, Every time)
  Whenever you come, you are welcome. (= No matter when)

- ◆ **wherever**
  Put your bag down **wherever** you want. (= at any place where)
  Wherever I go, I carry my phone with me. (= No matter where)

- ◆ **however**
  However far it is, I will go with you. (= No matter how)

EXERCISE

A Choose the correct one for each sentence.

1 (Who, Whoever) arrives first may be given a free ticket.

2 We should appreciate (whoever, whatever) those people do for us.

3 (Whenever, Whichever) you choose, you cannot take back your decision.

4 (Whoever, Whatever) spilled the milk has to clean it up.

5 Mike will be satisfied with (whoever, whatever) he receives on his birthday.

B Fill in the blank so that the two sentences have the same meaning.

1 Whoever runs it, this project has got to be completed by this Friday.

= No _____ runs it, this project has got to be completed by this Friday.

2 We will support whoever is elected as the leader.

= We will support _____ who is elected as the leader.

3 Whichever you open first, you will be happy with it.

= _____ you open first, you will be happy with it.

4 Whatever happens, I will not leave you.

= _____ happens, I will not leave you.

C Choose the correct word in the box and fill in the blank.

wherever	where	whenever	how	however

1 _____ he comes home after work, he takes a shower.

2 _____ expensive they might be, she has to buy the things she needs.

3 Buck, my dog, follows me _____ I go.

4 Online classes can let you study no matter _____ you are.

5 No matter _____ difficult the task is, he will manage to do it.

D Complete the sentence using the given words.

1 누구든지 가장 많은 경험을 가진 사람이 고용될 것이다. (the most, experience)

→ _____ will be hired.

2 네가 택한 길이 어떤 것이든 그 길이 너를 집으로 이끌 것이다. (path, take)

→ _____ will lead you home.

3 그가 아무리 배가 고파도 그는 식당에서 먹지 않을 것이다. (hungry)

→ _____, he will not eat at a restaurant.

Relatives **139**

WRITING CONNECTION

1 Grammar Check-up

A Choose the correct one.

1 I know a girl _____ speaks three languages fluently.

ⓐ which   ⓑ whose   ⓒ who   ⓓ whom

2 My grandparents live in a small town _____ there is no hospital.

ⓐ where   ⓑ when   ⓒ how   ⓓ why

3 His last book, _____ I did not read, is a bestseller these days.

ⓐ that   ⓑ which   ⓒ when   ⓓ whenever

4 I forgot the time _____ the meeting was going to start.

ⓐ when   ⓑ which   ⓒ where   ⓓ how

5 Nobody understands the reason _____ Maggie got the main role.

ⓐ whose   ⓑ which   ⓒ why   ⓓ where

6 Patrick, _____ I saw at the park yesterday, is a friend of my mom's.

ⓐ whom   ⓑ what   ⓒ which   ⓓ that

B Circle the inappropriate one between ⓐ and ⓑ. Then correct it.

1 Is this the book for <u>that</u> you were looking?   _____
　　　　　ⓐ　　　　　　　　　ⓑ

2 I know a boy <u>who</u> bike broke on the day when <u>he</u> bought it.   _____
　　　　　　　　　ⓐ　　　　　　　　　　　　　　　ⓑ

3 Global warming is a problem <u>that</u> everyone should take <u>it</u> seriously.   _____
　　　　　　　　　　　　　　　　　　ⓐ　　　　　　　　　　ⓑ

4 <u>Wherever</u> <u>do you</u> go, make sure you keep your passport with you.   _____
　　　ⓐ　　　ⓑ

5 <u>Whenever</u> the neighbors cook, the smell comes through the window, <u>that</u> makes
　　　ⓐ　　　　　　　　　　　　　　　　　　　　　　　　　　　　　　　　ⓑ
me hungry.   _____

2 Phrases to Sentences

A Complete the sentence by referring to the Korean translation.

1 저는 이 행사를 책임지고 있는 사람과 이야기하고 싶습니다. (the person, is in charge)

→ I would like to speak to _____ of this event.

2 네가 나에게 빌려준 그 책이 없어졌다. (lent)

→ _____ me is gone.

3 하나는 아버지가 배우인데 나를 자신의 파티에 초대했다. (actor)

→ Hana, _____, invited me to her party.

4 이 공을 빌렸던 사람이 누구든 가능한 빨리 돌려줘야 한다. (borrow)

→ _____ should return it as quickly as possible.

5 나는 항상 나 혼자서 독서할 수 있는 장소를 갖기를 원했다. (alone)

→ I have always wanted to have a place _____.

6 어제는 모든 것이 순조롭게 이루어졌는데 나의 행운의 날이었다. (go, smoothly)

→ Yesterday, _____, was my lucky day.

B Underline the error and rewrite the sentence.

1 James still remembers the days whose there were no personal computers.

→ _____

2 I cannot remember the person which I asked to keep an eye on my bag.

→ _____

3 Let's discuss that will happen next in this story.

→ _____

4 The heavy rain, which is unusual in this city, have destroyed my flowers.

→ _____

5 David keeps on telling the same story to whatever will listen.

→ _____

6 The company which my dad works is making a lot of profits these days.

→ _____

3 Sentence Practice

A Translate the Korean into English using the given words.

1 a. 여기가 내가 태어난 마을이야. (which, born in)

→ This is the town _____ .

b. 여기가 그 위대한 학자가 태어난 집이야. (in, the great scholar)

→ _____

2 a. 여러분의 주머니에 있는 것들을 꺼내서 전부를 책상 위에 올려 두세요. (have, what)

→ Take out _____ in your pockets and put everything on the desk.

b. 여러분의 가방에 있는 것을 꺼내서 전부를 책상 위에 올려 두세요. (bags)

→ _____

3 a. 그 남자는 이웃집에 사는데 우체국에서 일해. (live next door)

→ That man, _____ , works at the post office.

b. 내 사촌은 중국에 사는데 컴퓨터 공학을 가르쳐. (computer science)

→ My cousin, _____ .

4 a. 여기는 나의 부모님이 저녁 식사를 즐겨 하시는 음식점이다. (parents, dinner)

→ This is the restaurant _____ .

b. 여기는 내가 일요일마다 파이를 사는 디저트 가게이다. (dessert shop, some pies, on)

→ _____

B Unscramble the words to make a sentence.

1 네가 어제 만났던 그 남자는 내 삼촌이다.

(whom, the man, met, yesterday, you, is, my uncle)

→ _____

2 나는 이 병을 어떻게 열어야 하는지 알아내지 못하겠어.

(figure out, I, how, open, I, this bottle, should, cannot)

→ _____

3 그녀는 결국 2위를 했는데 그것은 그녀에게 아주 실망스러운 일이었다.

(ended up, she, very, second place, was, coming in, to her, disappointing, which)

→ _____

4 나는 누구도 나를 알아보지 못하는 곳으로 이사하고 싶다.

(recognizes, move to, where, nobody, want to, I, a place, me)

→ _____

ACTUAL TEST

> Answers **p. 24**

[1-4] 빈칸에 들어갈 알맞은 말을 고르시오.

1
> The girl _____ wore the funny hat attracted people's attention.

① are   ② who   ③ whom
④ whose   ⑤ which

2
> I know a family _____ house burned down in the fire.

① that   ② who   ③ which
④ whose   ⑤ what

3
> Is this the dog for _____ you are looking?

① who   ② that   ③ which
④ whose   ⑤ what

4
> My brother Tom, _____ hates fishing, decided to stay home.

① whoever   ② which
③ what   ④ when
⑤ who

[5-7] 두 문장이 같은 의미가 되도록 빈칸에 알맞은 말을 고르시오.

5
> He is hiding what he bought at the market.
> = He is hiding the thing _____ he bought at the market.

① that   ② what   ③ who
④ where   ⑤ whose

6
> No matter where Julia was, it was not like home.
> = _____ Julia was, it was not like home.

① Where   ② When   ③ Wherever
④ However   ⑤ Whenever

7
> I will show you how I found the answer.
> = I will show you the _____ I found the answer.

① what   ② however   ③ reason
④ way   ⑤ way how

[8-9] 밑줄 친 단어의 성격이 나머지 넷과 다른 것 하나를 고르시오.

8
① I think <u>that</u> more women should be politicians.
② A hammer is the tool <u>that</u> we need now.
③ Tell me something about her <u>that</u> I do not know.
④ He is not the honest man <u>that</u> he used to be.
⑤ I met someone <u>that</u> my brother went to school with.

9
① <u>What</u> are you talking about?
② He asked me <u>what</u> my name was.
③ <u>What</u> was the question again?
④ <u>What</u> you did to the poor man was wrong.
⑤ Tell me <u>what</u> the problem is.

10

> An orphanage is a place ___(A)___
> children ___(B)___ have no parents
> can live and be looked after.

	(A)	(B)
①	which	– who
②	where	– which
③	where	– who
④	in which	– whose
⑤	in which	– whom

11

> The dog ___(A)___ was hit by the car
> was immediately taken to a clinic,
> ___(B)___ he has been recovering.

	(A)	(B)		(A)	(B)
①	that	– which	②	which	– where
③	who	– where	④	whom	– where
⑤	which	– that			

12

> • Nate asks me about my sister
>   ___(A)___ he sees me.
> • ___(B)___ I do, my parents support
>   me.

	(A)	(B)
①	whenever	– Whatever
②	whenever	– Whenever
③	whenever	– Wherever
④	wherever	– Whenever
⑤	whatever	– Whatever

13
① The doctor that I wanted to see was off duty.
② Who is the person whom we need to thank?
③ I want to go to a place where I can relax.
④ Everything that you say seems to make sense.
⑤ It is hard to find people who hate chocolate.

14
① What is the reason why he quit his job?
② The dish that I ordered was very delicious.
③ Do you know the man whom he is talking to?
④ That man is the person whose son won a gold medal.
⑤ The woman who I spoke to at the meeting was very smart.

15

> The books that are on the shelf are bestsellers.

① The police admitted that they had made a mistake.
② Are you certain that the man you saw was Daniel?
③ Have you seen the lecture notes that I borrowed from Selina?
④ People believe that the new government will sincerely work for the people.
⑤ The survey showed that a majority of people think food is important.

16

I did not know <u>that</u> she was married.

① I am sorry, but that is all <u>that</u> I remember.
② An elephant is an animal <u>that</u> children love.
③ There is something <u>that</u> you should keep in mind.
④ Now I realize <u>that</u> he was lying to me all this time.
⑤ The man <u>that</u> was wearing a black coat was the host.

19 밑줄 친 부분과 바꿔 쓸 수 있는 것은?

<u>Whenever</u> I call him, he does not answer.

① Anything who
② Anything that
③ No matter how
④ No matter where
⑤ No matter when

[17-18] 어법상 <u>어색한</u> 문장을 고르시오.

17 ① Wendy lives in a house which is surrounded by trees.
② Drivers who drive recklessly are dangerous to society.
③ That is the same bag that I left on the bus yesterday.
④ Students who grades are good can receive scholarships.
⑤ This is my favorite dress, which I have had for ten years.

[20-21] 주어진 문장을 다시 쓸 때 빈칸에 알맞은 말을 고르시오.

20

There is no rose that does not have thorns.
→ There is no rose _____ has thorns.

① than   ② but
③ as   ④ that
⑤ who

18 ① I want to visit Brazil, where there is good coffee.
② I will not make friends with anyone whose heart is cold.
③ The situation in which we found ourselves in was terrible.
④ There were great works of art, many of which were not for sale.
⑤ It did not take long to get to our destination, which was five miles away.

21

Tony often wants to stay up late. That is usual with little children.
→ Tony often wants to stay up late, _____ is usual with little children.

① than   ② but
③ as   ④ that
⑤ who

[22-23] 우리말 뜻에 맞게 주어진 단어를 이용하여 문장을 완성하시오.

22
> 내 친구는 휴대 전화가 없었는데 마침내 하나 구입했다. (a cell phone)

→ My friend, _____,
  finally bought one.

23
> 공항에 도착했을 때 나는 내 여권을 잃어버렸다는 것을 알았는데 그것이 아주 짜증스러웠다. (passport, annoying)

→ When I got to the airport, I realized I
  had lost _____.

24 다음 문장을 어법에 맞게 고쳐 쓰시오.

> I don't like films whose has sad endings.

→ _____

25 다음 문장을 복합관계대명사를 이용하여 다시 쓰시오.

> No matter when you open that website, you will see an ad pop up first.

→ _____
  _____

[26-28] 우리말에 맞게 주어진 단어를 바르게 배열하여 문장을 쓰시오.

26
> 그들이 20년간 산 그 집은 수리가 필요하다. (where, the house, needs, for 20 years, they, repairs, have lived)

→ _____
  _____

27
> 내 친구 유나는 어머니가 일본인인데 조부모님을 만나러 일본에 갔다.
> (her grandparents, mother, went to, is, my friend Yuna, whose, to see, Japan, Japanese)

→ _____
  _____

28
> 누구도 그가 그 마을을 떠난 이유를 알지 못했다. (he, the village, nobody, why, left, knew, the reason)

→ _____
  _____

🎯 CHALLENGE!

Write your own answer using the given words.

01 What kind of friends do you want to have? (*who* or *whom*)

_____

_____

02 When is a day that has a special meaning to you? (*when*)

_____

_____

CHAPTER 11

Subjunctive Mood
가정법

UNIT 01

Subjunctives
가정법

UNIT 02

I wish/as if/It is time + Subjunctive
I wish/as if/It is time + 가정법

UNIT 03

Implied Subjunctive / Leaving Out *if*
if절 대용어구 / if의 생략

Subjunctives 가정법

Ⓐ Past Subjunctive

If I **had** a smartphone, I **could find** their house.
(= I do not have a smartphone, so I cannot find their house.)

- 「If + S + V (past), S + would/could/might + V」
  If he **were** not sick, he **could go out** with you.
  (= He is sick, so he cannot go out with you.)

Ⓑ Past Perfect Subjunctive

If she **had tried** harder, she **could have won** the writing contest.
(= She did not try harder, so she could not win the writing contest.)

- 「If + S + had p.p., S + would/could/might have + p.p.」
  If the weather **had not been** so hot, I **would have gone** to play baseball.
  (= The weather was so hot, so I did not go to play baseball.)

Ⓒ Mixed Subjunctive

If I **had learned** French at school, I **could speak** French now.
(= I did not learn French at school, so I cannot speak French now.)

- 「If + S + had p.p., S + would/could/might + V」
  If you **had not spent** that money, you **could go** to Mexico with us next month.
  (= You spent that money, so you cannot go to Mexico with us next month.)

First Conditional vs. Past Subjunctive

조건문	가정법 과거
발생 가능한 일을 가정	실현 가능성이 희박한 일을 가정
If I **pass** the test, Mom **will buy** me a laptop.	If I **passed** the test, Mom **would buy** me a laptop.
(시험에 통과할 가능성 있음)	(시험에 통과할 가능성 없음)

EXERCISE

A Choose the correct one for each sentence.

1 If I could read her mind, I (will, would) know exactly what gift to buy for her.

2 If I (am, were) you, I would apply to the program right now.

3 If we (have, had had) more money, we could have renovated the entire house.

4 It would be great if you (can, could) help us move our stuff.

5 If she (had not, did not) done volunteer work, she would not have known the pleasure of helping others.

B Correct the underlined part.

1 If she <u>knows</u> your wedding date, she would have gone to the wedding.

→ _____

2 If you told me not to talk about it, I <u>will keep</u> it as a secret.

→ _____

3 I would not have learned Spanish if I <u>did not move</u> to Columbia.

→ _____

4 We <u>can share</u> a taxi if I had known that you lived so close to me.

→ _____

5 If he <u>is not</u> so busy, he would spend more time with his children.

→ _____

C Fill in the blank using the given words.

1 If Ted _____ in the accident, he would be 20 years old now. (not, die)

2 If she _____ my advice, she would have been in trouble. (ignore)

3 If you knew the rules, you _____ the game. (will, enjoy)

4 If I had saved money, I _____ a cell phone now. (can, buy)

D Complete the sentence using the given words.

1 내가 너라면 오늘 밤에 따뜻한 코트 없이 밖에 나가지 않을 것이다. (will, go out)

→ _____, I _____ without a warm coat tonight.

2 그가 사실을 말했더라면 우리는 감옥에 갇혔을 것이다. (tell, will, be put)

→ If he _____ the truth, we _____ into jail.

3 어젯밤에 비가 오지 않았더라면 우리는 오늘 축구를 할 수 있을 텐데. (rain, soccer)

→ If it _____ last night, we could _____ today.

4 그가 서둘렀더라면 버스를 놓치지 않았을 텐데. (hurry, will, miss)

→ If he _____, he _____ the bus.

UNIT 02

I wish/as if/It is time + Subjunctive
I wish/as if/It is time + 가정법

A I wish + 가정법

현재·과거의 일에 대한 유감이나 아쉬움을 나타낼 때 쓴다.

cf. 과거의 일에 대한 유감이나 아쉬움을 과거에 가졌을 때 쓰며, '~이었다면 좋았을 텐데'라는 뜻이다.

B as if + 가정법

현재·과거의 사실과 반대되는 일을 가정할 때 쓴다.

cf. 주절이 현재에서 과거로 변해도 「as if + 가정법」의 시제는 변하지 않는다. 주절과 같은 시점의 가정이면 가정법 과거를, 주절보다 과거의 일을 가정하면 가정법 과거완료를 쓴다.

C It is (high) time + 가정법

현재 해야(했어야) 할 일을 하지 않은 것에 대한 유감을 나타낼 때 쓴다.

cf. 「It is time + to부정사」는 현재 '~할 시간이다'라는 뜻이다.

A I wish + Subjunctive

I **wish** he **were** still alive.
(= I'm sorry he is not alive anymore.)
I **wish** I **had listened** to my mom and **had studied** harder.
(= I'm sorry I did not listen to my mom and did not study harder.)

I wish + S + V (past) ~라면 좋을 텐데	I wish + S + had p.p. ~했더라면 좋을 텐데
현재 일에 대한 유감이나 아쉬움을 나타낼 때	과거 일에 대한 유감이나 아쉬움을 나타낼 때
I wish I **had** more free time. (= I'm sorry I don't have much free time.)	I wish Susan **had told** me about the party earlier. (= I'm sorry Susan did not tell me about the party earlier.)

cf. **I wished + S + had p.p.**
  I **wished** I **had been** more patient, but it is all in the past.

B as if + Subjunctive

He acts **as if** he **were** my boyfriend.
(In fact, he is not my boyfriend.)
She talks **as if** she **had seen** a dinosaur.
(In fact, she did not see a dinosaur.)

as if + S + V (past) 마치 ~인 것처럼	as if + S + had p.p. 마치 ~였던 것처럼
현재 사실과 반대되는 일을 가정	과거 사실과 반대되는 일을 가정
I felt **as if** I **were** left alone. (In fact, I was not left alone.)	Ricky talked **as if** he **could have read** the Arabic letters. (In fact, Ricky could not read the Arabic letters.)

C It is (high) time + Past Subjunctive

It is almost 9 o'clock. **It is time** we **had** dinner.

It is (high) time + S + V (past) ~해야 할 시간이다
현재 해야 할 일을 하지 않은 것에 대한 유감을 나타낼 때

It is time you **went** to bed. You have to get up early tomorrow.
It is (high) time we **wrapped up** today's work.

EXERCISE

A Choose the correct one for each sentence.

1 It is only Wednesday. I wish it (is, were) Friday today.

2 I wish I (worked, had worked) harder before I graduated.

3 Sally did not invite me to her party. I wish I (were, had been) invited.

4 I wished he (did not say, had not said) that to me, but his critical comments motivated me to work harder.

5 I wish I (read, had read) the book so that I would understand what he said.

B Fill in the blank with the proper words.

1 He smiles as if he _____ everything. In fact, he knows nothing.

2 Sena talks as if she _____ in Hong Kong. In fact, she had not lived there.

3 Jim acts as if he _____ it before. In fact, he did not do it before.

4 Josh is screaming as if he _____ a ghost. In fact, he does not see a ghost.

C Fill in the blank using the given word.

1 It is high time this road _____ completed. (be)

2 It is time we _____ breakfast. (have)

3 It is time to _____ a break. (take)

4 It is high time we _____ blaming each other. (stop)

5 It is time for us to _____ about our future careers. (think)

D Complete the sentence using the given words.

1 Tim이 나의 진짜 동생이면 좋을 텐데. 그는 너무 귀엽다. (real brother)

→ I wish Tim _____. He is so cute.

2 내가 나의 제일 친한 친구와 말다툼을 하지 않았었다면 좋을 텐데. (argue with)

→ I wish I _____ my best friend.

3 그는 마치 모든 정답을 찾은 것처럼 웃고 있다. (as if, find)

→ He is grinning _____ all the answers.

4 벌써 8시야. 네가 학교에 가야 할 시간이다. (high time)

→ It is already 8 o'clock. _____.

UNIT 03

Implied Subjunctive / Leaving Out *if*

if절 대용어구 / if의 생략

A if절 대용어구

if절 대신 명사구, 부정사구, 분사구문, 부사 등이 그 의미를 대신할 수 있다.

B if의 생략

if절의 동사가 were, had, should인 경우 if를 생략하고, 주어와 동사는 도치되어 「Were/Had/Should + 주어」 어순으로 쓴다.

C If it were not for + Noun

현재 사실과 반대되는 가정을 나타내며 '~이 없다면'이라는 뜻이다. 「But for + 명사」나 「Without + 명사」로 바꿔 쓸 수 있다.

cf. 과거 사실과 반대되는 가정을 할 때는 「If it had not been for + 명사」를 쓴다. '~이 없었다면, ~이 아니었더라면'이라는 뜻을 나타낸다.

A Implied Subjunctive

A true friend would help you when you are in trouble.
(= *If he were* a true friend, he would help you when you are in trouble.)

e.g. **To hear him talk**, you would consider him Korean.
(= *If you heard* him talk, you would consider him Korean.)
Having supernatural powers, I would save the world.
(= *If I had* supernatural powers, I would save the world.)
She ran like a bullet. **Otherwise**, she would have missed her bus.
(= *If she had not run* like a bullet, she would have missed her bus.)

B Leaving Out *if*

Were I Jerry, I would ask the teacher for help.
(= *If I were* Jerry, I would ask the teacher for help.)
Had we any friends in Busan, we would not have to find a hotel.
(= *If we had* any friends in Busan, we would not have to find a hotel.)
Should you fail this time, you would have to try it again.
(= *If you should* fail this time, you would have to try it again.)

C If it were not for + Noun

If it were not for your support, I would not succeed.
→ **Were it not for** your support, I would not succeed.
→ **But for** [Without] your support, I would not succeed.

cf. **If it had not been for** Dave, our team would not have come in first.

「S + insist/suggest/require/demand + that + S (+ should) + V」
주장, 제안, 요구 동사의 목적절에는 「should + 동사원형」을 쓰며, 이때 should는 보통 생략한다.
My boss **insisted** that I **(should) go** with him.
It is **required** that everyone **(should) fasten** their seatbelts.

EXERCISE

A Choose the correct one for each sentence.

1 A good master (will, would) take good care of his dog.

2 (If, Without) the Internet, the whole world would be in chaos.

3 (See, To see) her in person, you would think she is actually beautiful.

4 The buyer demanded that the goods (were, be) delivered by tomorrow.

5 I am broke. Otherwise, I (would be, would have been) willing to lend you some money.

B Rewrite the sentence by leaving out *if*.

1 If I were you, I would not do such a thing.

→ _____, I would not do such a thing.

2 If I had not moved to Seoul, I would have made more friends there.

→ _____ to Seoul, I would have made more friends there.

3 If I had a mentor, I would make better choices.

→ _____, I would make better choices.

4 If it should cost you anything, please let me know.

→ _____ you anything, please let me know.

C Rewrite the sentence so that the two sentences have the same meaning.

1 Were it not for his help, I could not finish my project.

→ If _____, I could not finish my project.

2 Had it not been for your advice, I could not have won the contest.

→ If _____, I could not have won the contest.

3 But for your help, we could not open a booth at the exhibition.

→ If _____, we could not open a booth at the exhibition.

4 Without his support, I could not have achieved success.

→ If _____, I could not have achieved success.

D Complete the sentence using the given words.

1 나는 자전거를 왼쪽으로 틀었다. 그렇지 않았다면 나는 바위에 부딪혔을 것이다. (hit)

→ I turned my bike to the left. _____, _____ the rock.

2 물과 공기가 없다면 우리는 생존할 수가 없을 것이다. (for)

→ Were _____ and air, we could not survive.

3 전기가 없다면 생활이 어떨까? (how, life)

→ _____ without electricity?

WRITING CONNECTION

 STEP 1 Grammar Check-up

A Choose the correct one.

1 If I miss the last bus, I _____ home.

   ⓐ walk   ⓑ walks   ⓒ will walk   ⓓ walked

2 If I _____ in Canada, I would speak English fluently.

   ⓐ am born   ⓑ were born   ⓒ being born   ⓓ had been born

3 If he _____ Chinese, he could have gotten a job in China.

   ⓐ speaks   ⓑ has spoken   ⓒ spoke   ⓓ had spoken

4 I wish I _____ a lot of money and could donate to people in need.

   ⓐ had   ⓑ has   ⓒ have   ⓓ had had

5 If I _____ the last person on the earth, would you marry me?

   ⓐ was   ⓑ were   ⓒ will be   ⓓ have been

B Circle the inappropriate one between ⓐ and ⓑ. Then correct it.

1 I wish I <u>have</u> said hello to Jenny, but I <u>have</u> no courage. _____
           ⓐ   ⓑ

2 If I <u>get</u> a call from Mike, I <u>go</u> out to meet him. _____
          ⓐ   ⓑ

3 <u>Had</u> I been abroad before, I would <u>have had</u> a different dream now. _____
   ⓐ   ⓑ

4 It is already midnight. It <u>is</u> high time he <u>goes</u> to bed. _____
                     ⓐ   ⓑ

5 If you <u>had made</u> a left turn, you <u>would find</u> the way. I am sorry you are lost.

        ⓐ   ⓑ

   _____

6 If I <u>bought</u> an extra sandwich, I <u>would have given</u> you one. But I did not.

       ⓐ   ⓑ

   _____

Phrases to Sentences

A Complete the sentence by referring to the Korean translation.

1 그녀가 약속을 지켰더라면 나는 그녀를 신뢰했을 텐데. (keep)

→ _____ her promise, I would have trusted her.

2 그가 더 진지했다면 인터뷰를 통과했을 텐데. (more serious)

→ _____, he would have passed the interview.

3 내가 대중 앞에서 연설을 잘 한다면 좋을 텐데. (be good at, make speeches)

→ I wish I _____ in public.

4 내가 그의 주소를 안다면 그를 방문할 텐데. (will, visit, know)

→ I _____ him if I _____ his address.

5 선생님은 정말로 중요한 소식인 것처럼 그 소식을 전했다. (as, be)

→ The teacher delivered the news _____ really important.

6 Anne은 안전벨트를 하고 있었다. 그렇지 않았더라면, 그녀는 다쳤을 것이다. (get injured)

→ Anne was wearing her seatbelt. _____, she would _____.

B Underline the error and rewrite the sentence.

1 If I spoke English fluently, I will not worry about the interview.

→ _____

2 Mina talks as if she knows lots of celebrities, but she does not.

→ _____

3 Jessica would come to the party if she did not fight with you yesterday.

→ _____

4 Not had it been for the map, we would not have found our way home.

→ _____

5 If he were born in better circumstances, he would be pursuing his dream now.

→ _____

6 If it were not of an elbow injury, she would play basketball.

→ _____

Subjunctive Mood **155**

3 Sentence Practice

A Translate the Korean into English using the given words.

1 a. Will은 너무 이기적이다. 그가 다른 사람들을 좀 더 생각하면 좋을 텐데. (wish, think)

→ Will is too selfish. I _____ more about others.

b. Peter는 너무 게으르다. 그가 부지런하면 좋을 텐데. (diligent)

→ Peter is too lazy. _____ .

2 a. 그 차가 그렇게 비싸지 않았더라면 우리는 그것을 샀을 텐데. (will, buy)

→ If the car _____ so expensive, we _____ it.

b. 그 드레스의 가격이 적절했더라면 나는 그것을 샀을 텐데. (price, reasonable, buy)

→ _____

3 a. 그는 마치 그가 영어를 이해하는 것처럼 고개를 끄덕였다. (as if, understand)

→ He nodded his head _____ .

b. 그 개는 마치 내 말을 이해하는 것처럼 나를 쳐다보았다. (look at, my words)

→ _____

B Unscramble the words to make a sentence.

1 내 다리가 부러지지 않았더라면 너와 스키 타러 갈 텐데.

(go, you, not, with, I, skiing, would, if, broken, my leg, had, I)

→ _____

2 내가 John이라면 공부보다는 야구를 선택할 텐데.

(John, baseball, if, choose, I, rather than, were, I would, studying)

→ _____

3 내가 수영을 배웠다면 지금 수영장에서 즐기고 있을 텐데.

(I, enjoying myself, in the pool, if, now, had, I, to swim, learned, be, might)

→ _____

4 의학적 치료는 네가 더 잘 치유되도록 도울 것이다.

(medical treatment, better, you, would, heal, help)

→ _____

5 집에 혼자 남겨지면 Michael은 하루 종일 컴퓨터 게임을 할 것이다.

(Michael, all day, being, play, left, computer games, would, alone)

→ _____

ACTUAL TEST

> Answers **p. 27**

[1-3] 빈칸에 들어갈 알맞은 말을 고르시오.

1

_____ I had more time, I could exercise after school.

① When   ② Whether   ③ That
④ As   ⑤ If

2

She would have been here earlier if she _____ the train.

① missed   ② has not missed
③ does not miss   ④ had not missed
⑤ did not miss

3

I wish I _____ something to drink. I am so thirsty.

① have   ② had
③ were having   ④ have had
⑤ had had

[4-5] 빈칸에 들어갈 말이 알맞게 짝 지어진 것을 고르시오.

4

• If we ____(A)____ in a city, we would eat out for dinner every night.
• The customer required that the sleeves ____(B)____ made longer.

(A)   (B)   (A)   (B)
① lived – be   ② live – be
③ lived – were   ④ live – were
⑤ lived – have been

5

• If you ____(A)____ Carl later, will you tell him to call me?
• If we had turned left at the intersection, we would not ____(B)____ lost now.

(A)   (B)   (A)   (B)
① see – have had   ② saw – been
③ see – be   ④ saw – be
⑤ see – have been

[6-7] 밑줄 친 부분이 어법상 어색한 문장을 고르시오.

6 ① A good student <u>would not do</u> such a thing.
② If you saw him at night, you <u>were</u> scared.
③ If you are looking for a cheap computer, you <u>should</u> go to Yongsan.
④ If I <u>had not spent</u> all my money, I would buy this jacket.
⑤ <u>Were</u> it not for the fans, we would not survive in this weather.

7 ① It is high time we <u>headed</u> home.
② He is poor, but he acts as if he <u>were</u> a rich guy.
③ He studied very hard. Otherwise, he <u>could not have caught up with</u> the class.
④ If it <u>were not</u> for her support, I could not have achieved my goal.
⑤ I would read more if there <u>were</u> no TV at home.

[8-10] 우리말에 맞게 빈칸에 알맞은 말로 짝 지어진 것을 고르시오.

8

네가 공부를 더 열심히 했다면 시험에서 좋은 결과를 얻었을 텐데.

→ If you _____ harder, you _____ good results on the test.

① study – would get

② studied – would have gotten

③ has studied – would get

④ had studied – would have gotten

⑤ had studied – would get

9

9시가 넘었다. 숙제를 시작했어야 할 시간이다.

→ It is past 9. It is _____ we _____ doing our homework.

① time – start   ② time – started

③ time for – start   ④ high – started

⑤ high time for – started

10

내가 그날 그녀의 주소를 받았더라면 지금 그녀의 집에 갈 수 있을 텐데.

→ _____ I gotten her address that day, I could _____ to her house now.

① Have – go   ② Have – have gone

③ Had – went   ④ Had – go

⑤ Had – have gone

[11-13] 두 문장이 같은 의미가 되도록 빈칸에 알맞은 말을 고르시오.

11

If it were a good movie, it would give you something to learn and think about.

= A good movie _____ you something to learn and think about.

① gave   ② gives   ③ will give

④ would give   ⑤ would have given

12

The trip was only for three days, so I could not visit you in Los Angeles.

= If the trip _____ longer, I _____ you in Los Angeles.

① were – would have visited

② were – would visit

③ had been – would have visited

④ had been – would visit

⑤ had been – visited

13

I would like to go shopping with you, but I am too busy to do that.

= I wish I _____ with you.

① go shopping   ② had gone shopping

③ will go shopping   ④ can go shopping

⑤ could go shopping

14 나머지 넷과 의미가 다른 하나는?

① Without water, nothing would survive on this planet.

② But for water, nothing would survive on this planet.

③ Were it not for water, nothing would survive on this planet.

④ If there were no water, nothing would survive on this planet.

⑤ Had it not been for water, nothing would have survived on this planet.

15 어법상 어색한 것은?

Nick skipped breakfast. Otherwise, he ①would ②not ③had ④been hungry ⑤now.

[16-17] 빈칸에 주어진 단어의 형태가 <u>다른</u> 하나를 고르시오.

16 ① If James ___(do)___ the laundry, he could have worn the shirt that day.

② If Tina ___(do)___ what I told her to do, the result would have been different.

③ If I ___(do)___ the opposite, I would not have made it to the Olympics.

④ If I ___(do)___ something wrong, it would show on my face.

⑤ If the students ___(do)___ a good job, the teacher would not have been so angry.

17 ① I wished we ___(give)___ him a second chance at that time.

② I wished someone ___(give)___ me this same advice sooner.

③ I wish the company ___(give)___ me some options, but it did not.

④ I wish he ___(give)___ me a necklace for my birthday next week.

⑤ I wish I ___(give)___ her my number; there was no way to contact her.

[18-19] 밑줄 친 부분을 바르게 고친 것을 고르시오.

18
> Peter spends money as if he <u>is</u> a millionaire.

① were　　　　② have been
③ has been　　④ had been
⑤ will be

19
> Ms. Brown suggested that Michael <u>would take</u> the expert course.

① could take　　② should take
③ might take　　④ had taken
⑤ took

20 문장이 의미하는 바가 알맞지 <u>않은</u> 것은?

① It is high time you let go of your past.
→ You did not let go of your past yet.

② I wish I could speak confidently in public.
→ I cannot speak confidently in public.

③ If I had known where you were, I would have found you.
→ I did not know where you were then.

④ It would have been nice if you had shared your food.
→ You did not share your food.

⑤ To hear him speak English, you would take him for a foreigner.
→ He is an English-speaking foreigner.

21 if절 전환이 알맞지 <u>않은</u> 것은?

① Should you find any problems with this computer program, please let me know.
→ If you should find any problems with this computer program, please let me know.

② Had he been at school, he would have had access to the computer.
→ If he was at school, he would have had access to the computer.

③ To hear him sing, you would take him for an opera singer.
→ If you heard him sing, you would take him for an opera singer.

④ Telling you the secret, I would become an unreliable person.
→ If I told you the secret, I would become an unreliable person.

⑤ A singing bird in the morning would mean good fortune.
→ If a bird sang in the morning, it would mean good fortune.

> Answers **p. 27**

[22-23] 우리말에 맞게 주어진 단어를 사용하여 빈칸에 알맞은 말을 쓰시오.

22
> 배가 아파. 핫도그를 먹지 않았더라면 좋았을 텐데.
> (wish, eat)

→ My stomach hurts. _____ the hotdog.

23
> 네가 자신만의 머물 곳을 찾아야 할 시간이다.
> (high, that)

→ _____ you got your own place to stay.

[24-25] 다음 문장을 어법에 맞게 고쳐 쓰시오.

24
> If Mina had not forgotten her bus card, she would not be late for school.

→ _____

_____

25
> If I had taken my parents' advice, I would have been happier now.

→ _____

_____

[26-28] 우리말에 맞게 주어진 단어를 바르게 배열하여 문장을 쓰시오.

26
> Alex는 마치 급하게 할 무언가가 있는 것처럼 빨리 먹는다.
> (something, he, Alex, had, as if, fast, urgent, eats, to do)

→ _____

27
> 만약 그의 조언이 없었더라면, 나는 그 사업을 시작하지 않았을 것이다.
> (it, advice, had not, if, his, would not, I, started, for, been, the business, have)

→ _____

_____

28
> 네가 다른 사람들에게 좀 더 예의가 있었으면 좋겠다.
> (were, to, wish, more, I, you, others, polite)

→ _____

🎯 CHALLENGE!

Write your own answer to the question.

01 If you had a billion won, what would you do?

_____

_____

02 Write one thing that you regret about what you did or what you did not do. (Use *I wish . . . .*)

_____

_____

CHAPTER 12

Agreement & Narration

일치와 화법

UNIT 01 **Number Agreement**
수일치

UNIT 02 **Tense Agreement**
시제 일치

UNIT 03 **Indirect Speech**
간접화법

Number Agreement 수일치

A With Singular Verbs

Each student **has** a locker.
Physics **was** one of the most difficult subjects for me.
Three years **seems** like a long time to me.
Watching movies **is** my only hobby.

- ◆ 「every/each + Noun」, -thing, -one, -body
  Nothing **has** changed.

- ◆ **Plural Names of Subjects, Countries, Diseases**
  The Philippines **is** made up of more than 7,000 islands.

- ◆ **Amounts and Quantities**
  Ten kilometers **is** not easy for a child to walk.

- ◆ **Gerunds and Noun Clauses as Subjects**
  Speaking English **is** essential to work at the airport.

B With Plural Verbs

Both my father and *my uncle* **are** going to visit me.
A number of students **are** in favor of having a school uniform.
The young usually **give** their seats to the elderly on the subway.

• a number of + 복수명사:
(많은 …) 복수 취급
the number of + 복수명
사: (…의 숫자) 단수 취급

- ◆ **A and B, a number of (people)**
  The professor *and* the poet **have** published their 5th book.
  cf. The professor and poet **has** published his 5th book.
      The number of students to quit school **has** risen during the past 3 years.

- ◆ **the + Adjective (= all Adjective people)**
  The injured **were** taken to the nearby hospital.

C With Singular or Plural Verbs

Most of the news **was** true.
All the people there **were** kind.
Half (of) the money **was** donated to charity.

- ◆ **most/all/half/some/ the rest/Fractions** + (of) ⎡ **+ Singular Nouns → Singular Verbs**
                                                    ⎣ **+ Plural Nouns → Plural Verbs**
  One-third of my friends **wear** glasses.

EXERCISE   **A** **Choose the correct one for each sentence.**

1   Each room (has, have) its own unique color.

2   Every student and every teacher (is, are) going to gather in the auditorium.

3   Ethics (is, are) concerned with what is morally right and wrong.

4   I think reading books (is, are) worthwhile.

5   Both her T-shirt and skirt (was, were) stained.

B **Choose the correct one in the box and fill in the blank.**

were	has	are	was

1   Ten years _____ passed since I saw him last.

2   All the classrooms _____ empty when I went to school at 7.

3   The number of festivals in Gangwondo _____ increased lately.

4   Almost 90 percent of the students _____ going on a field trip tomorrow.

5   The rest of the money _____ saved for the next event.

C **Correct the underlined part.**

1   Two-thirds of the students has received A's.   → _____

2   Monitoring the computer systems are Ryan's job.   → _____

3   The Netherlands were the winner of the World Cup last year. → _____

4   Five kilograms are hard to lose within a month.   → _____

5   The young has more opportunities to try new things than the old.

　　　　　　　　　　　　　　　　　　　　　　　　　　　　　→ _____

D **Complete the sentence using the given words.**

1   많은 학생들이 자원봉사 활동에 참가한다. (number, take part in)

→ _____ volunteer activities.

2   그 지휘자이자 작곡가는 새 앨범을 발표할 예정이다. (composer, be going to)

→ The conductor and _____ release a new album.

3   그 피자의 5분의 1만이 먹지 않은 채 남아 있다. (one-fifth)

→ Only _____ been left uneaten.

4   그 학생들 대부분이 그 게임을 어떻게 하는지 알고 있다. (most of)

→ _____ how to play the game.

Tense Agreement 시제 일치

A Agreement of Sequent Verb Tenses

A 시제 일치

주절의 시제가 현재이면 종속절에는 모든 시제가 올 수 있고, 주절의 시제가 과거이면 종속절에 과거나 과거완료 시제가 온다.

| She *thinks* | he **is** wise.
he **was** wise.
he **has been** wise.
he **will be** wise. | She *thought* | he **was** wise.
he **had been** wise.
he **would be** wise. |
| Main Clause | Subordinating Clause | Main Clause | Subordinating Clause |

e.g. I *think* that Frank seldom **tells** lies.
I *thought* that Frank seldom **told** lies.

He *promises* that he **will call** me later.
He *promised* that he **would call** me later.

She *does not know* that Philip's family **came** (**has come**) from Europe.
She *did not know* that Philip's family **had come** from Europe.

cf. We *have to* hurry because we **must** be there by 9 o'clock.
→ We *had to* hurry because we **must** be there by 9 o'clock.

cf. 주절의 시제가 현재에서 과거로 바뀌어도 조동사 must는 형태가 바뀌지 않는다.

B Exceptions

B 시제 일치의 예외

불변의 진리, 과학적 사실, 현재의 습관, 속담은 항상 현재시제로 쓰고 역사적 사실은 항상 과거시제로 쓴다.

People *did not know* that the Earth **goes** around the Sun.
I *learned* today that water **consists** of oxygen and hydrogen.
Paul *said* that he still **wakes up** at 5 o'clock every morning.
My grandmother *used to* say that a stitch in time **saves** nine.
The textbook *says* that *Apollo 11* **landed** on the moon in 1969.

No need for tense agreement in the subjunctive
I *think* that he **would buy** the jacket if he **had** enough money.
→ I *thought* that he **would buy** the jacket if he **had** enough money.

I *wish* I **had** more time before the test.
→ I *wished* I **had** more time before the test.

EXERCISE

A Choose the correct one for each sentence.

1 Everyone knew that he (is, was) kidding except for Stacy.

2 Ted was on the bed when his friends (come, came) to his house.

3 You (have to, had to) warm up before you exercise.

4 I heard that he (has, had had) a part-time job when he was in middle school.

5 I (wonder, wondered) whether he is serious or not.

6 Wendy liked the story of how her parents (met, had met) 15 years ago.

B Change the present tense sentence to the past tense sentence.

1 I do not believe that she is taking care of 60 dogs.

→ I did not believe that she _____ care of 60 dogs.

2 He promises that he will be waiting for me there.

→ He promised that he _____ for me there.

3 I think he received the package already.

→ I thought he _____ the package already.

4 She thinks she must protect her little brother all the time.

→ She thought she _____ her little brother all the time.

C Correct the underlined part.

1 The students do not know that World War II begins in 1939. → _____

2 Tom said that Italy bordered France. → _____

3 Louis kept saying that heaven helped those who help themselves.

→ _____

4 Mom said that Grandpa took a walk for 30 minutes after dinner every day.

→ _____

5 My little brother learned yesterday that ten times ten made one hundred.

→ _____

D Complete the sentence using the given words.

1 그녀는 다시 늦지 않을 거라고 약속했다. (will not, late)

→ She promised that she _____.

2 아무도 그가 법대에서 공부했었다고 생각조차 하지 않았다. (have studied)

→ Nobody even thought that _____ at law school.

3 나는 목성 주위를 도는 60개 이상의 달이 있다는 것을 몰랐다. (there, more)

→ I did not know that _____ 60 moons orbiting Jupiter.

Indirect Speech 간접화법

A Indirect Speech with Declarative Sentences

He said to me, "I am going on a trip this weekend." <direct>
①   ② ③ ④   ⑤

→ He **told** me **(that) he was** going on a trip **that** weekend.
<indirect>

① said to → told, said → said

② , → (that)

③ Change speaker (I → he/she)

④ Change tenses (Present/Future → Past, Past → Past perfect)

⑤ this → that, these → those, now → then, ago → before, here → there,
today → that day, tomorrow → the next (following) day

B Indirect Speech with Questions

She said to me, "When will you be home?" <direct>
→ She **asked** me when **I would be** home. <indirect>
Jennifer said to me, "Are you coming to my party?" <direct>
→ Jennifer **asked** me **if (whether) I was coming** to **her** party.
<indirect>

- **Wh-Questions**
「**ask + O + wh-word + S + V**」
They said to their mother, "Why shouldn't we do this?"
→ They **asked** their mother **why they shouldn't do that.**

- **Yes/No Questions**
「**ask + O + if (whether) + S + V**」
She said to me, "May I sit next to you?"
→ She **asked** me **if she might sit** next to **me.**

Use to-infinitives in indirect speech with imperative sentences
The guard said to them, "Watch out!"
→ The guard **told** them **to watch out.**
She said to me, "Don't close the door."
→ She **advised** me **not to close** the door.

A 평서문의 간접화법
전환
① 전달 동사를 바꾼다.
② 주절의 콤마와 인용 부호
를 없애고 that을 쓴다.
(that 생략 가능)
③ 인용 부호 안의 인칭대명
사를 전달자에 맞게 바꾼
다.
④ 인용 부호 안의 시제를 바
꾼다. (현재/미래 → 과거,
과거 → 과거완료)
⑤ 전달자의 시점에 맞게 대
명사 및 부사를 바꾼다.

B 의문문의 간접화법
전환
• 의문사가 있는 경우
「ask + 목적어 + 의문사 +
주어 + 동사」

• 의문사가 없는 경우
「ask + 목적어 + if
(whether) + 주어 + 동사」

EXERCISE

A Choose the correct one for each sentence.

1 She said, "The house is too cold inside."

→ She said (if, that) the house (is, was) too cold inside.

2 The minister announced, "The missing plane was discovered yesterday."

→ The minister announced that the missing plane (had, had been) discovered the day (before, ago).

3 My father said to me, "I should buy a new computer."

→ My father (said, told) me that he (should, has to) buy a new computer.

4 Mary said to them, "I live in Busan now."

→ Mary told them that she (lives, lived) in Busan (now, then).

B Fill in the blank to complete indirect speech sentence.

1 "What is your name?" he said to me.

→ He asked me _____ .

2 "How old is your sister?" he said to her.

→ He asked her _____ .

3 The police officer said to the boy, "Where are your parents?"

→ The police officer asked the boy _____ .

C Correct the underlined part.

1 I asked my brother it was raining.　　　　　　　　　→ _____

2 The lady asked me whether will I mind if she sat there.　→ _____

3 She told me buy some groceries on my way back home.　→ _____

4 The owner of the shop ordered his clerks do not doze off during working hours.　　　　　　　　　　　　　　　　　　　→ _____

D Complete the sentence using the given words.

1 선생님은 Jack에게 왜 그렇게 늦었는지 물었다. (why, so late)

→ The teacher asked Jack _____ .

2 Laura는 네가 이미 호주로 떠났다고 말했다. (already, leave for)

→ Laura said that you _____ Australia.

3 비행기 승무원은 소년에게 그가 영어를 할 수 있는지를 물었다. (can speak)

→ The flight attendant asked the boy _____ .

4 나의 어머니는 내게 시간을 낭비하지 말라고 충고하셨다. (advise, waste my time)

→ _____

WRITING CONNECTION

 Grammar Check-up

A Choose the correct one.

1 Three thousand won _____ all I have now.

ⓐ is   ⓑ are   ⓒ was   ⓓ were

2 The unemployed _____ to find new jobs.

ⓐ struggles   ⓑ struggle   ⓒ is struggling   ⓓ has struggled

3 We asked her where she _____ .

ⓐ had been   ⓑ has been   ⓒ is   ⓓ will be

4 They thought their parents _____ back before dinner.

ⓐ come   ⓑ will come   ⓒ have come   ⓓ would come

5 The children kept asking their teacher when they _____ lunch.

ⓐ will have   ⓑ have   ⓒ could have   ⓓ can have

6 The teacher asked the new student whether he _____ the instructions.

ⓐ understand   ⓑ understood   ⓒ can understand   ⓓ will understand

B Circle the inappropriate one between ⓐ and ⓑ. Then correct it.

1 Don't be scared. The dogs <u>growls</u> when <u>they</u> are hungry.   _____
                              ⓐ   ⓑ

2 Surfing in the ocean and rock-climbing <u>are</u> his <u>hobby</u>.   _____
                                        ⓐ   ⓑ

3 Each <u>sculpture</u> <u>weigh</u> a ton.   _____
          ⓐ   ⓑ

4 The designer and programmer <u>are</u> able <u>to help</u> you with your project.   _____
                              ⓐ   ⓑ

5 The number of people <u>lined</u> up at the ticket box <u>were</u> more than fifty.   _____
                        ⓐ   ⓑ

6 Tony did not seem <u>to understand</u> why his mom <u>tells</u> him to be quiet.   _____
                    ⓐ   ⓑ

2 Phrases to Sentences

A Complete the sentence by referring to the Korean translation.

1 그 케이크의 절반을 벌써 먹었다. (half)

→ _____ already been eaten.

2 선생님은 누가 영어를 유창하게 말하는지 알고 싶어 했다. (who, speak)

→ The teacher wanted to know _____ fluently.

3 많은 사람들이 해마다 그 축제에 온다. (number, come)

→ _____ to the festival every year.

4 2년은 그녀가 기다리기에는 긴 시간처럼 보인다. (seem like)

→ _____ for her to wait.

5 학생들 각각은 자신의 행동에 대해 책임이 있다. (each)

→ _____ responsible for his or her actions.

6 엄마는 나에게 그 다툼이 무엇에 관한 것이었는지 물어보셨다. (what, the fight)

→ My mom asked me _____ .

B Underline the error and rewrite the sentence.

1 I heard you will leave for Canada soon.

→ _____

2 Some of the money were spent to buy clothes.

→ _____

3 They learned that Korea becomes independent from Japan in 1945.

→ _____

4 Measles are a highly contagious disease caused by a virus.

→ _____

5 The arrival of new spring fashions have excited young shoppers.

→ _____

6 Dad couldn't make it to dinner because his office was usually busy on Mondays.

→ _____

3 Sentence Practice

A Translate the Korean into English using the given words.

1 a. 사람들이 우리가 공원에서 무엇을 하고 있는지 물었다. (what, do)

   → People asked us _____ in the park.

b. 그녀는 내가 그녀의 방에서 무엇을 하고 있는지 물었다. (do, in her room)

   → _____

2 a. 그 가수와 화가는 오랜 시간 친구로 지내오고 있다. (friends)

   → The singer and the artist _____ for a long time.

b. 그 배우와 그 여배우는 이번 영화에서 라이벌 관계이다. (rivals, film)

   → _____

3 a. 모두가 그가 그 사고에서 죽었다고 생각했다. (be killed)

   → Everyone _____ he _____ in the accident.

b. 모두가 그녀가 대학에서 피아노를 전공할 것이라고 생각했다. (major in, in college)

   → _____

4 a. 그는 나에게 젊을 때 가능한 한 많은 돈을 저축하라고 충고했다. (advise, save)

   → He _____ as much money as possible when young.

b. 부모는 그 어린 남자아이에게 식당에서 바르게 행동하라고 충고했다. (behave, properly)

   → _____

B Unscramble the words to make a sentence.

1 누군가가 내 개인 정보를 사용하고 있다면 저는 무엇을 해야 할까요?

(I, if, should, is using, what, do, my personal information, someone)

   → _____

2 간호사는 그에게 아침 식사를 했는지 물었다.

(whether, asked, the nurse, breakfast, him, he, had eaten)

   → _____

3 액션 영화를 보는 것이 내가 스트레스를 푸는 방법이다.

(is, the way, watching, I, action movies, my stress, relieve)

   → _____

ACTUAL TEST

[1-3] 빈칸에 들어갈 알맞은 말을 고르시오.

1
> Ten kilometers _____ equal to 1,000 meters.

① am   ② are
③ is   ④ was
⑤ were

2
> The United States _____ 50 states, including Alaska and Hawaii.

① have   ② are having
③ has   ④ had
⑤ have had

3
> Simon said what he told me yesterday _____ a lie.

① be   ② was
③ were   ④ has been
⑤ have been

[4-5] 빈칸에 들어갈 수 없는 말을 고르시오.

4
> _____ of the students are more interested in science than in social studies.

① Some   ② Most
③ A few   ④ Almost
⑤ All

5
> Half of the _____ has disappeared.

① water   ② people
③ cake   ④ money
⑤ information

[6-8] 밑줄 친 부분이 어법상 어색한 것을 고르시오.

6
① The rest of the money <u>was</u> saved for their trip.
② Three kilograms <u>is</u> a proper weight to lose in a month.
③ Not Alex but you <u>have to</u> go there and talk to them.
④ A number of suggestions <u>were</u> made by the students.
⑤ Physics <u>are</u> the knowledge of nature.

7
① A month <u>has</u> already passed since we entered this school.
② A number of students <u>want</u> to go to the amusement park instead of the zoo.
③ The rich <u>get</u> richer, and the poor <u>get</u> poorer.
④ Each room <u>need</u> to be painted again.
⑤ Where <u>is</u> the Maldives?

8
① Almost all of the students <u>are</u> familiar with the game.
② More than 90 percent of the water <u>is</u> polluted.
③ Everyone knew who he <u>is</u>, but no one said anything.
④ Five percent of the students at my school <u>wear</u> glasses.
⑤ Mathematics <u>was</u> one of my favorite subjects in high school.

9

> "Where have you been?" he said to me.
> → He asked me where I _____ .

① am   ② was   ③ have been

④ had been   ⑤ would have been

10

> I said to my sister, "Is it raining in Busan?"
> → I asked my sister _____ in Busan.

① that it was raining

② that was it raining

③ if was it raining

④ whether it was raining

⑤ whether was it raining

11

> "What time does the bus leave?" Mary said to the bus driver.
> → Mary asked the bus driver _____ .

① what time the bus left

② what time the bus leaves

③ what time the bus has left

④ what time does the bus leave

⑤ if the bus left at what time

12 화법을 바꿔 쓸 때 빈칸에 공통으로 들어갈 알맞은 말은?

> • She said to him, "I'm tired."
> → She _____ him that she was tired.
> • He said to her, "Get some rest."
> → He _____ her to get some rest.

① asked   ② advised   ③ talked

④ told   ⑤ said

[13-14] 어법상 어색한 것을 고르시오.

13

> I thought you have already left a month
>   ①   ②   ③   ④
> ago.
> ⑤

14

> The politician, as well as the journalists,
>   ①
> are expected to arrive around 1 p.m.
> ②   ③   ④   ⑤

15 빈칸에 들어갈 말이 알맞게 짝 지어진 것은?

> • My brother did not know that a whale ___(A)___ a mammal until I told him about it.
> • Half of the visitors ___(B)___ know where their seats are.

    (A)   (B)

① was – do not

② is – did not

③ was – does not

④ is – does not

⑤ is – do not

16 어법상 어색한 문장은?

① The banker found out that his client had visited earlier that day.

② I did not know that your family has moved out of the city.

③ You told me that the shop does not close until 5 p.m.

④ The teacher explained that Jupiter has a ring around it.

⑤ Dad promised that he would take me to the popular restaurant.

[17-19] 빈칸에 주어진 단어의 형태가 <u>다른</u> 하나를 고르시오.

17 ① I think either Eric or Michael ___(be)___ wrong.

② Everyone ___(be)___ waiting for summer vacation.

③ Andy is adventurous, and both of his children ___(be)___ as well.

④ The cell phone, I think, ___(be)___ the greatest invention of all time.

⑤ Keeping a secret ___(be)___ not easy for anyone.

18 ① Somebody ___(have)___ to do something about it.

② Everybody ___(have)___ a dream to meet someone special.

③ Most of the information in this file ___(have)___ been obtained from the Internet.

④ Some parts of this page ___(have)___ been torn off.

⑤ Comfortable clothes ___(have)___ became a trend for teenagers.

19 ① Sue refused to explain what she ___(do)___ yesterday.

② The children ___(do)___ a great job on their painting, which was done yesterday.

③ Nick would be somewhere else now if he ___(do)___ not apply for the job.

④ John seems to be alone all the time because he ___(do)___ not enjoy hanging out with his friends.

⑤ Tom asked me whether I ___(do)___ a good job on my presentation during science class.

20 화법 전환이 알맞지 <u>않은</u> 것은?

① Sally said, "I will take a shuttle bus to the airport."

→ Sally said she would take a shuttle bus to the airport.

② My friend said, "You need to see a doctor."

→ My friend said I needed to see a doctor.

③ The coach said to the players, "Do your best in the game."

→ The coach ordered the players to do their best in the game.

④ James said, "I have taken Spanish classes before."

→ James said he had taken Spanish classes before.

⑤ The wife said to her husband, "Please don't take any risks."

→ The wife begged her husband who didn't take any risks.

21 빈칸에 들어갈 수 있는 말로 알맞게 짝 지어진 것은?

> Ms. Smith asked her secretary _____ he had submitted the papers in time.

① if, what

② if, which

③ if, whether

④ whether, what

⑤ whether, which

[22-23] 다음 글을 읽고, 물음에 답하시오.

One of the main reasons my parents came to the U.S. was a desire to provide good educational and economic opportunities for us. <u>Both my brother and I was well aware</u> that they are working really hard for us. Our parents' efforts and sacrifice (A) (be) the sources of motivation for us to try to do our best. Like most immigrant children, we feel a strong sense of obligation to support our parents. I think the value we place upon family (B) (remain) higher than that of most other American children.

22 (A), (B)에 주어진 단어를 각각 알맞은 형태로 쓰시오.

(A) _____ (B) _____

23 밑줄 친 부분을 어법에 맞게 고쳐 쓰시오.

_____

[24-25] 다음 문장을 간접화법으로 바꿔 쓰시오.

24 Susan said to me, "Where will you be on Christmas?"

➡ _____

_____

25 Mr. Smith said to us, "Practice makes perfect."

➡ _____

_____

[26-28] 우리말에 맞게 주어진 단어를 바르게 배열하여 문장을 쓰시오.

26 모든 남자와 모든 여자가 그 사우나에서 두 개의 수건을 받는다.

(given, and, every, two towels, every, the sauna, man, is, woman, in)

➡ _____

_____

27 15킬로미터는 걸어가기에는 너무 멀다.

(walk, fifteen, is, too, kilometers, far, to)

➡ _____

28 간호사는 나에게 침대에 누우라고 말했다.

(me, the bed, the nurse, to, told, on, lie down)

➡ _____

🎯 CHALLENGE!

Write your own answer to the question.

01 What do you have in common with your best friend? (Use *both*.)

_____

_____

02 What is the gender ratio in your class?

_____

_____

* gender ratio 남녀 성비

CHAPTER
13

Sentence Arrangement
기타 구문

UNIT
01

Emphasis, Negation, & Parallel Structure
강조, 부정, 병렬 구조

UNIT
02

Apposition, Inversion, & Ellipsis
동격, 도치, 생략

Emphasis, Negation, & Parallel Structure

강조, 부정, 병렬 구조

A 강조

일반동사를 강조할 때는 조동사 do를 동사 앞에 쓰고, 다른 문장 요소를 강조할 때는 「It is (was) . . . that」을 쓴다.

A Emphasis

I **do** *understand* why my mom was so upset.
It **was** *the apple pie* **that** my grandmother used to make for us.

- **Verb emphasis with *do***
  Amy **did** *love* him, but she had to leave him.

- **Emphasis with *It is (was) . . . that***
  I met Tony in the library yesterday.
  → **It was** *I* **that (who)** met Tony in the library yesterday.
  → **It was** *Tony* **that (whom)** I met in the library yesterday.
  → **It was** *in the library* **that (where)** I met Tony yesterday.
  → **It was** *yesterday* **that (when)** I met Tony in the library.

B 부정

no, neither, none을 써서 '아무도 ~하지 않다'라는 의미로 전체부정을 나타낸다. 부분부정은 「not + all/always」 형태로 '모두 ~한 것은 아니다'라는 뜻을 나타낸다.

- neither: not . . . either
  none: no . . . one

B Negation

None of them has breakfast.
Not everyone likes the math class.

- **Complete negation: no one, none, neither, nothing**
  Neither of them answered the question.

- **Partial negation: not + all/every/both/always**
  Not both of them agreed with me.
  She is **not always** kind.

C 병렬 구조

등위접속사(and, but)나 상관접속사(both A and B, either A or B)로 연결된 두 개 이상의 단어, 구, 절은 문법적으로 같은 형태로 쓴다.

C Parallel Structure

Oliver likes to *cook* **and** *eat*.
The drama is suitable for **both** *children* **and** *adults*.

e.g. He has done the work **not only** *quickly* **but also** *perfectly*.
I would like to go **either** *camping* **or** *fishing*.

no + Noun (= not . . . any) 어떤 …도 없는 (아닌)
I have **no** plans for this weekend.
→ I do **not** have **any** plans for this weekend.
cf. 「no + 명사」가 주어로 쓰일 때는 「not + any 명사」로 바꿔 쓸 수 없다.

No food is left. (○)　　　Not any food is left. (✕)

EXERCISE

A Choose the correct one for each sentence.

1 I (do, does) like your gift.

2 Joe did (finish, finished) his homework.

3 We (do, did) have 20 rainy days in July last year.

4 (This, It) was Jim who made this sauce.

5 It was not a ring (who, that) Dan gave me for my birthday gift.

B Correct the underlined part.

1 Not answer is correct.　→ _____

2 She believes not one hates flowers, but some people do.　→ _____

3 He has two choices, but he does not like neither of them.　→ _____

4 I will try again because I do not have nothing to lose.　→ _____

5 He does not eat no meat these days.　→ _____

6 All not his books are interesting. Some of them are boring.　→ _____

7 The clerk is always not nice to her customers. She is unfriendly sometimes.

→ _____

C Fill in the blank using the given word.

1 Mary enjoys hiking, swimming, and _____ her bicycle. (ride)

2 The students were asked to write their reports quickly, _____, and thoroughly. (accurate)

3 I was surprised by both his modesty and _____. (kind)

4 My cat likes not only _____ with a ball but also chasing my dog. (play)

D Complete the sentence using the given words.

1 Jacob은 돈뿐 아니라 명성도 원한다. (not only, fame)

→ Jacob wants _____.

2 모든 소년이 스포츠를 보는 것과 하는 것을 좋아하는 것은 아니다. (every, like)

→ _____ to watch and play sports.

3 내가 구급약 상자를 보관하는 곳은 바로 이 서랍 안이다. (drawer, that)

→ _____ I keep a first-aid kit.

4 나는 너의 도움에 정말 감사한다. (do, appreciate)

→ I _____.

02

Apposition, Inversion, & Ellipsis 동격, 도치, 생략

A 동격
명사 뒤의 명사(구,절)가 앞의 명사를 보충 설명한다. 이때 콤마(,), that, of, to부정사 등으로 이어진다.

B 도치
부사(구)를 강조하기 위해 문두에 오면 주어와 동사가 도치된다.
부정어가 문두에 오면 be동사 또는 조동사가 도치되며, 일반동사 문장에서는 do를 조동사 대신 쓴다.

C 생략
반복되는 부분이나 생략되어도 의미 파악이 가능한 부분은 생략한다.
• and, but, or로 연결된 문장에서 반복되는 부분 생략
• 부사절에서 접속사 뒤의 「S + be동사」 생략
• 비교급에서 as, than 뒤에서 반복되는 부분 생략
• 목적격 관계대명사 생략
• 목적어 역할의 명사절을 이끄는 접속사 that 생략

A Apposition

Matt, **my best friend**, is a very good dancer. <Noun + Noun>
The fact **that he is the son of the owner** is often forgotten.
<Noun + that + S + V>
I am considering *the possibility* **of studying** abroad.
<Noun + of + Noun>
He had no *desire* **to be the next king** after his father.
<Noun + to infinitive>

B Inversion

Here *comes* the bus!
Never *does* he borrow money.

◆ **Inversion with adverbial phrases of place**
Along the street *walked* John.

cf. 「**Adverbial phrases + S (Pronoun) + V**」
Here she *comes*! (○)   Here comes she! (×)

◆ **Inversion with negative expressions**
Not only *was* the movie boring, but it was also violent.

C Ellipsis

She is here on Monday **but** (she is) out for the rest of the week.
I like listening to music **while** (I am) studying.
His brother, Dan, sings better **than** he (does).
They are the people (that) I went to school with.
Ellie thought (that) her success in business was fortunate.

After *so, neither, nor*
• 「**so** + V + S」 ···도 그렇다
  I am a baseball fan. — **So** *am* I.
  She cooks often, and **so** *does* he.
• 「**neither/nor** + V + S」 ···도 그렇지 않다
  I cannot eat shrimp. — **Neither** 〔**Nor**〕 *can* I.
  She was not late, and **neither** 〔**nor**〕 *was* he.

178 Chapter 13

EXERCISE

A Unscramble the words to complete the sentence.

1 _____, _____, punched the goalkeeper in the back.
(soccer player, Robin, a hot-tempered)

2 _____, _____, visits my house often.
(my neighbors, of, Mrs. Robinson, one)

3 _____ does not make any difference.
(the son of a rich man, the fact, he, that, is)

4 Think about how low _____ are.
(of, the lottery, the odds, winning)

B Choose the correct words for each sentence.

1 Into the classroom (walked the teacher, did the teacher walked).

2 Never (sleep I, do I sleep) in class.

3 Down (came the rain, the rain came) and washed the spider out.

4 Little (knew I, did I know) about him when we were in elementary school.

5 Not only (is Sam, Sam is) a great leader, but also he is a warm-hearted friend.

C Put parentheses ( ) around the words that can be omitted.

1 He was, and he will remain, the greatest basketball player.

2 I will have to go this way, and you will have to go that way.

3 My mom enjoys reading books while she is drinking coffee on Sunday.

4 I ate much more food at the buffet than he did.

5 Did Kate return the books that she borrowed last week?

6 I wish I had known that James moved to another school.

D Complete the sentence using the given words.

1 첫 번째는 사랑이 오고, 그 다음 결혼이 온다. (come, marriage)
→ First _____, and then _____.

2 Thomas는 우리 반에서 가장 똑똑한 학생인데 책을 많이 읽는다. (the brightest)
→ _____, _____, reads a lot of books.

3 백만 년 후에도 나는 내 고향에 돌아가지 않을 것이다. (will, go back)
→ Not in a million years _____ to my hometown.

WRITING CONNECTION

 STEP 1 Grammar Check-up

A Choose the correct one.

1 Tom _____ the answer, but he remained silent.
ⓐ knows   ⓑ does know   ⓒ did know   ⓓ will know

2 _____ did he show the scar on his back.
ⓐ What   ⓑ Any   ⓒ Some   ⓓ Never

3 Peter saw a snake coiling on a rock while _____ home.
ⓐ walk   ⓑ to walk   ⓒ walking   ⓓ walked

4 The fact _____ she is a college professor is not relevant to this case.
ⓐ that   ⓑ which   ⓒ what   ⓓ of

5 Only in this way _____ how to build good relationships.
ⓐ could learn Ella   ⓑ could Ella learn   ⓒ Ella could learn   ⓓ Ella learn could

B Circle the inappropriate one between ⓐ and ⓑ. Then correct it.

1 Jason insists that he does finish his homework last night.   _____
              ⓐ   ⓑ

2 He did not come to school in time, nor he did bring any of his books.
         ⓐ   ⓑ
                                                              _____

3 His desire to becoming a successful politician blinded his judgement.
                    ⓐ   ⓑ
                                                              _____

4 It was at this school which she taught us math for five years.   _____
         ⓐ   ⓑ

5 Under no circumstances I will ever talk to him again.   _____
              ⓐ   ⓑ

6 The rumor which David was in the hospital turned out to be false.   _____
              ⓐ   ⓑ

2 Phrases to Sentences

A Complete the sentence by referring to the Korean translation.

1 Neal은 수학 천재인데 그 문제를 20분 안에 풀었다. (genius)

→ _____, _____, solved the question within 20 minutes.

2 나를 우울하게 만드는 것은 바로 이 끔찍한 날씨이다. (it, make)

→ _____ this awful weather _____ me gloomy.

3 우리는 루브르 박물관에 가지 않았고 모나리자도 보지 않았다. (we, see)

→ We did not go to the Louvre, nor _____ the *Mona Lisa*.

4 역 안에는 수십 명의 집 없는 사람들이 산다. (dozens of, homeless)

→ Inside the station _____ people.

5 그들 둘 다 대학에 가는 것에는 관심이 없었다. (neither)

→ _____ was interested in going to university.

6 Wilson 선생님은 정말로 너를 이해했고, 나도 마찬가지였다. (do)

→ Mr. Wilson _____ understand you, and _____ I.

B Underline the error and rewrite the sentence.

1 Here come the rain!

→ _____

2 Not of these shirts fits me perfectly.

→ _____

3 She packed her suitcase, open the door, and ran down the stairs.

→ _____

4 He would rather die than to surrender to the enemy.

→ _____

5 Students were asked to do their assignments accurately and precise.

→ _____

6 Little thought she that Jake would call her again.

→ _____

3 Sentence Practice

A Translate the Korean into English using the given words.

1 a. 그녀는 가족들과 저녁을 먹고 TV를 본다. (eat, watch)

→ She _____ supper and _____ TV with her family.

b. 그는 샤워를 하고, 아침을 먹고, 자전거를 타고 학교에 간다. (take, have, ride his bike)

→ _____ to school.

2 a. 방을 이렇게 엉망으로 만든 것은 바로 Jake였다. (who, make)

→ _____ the room messy like this.

b. 그 공을 차서 유리창을 깬 것은 바로 Ashley였다. (kick the ball)

→ _____ and broke the window.

3 a. 나는 그녀에게 좀 더 주의해 달라고 정말로 부탁했다. (do, ask, more careful)

→ I _____ to _____ .

b. 나는 그에게 나를 도와 달라고 정말로 요청했다. (do, ask, help)

→ _____

4 a. 내가 물에 대한 두려움을 극복하리라고는 전혀 기대하지 못했다. (expect, overcome)

→ Never _____ my fear of water.

b. 그는 손가락 하나도 움직이지 않았다. (finger, move)

→ Not _____ .

B Unscramble the words to make a sentence.

1 극장까지 5번 버스를 타거나 걸어갈 수 있다.

(the number 5 bus, walk to, take, either, you, or, can, the theater)

→ _____

2 Emma가 그 노래를 부른 것은 바로 그녀의 이모의 결혼식이었다.

(that, at, it was, her aunt's wedding, the song, sang, Emma)

→ _____

3 우리는 Jimmy의 생일 파티에서 정말 즐거운 시간을 가졌다.

(Jimmy's, a good time, we, have, at, did, birthday party)

→ _____

ACTUAL TEST

> Answers **p. 32**

[1-3] 빈칸에 들어갈 알맞은 말을 고르시오.

1
> My father is very healthy. He neither
> smokes nor _____.

① drink   ② to drink
③ drank   ④ have drunk
⑤ drinks

2
> Trust me. I _____ take my cold
> medicine yesterday.

① will   ② does   ③ am doing
④ did   ⑤ have done

3
> It was Mary _____ received the
> phone call.

① that   ② whom   ③ if
④ what   ⑤ which

4 두 문장의 의미가 같을 때 빈칸에 들어갈 말로 알맞은
것은?

> She is not a singer. She is not a nurse
> either.
> = She is _____ a singer nor a
> nurse.

① too   ② as   ③ either
④ nor   ⑤ neither

[5-6] 대화의 빈칸에 들어갈 알맞은 말을 고르시오.

5
> A: I haven't eaten anything.
> B: _____

① So am I.   ② Me, too.
③ Neither have I.   ④ So have I.
⑤ Nor have I.

6
> A: I found the yoga class too difficult
>   for beginners.
> B: _____

① So did I.   ② So am I.
③ Neither am I.   ④ Neither do I.
⑤ Neither did I.

[7-8] 어법상 <u>어색한</u> 문장을 고르시오.

7
① He makes and spends a lot of money.
② I did saw the president in the lobby!
③ Roy is going south and Sara north.
④ Never have I seen such cute puppies.
⑤ Into the classroom walked the famous
   girl group.

8
① The fact that she rejected his offer is
   shocking to me.
② Never have I met such a selfish person.
③ Under the table lies Charlie, our dog.
④ Little I knew about her when we lived
   next door to each other.
⑤ It was Mr. Jones that taught us English
   for two years.

9

> At the acting school, I ① learned how
> ② to read, how ③ to stand, how
> ④ to cry, and ⑤ to talk with fans.

10

> ① No sooner ② we had lied down
> ③ to sleep ④ than there ⑤ was a
> knock on the door.

11

> I do not ① think ② neither ③ of us
> ④ will ⑤ get the prize.

12

> 너는 내가 전화를 하지 않았다고 말하지만 나는
> 그날 너에게 정말로 전화했다.
> → You say I did not call you, but I
> _____ call you that day.

① do   ② do not
③ did   ④ did not
⑤ does

13

> 우리는 수지가 그렇게 긴장하는 것을 결코 본 적이
> 없었다.
> → Never _____ Suzie so
> nervous.

① we had seen   ② had we seen
③ had seen we   ④ have we seen
⑤ we have seen

14

> The snowballs that the children made
> rolled down the hill.

① Down the hill rolled the snowballs that
the children made.
② Down the hill the snowballs rolled that
the children made.
③ Down the hill the snowballs that rolled
the children made.
④ Down the hill rolled that the snowballs
the children made.
⑤ Down the hill did roll the snowballs
that the children made.

15

> His comments made me happy.

① It is his comments that made me happy.
② It is his comments what made me happy.
③ It was his comments that made me
happy.
④ It was his comment what made me
happy.
⑤ That was his comments which made me
happy.

16

> The new coat looks good on you.

① The new coat do looks good on you.
② The new coat do look good on you.
③ The new coat does looks good on you.
④ The new coat does look good on you.
⑤ The new coat is looks good on you.

17 생략된 부분을 포함하고 있지 <u>않은</u> 문장은?

① I have sun allergies and Ashley, too.

② Let me know how the meeting went if possible.

③ I want to tell him about his mistakes now, but I'd rather not.

④ Taking a nap is good for lowering your blood pressure.

⑤ Everything James said was not true.

18 빈칸에 들어갈 수 <u>없는</u> 것은?

> There _____ went.

① he ② they

③ she ④ it

⑤ a dog

19 두 문장의 의미가 같지 <u>않은</u> 것은?

① Neither your car nor my car is fast enough.

= Your car and my car are not fast enough.

② Jason has not forgotten everything that we did together.

= Jason remembers some of the things we did together.

③ He did not find either the map or the compass.

= He did not find the map and the compass.

④ Neither the secretary nor the guard has the keys to the door.

= The secretary and the guard both have the keys to the door.

⑤ None of the people at the audience made a sound.

= Nobody in the audience made a sound.

20 우리말 해석이 알맞지 <u>않은</u> 것은?

① The desire to be special can make you suffer.

→ 특별하고자 하는 바람이 너를 고통스럽게 할 수 있다.

② Just thinking about the possibility of marrying him made her blush.

→ 그와 결혼할 가능성에 관해 생각하는 것만으로 그녀는 얼굴이 붉어졌다.

③ It takes courage to overcome the difficulty of fitting in with new peers.

→ 어려움을 극복하는 데 용기가 필요하기 때문에 새로운 동료들과 어울려야 한다.

④ We should not forget the fact that we are running out of money.

→ 우리는 돈이 떨어지고 있다는 사실을 잊지 말아야 한다.

⑤ I have always had a dream that my family will all get together.

→ 나는 내 가족들이 모두 함께 모이게 되는 꿈을 항상 갖고 있다.

21 괄호 친 부분 중 생략할 수 <u>없는</u> 것은?

① Jason likes pizza and Jacob (likes) noodles.

② Do not open your mouth to talk when (you are) eating.

③ I fell asleep only after (I saw) the moon in the night sky.

④ Fruits are good for your health and (they are) also delicious.

⑤ When Tom got to the hall, he found (that) the concert had been canceled.

[22-23] 다음 문장을 어법에 맞게 고쳐 쓰시오.

22 Sally likes neither watching movies nor listens to music.

→ _____

_____

23 It was at that moment that I achieved my goal that being a curator.

→ _____

_____

24 두 문장의 의미가 같도록 빈칸에 알맞은 말을 쓰시오.

Tom is sometimes kind to me and sometimes not.

= Tom is _____ _____ kind to me.

25 밑줄 친 부분을 강조하는 문장으로 바꿔 쓰시오.

The shop did <u>not</u> open <u>until 2 o'clock</u>.

→ _____

[26-28] 우리말에 맞게 주어진 단어를 바르게 배열하여 문장을 쓰시오.

26 나의 부모님은 그 콘서트에 가실 것이고, 나도 마찬가지이다.
(I, and, are, so, my parents, am, to, going, the concert)

→ _____

_____

27 David는 휴가 중에 회의가 연기되었다는 소식을 들었다.
(had been, while, the news, postponed, that, David, the meeting, on vacation, heard)

→ _____

_____

28 나는 그렇게 무례한 종업원은 결코 본 적이 없다.
(have, such, I, rude, seen, waiter, a)

→ Never _____ .

🎯 CHALLENGE!

Write your own answer to the question.

01 What did you do after you woke up this morning? (Write more than two things using *and*.)

_____

_____

02 What makes your life meaningful? (Use *It is . . . that* form.)

_____

_____

원형	과거형	과거분사형
arise (일어나다)	arose	arisen
awake (깨어나다)	awaked / awoke	awaked / awoken
be (~이다, 있다)	was / were	been
bear (낳다)	bore	born
beat (이기다, 치다)	beat	beaten
become (~이 되다)	became	become
bend (굽히다)	bent	bent
bind (묶다)	bound	bound
bite (물다)	bit	bitten
blow (불다)	blew	blown
break (깨뜨리다)	broke	broken
bring (가져오다)	brought	brought
broadcast (방송하다)	broadcast / broadcasted	broadcast / broadcasted
build (짓다)	built	built
burn (타다)	burnt / burned	burnt / burned
cast (던지다)	cast	cast
catch (잡다)	caught	caught
choose (고르다)	chose	chosen
come (오다)	came	come
cost (비용이 들다)	cost	cost
creep (기다, 살금살금 움직이다)	crept	crept
dig (파다)	dug	dug
dream (꿈꾸다)	dreamed / dreamt	dreamed / dreamt
drink (마시다)	drank	drunk
fall (떨어지다)	fell	fallen
feed (먹이를 주다)	fed	fed
feel (느끼다)	felt	felt
fight (싸우다)	fought	fought
fly (날다)	flew	flown
forget (잊다)	forgot	forgotten
forgive (용서하다)	forgave	forgiven
freeze (얼다)	froze	frozen
grow (자라다)	grew	grown
hide (숨기다)	hid	hidden
hold (붙들다)	held	held

원형	과거형	과거분사형
lay (눕히다)	laid	laid
lead (인도하다)	led	led
learn (배우다)	learned / learnt	learned / learnt
lend (빌려주다)	lent	lent
let (~하게 하다)	let	let
lie (눕다)	lay	lain
mean (의미하다)	meant	meant
mistake (오해하다)	mistook	mistaken
pay (지불하다)	paid	paid
read (읽다)	read	read
ride (타다)	rode	ridden
ring (울리다)	rang	rung
rise (오르다)	rose	risen
seek (찾다)	sought	sought
send (보내다)	sent	sent
shake (흔들다)	shook	shaken
shine (빛나다)	shone / shined	shone / shined
show (보여주다)	showed	shown / showed
shut (닫다)	shut	shut
sink (가라앉다)	sank / sunk	sunk / sunken
slide (미끄러지다)	slid	slid / slidden
smell (냄새가 나다)	smelled / smelt	smelled / smelt
spend (소비하다)	spent	spent
spill (엎지르다)	spilled / spilt	spilled / spilt
spread (펼치다)	spread	spread
steal (훔치다)	stole	stolen
strike (치다)	struck	stricken / struck
swear (맹세하다)	swore	sworn
swim (수영하다)	swam	swum
teach (가르치다)	taught	taught
tell (말하다)	told	told
throw (던지다)	threw	thrown
understand (이해하다)	understood	understood
wake (잠이 깨다)	woke	woken
wear (입다)	wore	worn

Time
FOR
GRAMMAR
Fourth Edition

Time for Grammar is the unique English grammar practice book, helping students learn English grammar in easy and fast ways. This fourth edition of *Time for Grammar* focuses more on practicing English grammar. Students learn practical and usable English grammar with up-to-date, interesting English expressions.
Now it's time for grammar!

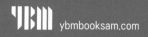

Time
FOR
GRAMMAR
Workbook

EXPERT

Time FOR GRAMMAR

Fourth Edition

Workbook

CONTENTS

CHAPTER 01	Sentence Patterns 문장의 형식	2
CHAPTER 02	Perfect Aspect 완료 시제	8
CHAPTER 03	Modals 조동사	12
CHAPTER 04	Passives 수동태	16
CHAPTER 05	To-infinitives to부정사	22
CHAPTER 06	Gerunds 동명사	32
CHAPTER 07	Participles 분사	36
CHAPTER 08	Comparisons 비교	42
CHAPTER 09	Conjunctions 접속사	48
CHAPTER 10	Relatives 관계사	52
CHAPTER 11	Subjunctive Mood 가정법	60
CHAPTER 12	Agreement & Narration 일치와 화법	66
CHAPTER 13	Sentence Arrangement 기타 구문	72

UNIT
01
S + V & S + V + C
1형식과 2형식

A 괄호 안에서 알맞은 말을 고르시오.

1 Lightning (occurred / occurred to) without rain.

2 The artwork (looks / looks like) real and even alive from a distance.

3 A flying fish (appeared / appeared at) above the water.

4 Your bag smells like the (sea / salty) because you put many seashells in it.

5 When bananas turn yellow, they taste really (sweet / sweetly).

B 밑줄 친 부분을 바르게 고쳐 쓰시오.

1 The plane <u>was arrived</u> an hour later than the expected arrival time.

→ _____

2 My brother became <u>sickness</u> after eating raw seafood.   → _____

3 If you add too much sauce, it could taste <u>strongly</u>.   → _____

4 The students know what <u>was happened</u> in the gym.   → _____

5 Brad's forehead <u>felt like</u> hot, so I put a wet towel on it.   → _____

C 빈칸에 들어갈 말을 골라 알맞은 형태로 쓰시오.

terrific	grow up	weird	turn

1 The milk _____ sour after we got back from our vacation.

2 When my father cooked sausages, they smelled _____.

3 Mike and I _____ in the same neighborhood.

4 After three hours of singing, Jack's voice sounded _____.

D 어법상 잘못된 부분을 고쳐 문장을 다시 쓰시오.

1 Some people believe that UFOs are appeared around the world.

→ _____

2 If there is no one at the station, the train will leave at earlier than usual.

→ _____

3 The sky suddenly got darken, and heavy rain started to pour.

→ _____

4 The instructions that my teacher gave to me seem easily to follow.

→ _____

E 우리말과 같은 뜻이 되도록 괄호 안의 말을 바르게 배열하시오.

1 처음에 그의 계획은 비현실적인 것 같았다.

(unrealistic, his plan, at first, seemed)

→ _____

2 어떤 치즈는 나에게 냄새가 역겹지만 나의 언니는 동의하지 않는다.

(disagrees, smells, my sister, to me, some cheese, but, disgusting)

→ _____

3 매일 아침 그녀의 개를 산책시키는 것은 그녀의 일상이 되었다.

(routine, every morning, her dog, her daily, walking, became)

→ _____

F 우리말과 같은 뜻이 되도록 주어진 말을 이용하여 문장을 완성하시오.

1 그의 최신 책은 일주일 내로 베스트셀러가 되었다. (become, a bestseller)

→ His latest book _____ within a week.

2 무대가 조명으로 비춰졌을 때 관객들은 조용히 있었다. (the audience, stay, silent)

→ _____ when the stage was lit.

3 나는 내 친구들이 깜짝 파티를 열어줬을 때 행복했다. (feel, happy)

→ _____ when my friends held a surprise party for me.

4 Ted는 팀 구성원으로 선택되어서 기뻐 보였다. (Ted, look, pleased)

→ _____ when he was chosen as a team member.

UNIT
02

S + V + O & S + V + I.O. + D.O.

3형식과 4형식

A 괄호 안에서 알맞은 것을 고르시오.

1　Upon entering (the building / into the building), he went straight to his office.

2　It is not easy to (explain / explain about) the problem with this project.

3　The club members suggested (practicing / to practice) after school every day.

4　My mom gave a list of groceries (of / to) me before I left home.

5　I thought they were siblings because they (resemble / resemble with) each other.

B 밑줄 친 부분을 바르게 고쳐 쓰시오.

1　David refused <u>listening</u> to Jack's excuses.　　　　→ _____

2　Ben gave up on <u>to call</u> the store as the line was busy all morning.

　　　　　　　　　　　　　　　　　　　　　　　　　→ _____

3　Sue enjoys <u>to spend</u> time at the gym during her lunch break.

　　　　　　　　　　　　　　　　　　　　　　　　　→ _____

4　She tried to reach Tom to ask a favor <u>with</u> him.　→ _____

5　I need to <u>discuss about</u> the schedule in person.　→ _____

C 두 문장이 같은 뜻이 되도록 빈칸에 알맞은 말을 쓰시오.

1　Dan's parents bought him a suit for graduation.

　→ Dan's parents bought _____ for graduation.

2　Did you offer him the job because you think highly of his computer skills?

　→ Did you offer _____ because you think highly of his computer skills?

3　When we arrived at the house, Mary had prepared us a cozy room.

　→ When we arrived at the house, Mary _____.

4　When the audience applauded, the singer sang them another song.

　→ When the audience applauded, the singer sang _____.

D 다음 문장에서 어법상 <u>잘못된</u> 부분을 고쳐 문장을 다시 쓰시오.

1 Nick fell in love with Suzy at first sight and married with her last year.

→ _____

2 If you avoid to go to the dentist, your toothache will get worse in no time.

→ _____

3 The pharaohs of Egypt built pyramids to themselves for religious purposes.

→ _____

E 우리말과 같은 뜻이 되도록 괄호 안의 말을 바르게 배열하시오.

1 그는 우리에게 그의 강아지의 사진을 좀 보여주었다. (some photos of, he, us, his puppy, showed)

→ _____

2 그는 신입 작가들을 만나기 위해 도서전에 자주 참석한다. (meet, attends, to, the book fair, new authors, often, he)

→ _____

3 내가 그의 집에 방문했을 때, 그는 나에게 미트볼을 요리해 주었다. (when, meatballs, visited, cooked, me, he, for, I, his home)

→ _____

4 나에게 기타 치는 법을 가르쳐주는 것은 어때? (me, don't you, play, how to, the guitar, why, teach)

→ _____

F 우리말과 같은 뜻이 되도록 주어진 말을 이용하여 문장을 완성하시오.

1 우리 할아버지는 그가 가장 좋아하는 시계를 나에게 남기셨다. (leave, me, his favorite watch)
→ My grandfather _____ .

2 너는 새 침대를 네 방 어디에 두고 싶니? (want, put, the new bed)
→ Where do you _____ in your room?

3 선수들은 그들의 주장의 슈팅 스킬을 부러워했다. (envy, their captain, his shooting skills)
→ The players _____ .

4 Sam은 그의 등 통증 때문에 한동안 요가 하는 것을 멈추었다. (stop, do, yoga)
→ Sam _____ for a while because of his back pain.

UNIT

03　S + V + O + O.C.

5형식

A　괄호 안에서 알맞은 것을 고르시오.

1　The athlete never gives up on a race, so people call (her / to her) a fighter.

2　Emily saw her brother (waited / waiting) on the bench.

3　We made Ben (feel / to feel) welcome and comfortable at our house.

4　The director made Carl (the hero / to the hero) of the movie.

5　The coach expects her football team (advanced / to advance) to the finals.

B　밑줄 친 부분을 바르게 고쳐 쓰시오.

1　The tour guide advised us <u>watch</u> our step inside the cave.

→ _____

2　The woman heard wolves <u>to howl</u> while she walked in the forest.

→ _____

3　I let the girl <u>to come</u> in and warm herself by the fireplace. → _____

4　The police had no evidence to prove the man <u>innocence</u>. → _____

5　He watched a few boys <u>taken</u> the cookies without asking. → _____

C　빈칸에 들어갈 말을 골라 알맞은 형태로 쓰시오.

solve	paint	open	crash

1　I saw a drone _____ on the ground.

2　She made me _____ the math problems in an hour.

3　The teacher asked his students _____ their textbooks.

4　She bought a second-hand boat and had it _____ .

D 밑줄 친 부분을 바르게 고쳐 쓰시오.

1 They appointed Mr. Parker <u>as</u> the new manager.

→ _____

2 Jim had his cell phone <u>check</u> by the repairman because it would not turn on.

→ _____

3 He encouraged the man <u>make</u> a speech in front of the crowd.

→ _____

E 우리말과 같은 뜻이 되도록 주어진 말을 바르게 배열하시오.

1 그녀는 그녀의 선생님을 인생의 롤 모델로 여긴다. (considers, her teacher, she, in, her life, a role model)

→ _____

2 체육 선생님은 학생들이 오후 네 시까지 축구를 연습하도록 허락해 주었다.

(until 4 p.m., the students, soccer, the P.E. teacher, to practice, allowed)

→ _____

3 그들은 내가 그 제안을 수락하길 요청했다. (to accept, they, me, the offer, asked)

→ _____

4 만약 우리가 토요일 경기를 취소한다면, 모두 우리를 약하다고 생각할 것이다. (everyone, we, cancel, think, on Saturday, us, the game, if, weak, will)

→ _____

F 우리말과 같은 뜻이 되도록 주어진 말을 이용하여 문장을 완성하시오.

1 나는 Peter에게 축제에서 내 공연을 녹화하는 것을 상기시켰다. (remind, Peter, film)

→ I _____ my performance at the festival.

2 그들은 비둘기들이 식탁 아래의 빵 부스러기를 쪼아 먹는 것을 보았다. (watch, the pigeons, peck)

→ They _____ the bread crumbs under the table.

3 Peterson 선생님은 나를 한 시간 동안 기다리게 만들었다. (make, me, wait)

→ Mr. Peterson _____ for an hour.

UNIT
01

Present Perfect
현재완료

A   괄호 안에서 알맞은 말을 고르시오.

1   I have (made, making) some egg sandwiches for the picnic.

2   He (has finished, finished) writing his novel in 1892.

3   My sister (has been, were) ill since yesterday.

4   They (have been, are) friends with each other for 10 years.

5   She (has visited, visited) her friends in Taiwan last year.

6   He (has gotten, got) a job offer from a design company a few days ago.

B   괄호 안에 주어진 단어를 이용해 현재완료진행 시제로 만드시오.

1   I _____ a blue bag with a small pocket. (look for)

2   We _____ the best sneakers in the nation. (make)

3   She _____ two plates of vegetables every day for a month. (eat)

4   He _____ to be an accountant since last year. (study)

5   How many years _____ you _____ in the city? (live)

C   밑줄 친 부분을 바르게 고쳐 쓰시오.

1   He has been <u>worked</u> as a journalist for 8 years.   → _____

2   How long <u>did</u> you been staying in Seoul?   → _____

3   Mary <u>has dreamed</u> about being a movie star last night.   → _____

4   I have never <u>visit</u> Julie's house before.   → _____

5   David and Victoria have <u>be dating</u> for a month.   → _____

6   I <u>lost</u> my watch. I will check my room right now.   → _____

7   He <u>had fought</u> with his sister. He still does not talk to her. → _____

D 주어진 문장과 같은 의미가 되도록 문장을 완성하시오.

1 It has snowed for a week. It is still snowing.

→ _____ for a week.

2 My brother started playing the game an hour ago. He is still playing it.

→ _____ for an hour.

3 Jake started doing a part-time job three months ago. He is still doing it.

→ _____ for three months.

E 우리말과 같은 뜻이 되도록 괄호 안의 말을 바르게 배열하시오.

1 그녀는 지난주 이후로 그 드라마를 시청해오고 있다. (watching, last, since, she, week, been, the drama, has)

→ _____

2 나는 인도 음식을 몇 번 먹어 본 적이 있다. (times, I, food, Indian, eaten, a few, have)

→ _____

3 민수는 브라질에 그의 친척들을 만나러 가고 없다. (has, Minsu, to, his, relatives, Brazil, gone, to see)

→ _____

4 팬들은 그의 콘서트를 보기 위해 두 시간째 기다리는 중이다. (two hours, his, been, have, the fans, waiting, for, to, concert, see)

→ _____

F 괄호 안의 말을 이용하여 우리말을 영어로 쓰시오.

1 학생들은 이틀 동안 기말고사를 보는 중이다. (take their final exams, for)

→ _____

2 그들은 마침내 그 그룹 프로젝트를 완성했다. (finally, complete, the group project)

→ _____

3 강아지 한 마리가 내가 본 후 계속 나무 아래에 앉아있는 중이다. (a puppy, since)

→ _____

4 우리는 몇 년 동안 좋은 사이로 지내 오는 중이다. (have, relationship, several)

→ _____

Past Perfect / Future Perfect

과거완료/미래완료

A 괄호 안에서 알맞은 말을 고르시오.

1 When we graduated from middle school, we (knew, had known) each other for six years.

2 The training (had been finished, will have been finished) tomorrow.

3 Adam (had been, will be) watching TV when I called him.

4 We (had painted, will have painted) the house by the time Mom returns.

5 She (had used, will have used) the car for 20 years by next Monday.

6 Martin (will have gone, had gone) fishing when Carl stopped by his house.

B 주어진 단어를 이용해 과거완료진행 또는 미래완료진행 시제로 만드시오.

1 Nick was out of breath. He _____ for an hour. (run)

2 By this Friday, Jim _____ at the company for four years. (work)

3 My sister _____ when I knocked on the door. (sleep)

4 Mr. Choi _____ for 10 years by next year. (teach)

5 She _____ yoga for years until last year. (learn)

C 밑줄 친 부분을 바르게 고쳐 쓰시오.

1 I <u>lived</u> in this city for six years by next month. → _____

2 He <u>has gone</u> to Italy for business when I went to his office. → _____

3 By the end of this semester, I will <u>be taken</u> three exams. → _____

4 We <u>have been</u> playing tennis for an hour when the rain started.

→ _____

5 Chris <u>would be</u> working as a cook for two years next week.

→ _____

6 Nate wondered if I <u>have been</u> to Paris. → _____

7 How long <u>have you been</u> waiting until the bus came? → _____

D 주어진 문장과 같은 의미가 되도록 문장을 완성하시오.

1 I started to bake a chocolate cake at 2. I think I will finish it by 4.

→ _____ by 4.

2 Ellen had started doing her homework at 5 p.m. She was still doing it at 7.

→ _____ for two hours.

3 Jane has studied Korean for a year. She will study Korean next year.

→ _____ for two years next year.

E 우리말과 같은 뜻이 되도록 괄호 안의 말을 바르게 배열하시오.

1 관광객들은 그때까지는 공항에 도착해 있을 것이다. (by then, the tourists, the airport, will, at, have, arrived)

→ _____

2 이번 여름이면 그 댄스 그룹은 세 번째 공연을 했을 것이다. (this, the dance group, by, three times, will, performed, have, summer)

→ _____

3 그녀가 집에 왔을 때, 그녀의 아들은 친구들을 만나러 나가고 없었다. (got, when, she, had, gone out, to meet, his friends, home, her son)

→ _____

4 내가 이모 댁에 들렀을 때, 그녀는 쿠키를 굽는 중이었다. (baking, had been, stopped by, she, I, cookies, when, aunt's house, my)

→ _____

F 괄호 안의 말을 이용하여 우리말을 영어로 쓰시오.

1 Jim은 올해 말이면 새로운 일을 시작했을 것이다. (career, by the end of)

→ _____

2 Jina는 다섯 시가 되면 그녀의 숙제를 두 시간째 하는 중일 것이다. (her homework, by)

→ _____

3 그는 오랫동안 밖에서 일하고 있었기 때문에 매우 피곤했다. (work outside, for a long time)

→ _____

UNIT
01

can, may, must, should
조동사의 종류와 용법

A 괄호 안에서 알맞은 말을 고르시오.

1 (Must, May) I use your pen?

2 Everyone (ought to not, ought not to) talk in the theater.

3 It (cannot, have to not) be true that your dog can sing.

4 You will (can, be able to) learn about different cultures.

5 You (may, must) fasten your seatbelt when you ride in a car.

6 You (should, might) be careful when you use a knife.

7 You (must, can) sit here if you want.

B 빈칸에 알맞은 말을 골라 쓰시오.

| was able to | must not | may | cannot | don't have to |

1 That _____ be Mr. Lee. He has gone to Sydney.

2 _____ I open the window? It is too hot inside.

3 She _____ play the guitar when she was a teenager.

4 You _____ eat cold food when you have a stomachache.

5 I already have a fancy table. I _____ buy a new one.

C 우리말과 일치하도록 밑줄 친 부분을 바르게 고쳐 쓰시오.

1 Olivia <u>might be</u> a doctor.   → _____
 (Olivia는 의사임에 틀림없다.)

2 You <u>must not bring</u> a gift for the party.   → _____
 (너는 그 파티에 선물을 가져올 필요가 없다.)

3 Ryan <u>will can finish</u> this project tomorrow.   → _____
 (Ryan은 내일 이 프로젝트를 끝낼 수 있을 것이다.)

D 주어진 두 문장이 같은 의미가 되도록 빈칸에 알맞은 말을 쓰시오.

1 You may stay at my house as long as you want.

→ You _____ stay at my house as long as you want.

2 You don't need to wait for me.

→ You don't _____ _____ wait for me.

3 They could come up with a plan after their long discussion.

→ They _____ _____ _____ come up with a plan after their long discussion.

E 우리말과 같은 뜻이 되도록 괄호 안의 말을 바르게 배열하시오.

1 너는 약을 먹고 쉬어야 한다. (take, must, you, some medicine, get, and, some rest)

→ _____

2 그녀의 무례한 태도는 받아들여질 리가 없다. (cannot, her, rude, accepted, attitude, be)

→ _____

3 너는 길에 침을 뱉으면 안 된다. (not, you, on the street, should, spit)

→ _____

4 내가 너의 연필을 써도 될까? (I, your, may, pencil, use)

→ _____

F 괄호 안의 말을 이용하여 우리말을 영어로 쓰시오.

1 그는 그 대회에 참가할 수 있을 것이다. (will, able, participate in, the competition)

→ _____

2 너는 내 보고서를 출력해 줄 수 있니? (print, report)

→ _____

3 그녀는 자신의 딸의 의견에 동의하지 않을지도 모른다. (agree with, opinion)

→ _____

4 학생들은 수업에 제시간에 와야만 한다. (have, be on time, for class)

→ _____

UNIT
02

Other Expressions with Modals

조동사의 관용적 표현

A 괄호 안에서 알맞은 말을 고르시오.

1 You would (rather, better) take a taxi.

2 There used (to be, to being) a huge park in the town.

3 She heard what we said. We (should, may) have whispered.

4 As you have a bad cold, you (had not better, had better not) go to the gym.

5 We (may as well, used to) try the local food this time.

6 Someone (should, must) have taken my package. It is not here.

B 빈칸에 알맞은 말을 골라 쓰시오.

must have been   had better take   may as well make   used to go

1 You _____ the subway to be on time.

2 Jack did not come to school. He _____ ill.

3 They _____ camping every weekend.

4 You _____ a call as send a message.

C 밑줄 친 부분에 유의하여 문장을 해석하시오.

1 He <u>must have sold</u> his precious car.

→ _____

2 You <u>may as well</u> put on sunscreen before going outside.

→ _____

3 They <u>should have noticed</u> the changed plan.

→ _____

4 The professor <u>cannot have proved</u> his theory.

→ _____

5 He <u>used to</u> work at a restaurant in France.

→ _____

D 우리말과 일치하도록 밑줄 친 부분을 바르게 고쳐 쓰시오.

1 너는 너의 치마를 다시 입느니 세탁하는 게 낫겠다.

You <u>had better</u> wash your skirt as wear it again. → _____

2 이 장소에는 오래된 사원이 있었다.

There <u>was used to</u> be an old temple on this site. → _____

3 나는 낮잠을 자느니 산책을 가겠다.

I <u>could rather</u> take a walk than take a nap. → _____

E 우리말과 같은 뜻이 되도록 괄호 안의 말을 바르게 배열하시오.

1 너는 부모님과 함께 너의 관심사에 대해서 이야기하는 게 좋을 것이다. (talk about, you, with, your parents, had, your interests, better)

→ _____

2 나는 우울할 때 피아노를 치곤 했다. (I, felt down, I, play, used, the piano, to, when)

→ _____

3 나는 차라리 온라인으로 잡지를 사겠다. (I, online, would, a magazine, rather, buy)

→ _____

4 개들이 그의 발자국을 놓친 것이 틀림없다. (lost, of, must, track, the dogs, have, him)

→ _____

F 괄호 안의 말을 이용하여 우리말을 영어로 쓰시오.

1 너는 약을 먹기 전에 뭔가를 먹는 게 낫겠다. (may, before, take medicine)

→ _____

2 그 의사가 환자에게 거짓말을 했을 리가 없다. (cannot, lie, his patient)

→ _____

3 너는 경찰에게 네가 본 것에 대해 말했어야 했는데. (should, tell, what you saw)

→ _____

4 그는 과거에 유명한 영화배우였을 수도 있다. (may, famous, before)

→ _____

UNIT
01

Passive Voice

수동태의 형태와 시제

A 괄호 안에서 알맞은 말을 고르시오.

1 My friend (injured, was injured) in a car accident.

2 My grandfather (appeared, was appeared) in my dream last night.

3 A new novel (is writing, is being written) by her.

4 Dinner (consists of, is consisted of) steak, salad, and drinks.

5 His idea (has ignored, has been ignored) for years.

6 The flowers (do plant, are planted) by the gardener.

7 The classroom (was cleaning, was being cleaned) yesterday.

B 밑줄 친 부분을 바르게 고쳐 쓰시오.

1 The World Cup <u>holds</u> every four years. → _____

2 The plates are being <u>wash</u> now. → _____

3 The specialist will <u>be arrived</u> here soon. → _____

4 The building <u>has built</u> since April. → _____

5 Before you <u>are cooked</u> the chicken, add some spices. → _____

6 The window <u>is broken</u> when we moved here. → _____

C 괄호 안에 주어진 단어를 알맞은 형태로 쓰시오.

1 Her family _____ here next month. (will, stay)

2 Alice _____ her grandma. (resemble)

3 A pizza _____ when I came home. (deliver)

4 The flight _____ a month ago. (book)

5 These photos _____ by a reporter last week. (take)

6 Maple trees _____ almost everywhere in this city. (can, find)

D 다음 문장을 수동태로 바꿔 쓰시오.

1 Brian repairs these machines.

→ _____

2 She wears the black dress on special days.

→ _____

3 Mom is watering the flowers.

→ _____

4 I am going to send the postcards to my parents.

→ _____

E 우리말과 같은 뜻이 되도록 괄호 안의 말을 바르게 배열하시오.

1 나는 의사에 의해 진찰을 받고 있는 중이다. (examined, I, by, the doctor, am, being)

→ _____

2 너는 결혼식에 초대되었니? (you, invited, the wedding, are, to)

→ _____

3 그의 그림들이 곧 전시될 것이다. (be, his paintings, exhibited, soon, going to, are)

→ _____

F 괄호 안의 말을 이용하여 우리말을 영어로 쓰시오.

1 이 휴대 전화는 지난달부터 사용되어 왔다. (this cell phone, use, since)

→ _____

2 정치 뉴스는 매일 아침 Jessica에 의해 보도된다. (the political news, report, every morning)

→ _____

3 이 책은 2018년에 개정되었다. (this book, revise)

→ _____

4 카페는 다음 주 월요일에 문을 닫을 것이다. (café, will, close)

→ _____

UNIT 02 Passives of S + V + I.O. + D.O. / S + V + O + O.C.

4형식·5형식 문장의 수동태

A 괄호 안에서 알맞은 말을 고르시오.

1 The boy was told (stretch, to stretch) his legs.

2 I am being (taught, taught to) Spanish by my neighbor, Brian.

3 He was elected (president, as president) in 1980.

4 A funny video (was shown, showed) to us by the teacher.

5 She was seen (to, of) leave the house by her neighbor.

6 Healthy meals were cooked (of, for) me by Dad.

7 The students are made (for, to) wear uniforms.

B 밑줄 친 부분을 바르게 고쳐 쓰시오.

1 The girl was <u>told help</u> people in need.   → _____

2 A doll was <u>made of</u> me by my mother.   → _____

3 She was <u>heard talked</u> on the phone last night.   → _____

4 The house was <u>built to</u> Robert by them.   → _____

5 Claire was <u>made finish</u> her homework.   → _____

C 다음 문장을 수동태로 고칠 때 빈칸에 알맞은 말을 쓰시오.

1 The interviewer asked Rachel about her work experience.

→ Rachel _____ about her work experience by the interviewer.

2 The boy made the teacher very upset.

→ The teacher _____ by the boy.

3 She gave her brother sweet desserts.

→ Her brother _____ sweet desserts by her.

4 Tony brought some classmates the gifts.

→ The gifts _____ some classmates by Tony.

D 밑줄 친 단어를 주어로 하는 수동태 문장으로 바꿔 쓰시오.

1 I heard him shout in a loud voice.

→ _____

2 He asks me many questions whenever we meet.

→ _____

3 My parents bought me new sneakers.

→ _____

4 Mr. Jackson made me mop the kitchen floor.

→ _____

E 우리말과 같은 뜻이 되도록 괄호 안의 말을 바르게 배열하시오.

1 그 학생들은 자신들의 이름을 적도록 시켜졌다. (the students, to, made, their names, were, write down)

→ _____

2 나는 그녀에 의해 그 소포를 보내라는 요청을 받았다. (I, to, was, asked, by, send, her, the package)

→ _____

3 그는 그의 나라에서 가장 영향력 있는 사람들 중의 하나로 여겨진다. (is, he, considered, people, one, of, in his country, the most powerful)

→ _____

F 괄호 안의 말을 이용하여 우리말을 영어로 쓰시오.

1 크리스마스 카드는 내 친구들에 의해 나에게 보내질 것이다. (will, send)

→ _____

2 그가 버스를 타는 것이 우리에 의해 목격되었다. (see, take a bus)

→ _____

3 이 머그 잔은 나의 할머니를 위해 삼촌에 의해 만들어졌다. (mug, grandma, my uncle)

→ _____

4 나는 친한 친구들에 의해 Alex라고 불린다. (call, close friend)

→ _____

UNIT
03

Other Passive Forms

주의해야 할 수동태

A 괄호 안에서 알맞은 말을 고르시오.

1 Andy is pleased (with, of) his success.

2 My dog was not (run over, run over by) a bus.

3 During winter, the city is covered (in, with) snow.

4 She is not scared (by, of) blood.

5 My kids are (taken care, taken care of) by a nanny.

6 The appointment was (put off, put off by) because of the storm.

7 The man was (looked by down on, looked down on by) his neighbors.

B 빈칸에 알맞은 말을 골라 쓰시오.

with	to	at	about	of

1 I was surprised _____ your answer.

2 My aunt was married _____ a German.

3 The furniture is made _____ wood.

4 We are worried _____ your health.

5 David is satisfied _____ his new bike.

C 밑줄 친 부분을 바르게 고쳐 쓰시오.

1 Her room is <u>filled with by</u> many books. → _____

2 Jason was <u>bring up</u> in New York. → _____

3 The singer is well <u>known by</u> middle-aged people. → _____

4 Henry is <u>thought be</u> a Canadian. → _____

5 The team is <u>composed with</u> 11 players. → _____

6 I was <u>disappointed to</u> his behavior. → _____

D 주어진 단어를 주어로 하는 수동태 문장으로 바꿔 쓰시오.

1 People say that the sports star is living in Paris.

→ It _____.

2 They thought that the class was canceled.

→ The class _____.

3 Cindy turned in her essay yesterday.

→ The essay _____.

E 우리말과 같은 뜻이 되도록 괄호 안의 말을 바르게 배열하시오.

1 그 박스는 여러 가지 맛의 초콜릿으로 가득하다. (filled, chocolate, many flavors of, is, the box, with)

→ _____

2 음식이 자원봉사자들에 의해 노숙자들에게 나눠질 것이다. (be, the volunteers, the food, the homeless, handed out, by, to, will)

→ _____

3 그는 마을에서 가장 정직한 사람들 중의 하나로 믿어진다. (he, believed, it, of, in town, one, is, is, that, the most honest, people)

→ _____

F 괄호 안의 말을 이용하여 우리말을 영어로 쓰시오.

1 그녀가 사회 문제에 관심이 있니? (interest, social issues)

→ _____

2 내 컴퓨터가 John에 의해 꺼졌다. (turn off)

→ _____

3 그 거리는 많은 방문객들로 붐빈다. (crowd, a lot of visitors)

→ _____

4 그는 항상 많은 친구들에 의해 둘러싸여 있다. (surround)

→ _____

UNIT
01

Substantive To-infinitives

to부정사의 명사적 용법

A 괄호 안에서 알맞은 말을 고르시오.

1 (Spread, To spread) rumors is not good manners.

2 My dream is (go, to go) to space.

3 I decided (to join, joining) the school band.

4 (It, That) is difficult to kick a bad habit.

5 He found (it, that) impossible to get to work on time.

6 I think it frightening (walk, to walk) alone in the dark.

B 밑줄 친 부분에 유의하여 문장을 해석하시오.

1 I do not know <u>how to pronounce</u> the word.

→ _____

2 The kid was not sure <u>whom to trust</u>.

→ _____

3 He advised me to write down <u>what to do</u> today.

→ _____

4 Mom did not tell me <u>where to buy</u> it.

→ _____

5 Can you tell me <u>when to push</u> the button?

→ _____

C 주어진 단어와 to부정사를 이용해 빈칸에 알맞은 말을 쓰시오.

1 _____ breakfast is good for your health. (eat)

2 Henry found it hard _____ a secret. (keep)

3 I do not know how _____ the machine. (use)

4 My plan is _____ 20 books a year. (read)

5 It is bad for your ears _____ to music too loud. (listen)

D 밑줄 친 부분을 바르게 고쳐 문장을 다시 쓰시오.

1 She was very angry and refused <u>speak</u> to me.

→ _____

2 <u>That</u> is important to do your best.

→ _____

3 I hope <u>seeing</u> you again.

→ _____

4 It is necessary <u>understand</u> different cultures.

→ _____

E 우리말과 같은 뜻이 되도록 괄호 안의 말을 바르게 배열하시오.

1 너의 약속을 지키는 것은 중요하다. (important, to, is, it, keep, your promises)

→ _____

2 그는 사진작가가 되기로 결심했다. (decided, he, a photographer, to, become)

→ _____

3 나는 도서관에서 시끄럽게 구는 것은 무례하다고 생각한다. (I, it, rude, think, be, noisy, to, in the library)

→ _____

F 괄호 안의 말을 이용하여 우리말을 영어로 쓰시오.

1 내 꿈은 유명한 스포츠 스타가 되는 것이다. (become, famous, sports star)

→ _____

2 그는 나쁜 일을 잊는 것이 어렵다는 것을 알았다. (find, difficult, the bad things)

→ _____

3 나는 어디에 열쇠를 놓아야 할지 생각하는 중이다. (think about, where, put)

→ _____

4 이 프로젝트를 다음 주까지 끝내는 것은 쉽지 않을 것이다. (it, finish, by next week)

→ _____

Adjective & Adverbial To-infinitives

to부정사의 형용사적·부사적 용법

A 괄호 안에서 알맞은 말을 고르시오.

1 I have a lot of things (doing, to do) after school.

2 Nicky is looking for someone (to dance, to dance with).

3 We (are, are to) move to a big city next month.

4 I was shocked (seeing, to see) my old friend.

5 You have to walk for 30 minutes (burn off, to burn off) calories.

6 A small bag would be easy (to carry, carried).

B 밑줄 친 부분에 유의하여 문장을 해석하시오.

1 Thomas <u>is to arrive</u> in Sydney tomorrow.

   → _____

2 There are enough chairs <u>to sit on</u>.

   → _____

3 I am sorry <u>to have hurt</u> your feelings.

   → _____

4 He woke up early <u>to catch</u> the plane.

   → _____

C 두 문장의 의미가 같도록 빈칸에 알맞은 말을 쓰시오.

1 We have to wash our hands before eating.

   = We are _____ our hands before eating.

2 Many people visit Paris in order to see the Eiffel Tower.

   = Many people visit Paris _____ the Eiffel Tower.

3 He is going to watch a movie with his family tonight.

   = He is _____ a movie with his family tonight.

D 밑줄 친 부분을 바르게 고쳐 문장을 다시 쓰시오.

1 She grew up be to a nurse.

→ _____

2 I am so lucky having a chance to participate in this festival.

→ _____

3 Do you have a piece of paper to write?

→ _____

4 He must be nervous bite his lips.

→ _____

E 우리말과 같은 뜻이 되도록 괄호 안의 말을 바르게 배열하시오.

1 나는 수박을 자를 칼이 필요하다. (I, a knife, with, need, the watermelon, cut, to)

→ _____

2 그들은 다시는 만날 수 없는 운명이다. (never, they, to, are, again, meet)

→ _____

3 나는 사고를 목격해서 충격을 받았다. (I, the accident, to, was, witness, shocked)

→ _____

4 그녀는 신문 기사를 좀 읽기 위해 컴퓨터를 켰다. (turned on, she, read, the computer, some news articles, to)

→ _____

F 괄호 안의 말을 이용하여 우리말을 영어로 쓰시오.

1 경기에 이기기 위해서 너는 열심히 연습해야 한다. (must, practice hard, the match)

→ _____

2 앉을 수 있는 여분의 의자가 있나요? (have, an extra chair, sit on)

→ _____

3 밖에서 놀기 전에 너는 쓰레기를 버려야 한다. (be, take out, the garbage)

→ _____

4 그녀는 시험에 불합격해서 슬픈 것임에 틀림없다. (must, fail, the test)

→ _____

UNIT
03
Subject, Tense, and Voices of To-infinitives
to부정사의 의미상의 주어, 시제, 태

A 괄호 안에서 알맞은 말을 고르시오.

1   It was rude (for her, of her) not to thank him.

2   It is important (for him, of him) to believe in himself.

3   It was thoughtful (for you, of you) to give me a ride home.

4   They seem (to work, to have worked) together in the past.

5   It was not easy (for adults, of adults) to learn a new language.

6   I am so sorry (to cancel, to have canceled) my appointment yesterday.

B 괄호 안에 주어진 단어를 알맞은 형태로 고쳐 쓰시오.

1   It was generous _____ to help the poor people. (he)

2   It is brave _____ to travel alone. (you)

3   It is natural _____ to feel sleepy after eating too much. (you)

4   It was difficult _____ to walk up the stairs to the 10th floor. (I)

5   It is necessary _____ to learn Internet etiquette. (we)

6   It was careless _____ to leave her bag on the bus. (she)

C 두 문장의 의미가 같도록 빈칸에 알맞은 말을 쓰시오.

1   It was believed that the Earth was flat.

    = The Earth was believed _____.

2   It seems that she is suspicious of me.

    = She seems _____ suspicious of me.

3   It appears that you were sick and tired of doing that.

    = You appear _____ sick and tired of doing that.

4   It is said that the man lived to be over 100 years old.

    = The man is said _____ to be over 100 years old.

D 밑줄 친 부분을 바르게 고쳐 문장을 다시 쓰시오.

1 It was sweet <u>for you</u> to send me flowers.

→ _____

2 It was easy <u>of him remember</u> numbers.

→ _____

3 The conference is scheduled <u>to hold</u> in Seoul.

→ _____

4 He seems <u>to have be</u> a member of the club last year.

→ _____

E 우리말과 같은 뜻이 되도록 괄호 안의 말을 바르게 배열하시오.

1 그가 자신의 실수를 인정한 것은 현명했다. (wise, it, was, his, him, to, of, mistake, admit)

→ _____

2 그들이 거리에서 노는 것은 위험하다. (it, in the street, is, for, dangerous, them, play, to)

→ _____

3 그는 내가 지난여름에 했던 일을 알고 있었던 것 같다. (last summer, he, seems, to, known, have, what I did)

→ _____

F 괄호 안의 말을 이용하여 우리말을 영어로 쓰시오.

1 그녀가 마라톤을 완주하는 것은 불가능하다. (impossible, finish a marathon)

→ _____

2 네가 사실을 말한 것은 정직했다. (honest, tell the truth)

→ _____

3 그녀는 그 설명을 이해하는 것 같았다. (seem to, understand, the explanation)

→ _____

4 칼은 어린이가 사용하면 안 된다. (knives, use)

→ _____

UNIT
04

Infinitives as Object Complements

목적격 보어로 쓰이는 부정사

A 괄호 안에서 알맞은 말을 고르시오.

1 Mom wanted me (being, to be) a good boy.

2 I heard someone (walking, to walk) up the stairs.

3 Matthew persuaded me (agree, to agree) with his idea.

4 The coach encourages us (achieve, to achieve) our goals.

5 I helped the kid (find, finding) his way back home.

6 Mr. Lee got me (move, to move) the sofa next to the table.

7 My grandfather made me (hammer, to hammer) a nail into the wall.

B 괄호 안에 주어진 단어를 알맞은 형태로 쓰시오.

1 He ordered me _____ the graffiti from the wall. (remove)

2 Do not let the children _____ near the fire. (go)

3 I watched Tommy _____ the hospital. (enter)

4 My mom got me _____ the dishes. (wash)

5 She allowed me _____ a belly dancing class. (take)

6 He made the boy _____ the snow in front of the house. (clean)

C 빈칸에 알맞은 말을 골라 쓰시오.

buy	stand	screaming	to take	to prepare

1 I hear someone _____ for help.

2 The teacher makes us _____ in line.

3 Could you help me _____ for the party?

4 She advised me _____ a deep breath.

5 My parents did not let me _____ a new cell phone.

D 밑줄 친 부분을 바르게 고쳐 문장을 다시 쓰시오.

1 My sister will not allow me <u>wear</u> her clothes.

→ _____

2 The good news made me <u>feeling</u> happy.

→ _____

3 The doctor told me <u>not drink</u> or eat anything for two hours.

→ _____

4 She heard the boys <u>to talk</u> about her behind the tree.

→ _____

E 우리말과 같은 뜻이 되도록 괄호 안의 말을 바르게 배열하시오.

1 나는 누군가 내 이름을 부르는 것을 들었다. (I, somebody, my name, call, heard)

→ _____

2 경찰은 그 남자가 주머니에 있는 모든 것을 꺼내게 했다. (the police, the man, had, take, out of his pockets, everything)

→ _____

3 나는 점원에게 가장 인기 있는 모델을 추천해달라고 요청했다. (the most popular model, I, asked, to, the clerk, recommend)

→ _____

F 괄호 안의 말을 이용하여 우리말을 영어로 쓰시오.

1 아버지는 내가 저녁 9시 이후에 외출하는 것을 허락하지 않으신다. (let, go out)

→ _____

2 나는 돌고래 떼가 바다에서 수영하고 있는 것을 보았다. (see, a group of dolphins)

→ _____

3 많은 사람들이 내가 이 프로젝트를 완성하는 것을 도와줬다. (help, complete)

→ _____

4 그녀의 나쁜 건강이 그녀로 하여금 꿈을 포기하게 했다. (poor health, cause, give up)

→ _____

UNIT
05

Common Structures of Infinitives
to부정사의 주요 구문

A 괄호 안에서 알맞은 말을 고르시오.

1 (Tell, To tell) the truth, I am afraid of heights.

2 He is not (rich enough, enough rich) to buy a house.

3 (To make, Making) matters worse, it started to snow.

4 He is too tired (to get, getting) up early in the morning.

5 The restaurant is (enough large, large enough) to hold 100 people.

6 The dress is too small for me (to wear, wearing).

B 밑줄 친 부분에 유의하여 문장을 해석하시오.

1 My mom is <u>too busy to spend time</u> with me.

→ _____

2 <u>Strange to say</u>, I saw a ghost last night.

→ _____

3 He is <u>strong enough to remain calm</u> in this situation.

→ _____

4 <u>To be honest with you</u>, I do not remember what she said.

→ _____

C 밑줄 친 부분을 바르게 고쳐 쓰시오.

1 Chris is, <u>so speak</u>, a walking dictionary.　　　→ _____

2 You are not <u>enough old</u> to travel alone.　　　→ _____

3 He is <u>enough tall</u> to become a basketball player.　　→ _____

4 The deer is too weak <u>protecting</u> itself from other animals.

→ _____

5 <u>To being frank with you</u>, I am very nervous.　　→ _____

D 두 문장의 의미가 같도록 빈칸에 알맞은 말을 쓰시오.

1 The food is too spicy for me to eat.

= The food is _____.

2 He is so young that he cannot ride a roller coaster.

= He is _____.

3 She practiced hard enough to win the game.

= She practiced _____.

4 She is so old that she can watch those kinds of movies.

= She is _____.

E 우리말과 같은 뜻이 되도록 괄호 안의 말을 바르게 배열하시오.

1 이 도시는 혼자 걸어서 돌아다닐 만큼 충분히 안전하지 않다. (this city, is, safe, alone, not, enough, to, walk around in)

→ _____

2 그 영화는 너무 무서워서 나는 그것을 볼 수 없었다. (the movie, was, for, to, too, watch, scary, me)

→ _____

3 사실대로 말하면, 나는 유럽에 가본 적이 없다. (to, I have, been, to, Europe, the truth, tell, never)

→ _____

F 괄호 안의 말을 이용하여 우리말을 영어로 쓰시오.

1 그의 연설이 너무 어려워서 내가 이해할 수가 없다. (his speech, too, difficult, understand)

→ _____

2 그는 친구들에게 조언을 해 주기에 충분히 현명하다. (wise, enough, give advice)

→ _____

3 공정하게 판단하면, 그녀는 그 일을 할 자격이 없다. (justice, qualified for)

→ _____

4 설상가상으로, 나는 마지막 버스를 놓쳤다. (worse, miss, last bus)

→ _____

UNIT

01 Functions & Usage of Gerunds

동명사의 역할과 쓰임

A 괄호 안에서 알맞은 말을 고르시오.

1 I am afraid of (talk, talking) with strangers.

2 The thing I hate most is (get, getting) up early.

3 Do you mind (he, his) joining our rock band?

4 (Climb, Climbing) mountains is one of his hobbies.

5 She is considering (going not, not going) to the meeting.

6 Mr. Lee suggested (to go, going) camping with his friends.

7 He was worried about (punishing, being punished) by the teacher.

B 밑줄 친 부분을 바르게 고쳐 쓰시오.

1 Tina has not given up on <u>to look for</u> her missing cat.　→ _____

2 I do not mind <u>he</u> coming here.　→ _____

3 He is sure of <u>being</u> seen her before.　→ _____

4 <u>Eating not</u> breakfast can make you gain weight.　→ _____

5 Tim is nervous about <u>make</u> a mistake.　→ _____

6 I usually enjoy <u>to eat</u> spicy food.　→ _____

C 두 문장의 의미가 같도록 빈칸에 알맞은 말을 쓰시오.

1 I am happy that I am invited to your birthday party.

= I am happy about _____ to your birthday party.

2 Do you mind if I close the window?

= Do you mind _____ the window?

3 He is proud that he got a high score on the English test.

= He is proud of _____ a high score on the English test.

D 밑줄 친 부분을 바르게 고쳐 문장을 다시 쓰시오.

1 I am not good at <u>make</u> speeches.

→ _____

2 Dad does not like <u>I</u> coming home late at night.

→ _____

3 Mark enjoyed <u>to be</u> photographed by others.

→ _____

4 He denied <u>having married</u> before.

→ _____

E 우리말과 같은 뜻이 되도록 괄호 안의 말을 바르게 배열하시오.

1 내가 가장 좋아하는 활동 중 하나는 만화책을 읽는 것이다. (is, my favorite activities, reading, one of, comic books)

→ _____

2 그녀는 내가 늦는 것을 걱정했다. (worried, she, was, being, me, about, late)

→ _____

3 그는 형편없이 대접받은 것을 불평했다. (been, poorly, of, complained, he, having, treated)

→ _____

F 괄호 안의 말을 이용하여 우리말을 영어로 쓰시오.

1 Eric은 주말마다 토크쇼를 보는 것을 즐긴다. (enjoy, watch, the talk show)

→ _____

2 나는 나의 두려움을 극복했던 것이 자랑스럽다. (proud of, overcome, fears)

→ _____

3 설탕을 지나치게 많이 먹는 것은 너의 건강에 좋지 않다. (too much sugar, health)

→ _____

4 그녀는 다른 사람들에게 비난 받는 것을 좋아하지 않는다. (blame, others)

→ _____

Gerunds vs. To-infinitives

동명사와 to부정사

A 괄호 안에서 알맞은 말을 고르시오.

1 I have difficulty (to sleep, sleeping) at night because I drink too much coffee.

2 I did not expect (to meet, meeting) you here.

3 He finally finished (to write, writing) the report.

4 She suggested (to eat out, eating out) at least once a week.

5 Stop (to complain, complaining) and do what you have to do.

B 밑줄 친 부분에 유의하여 문장을 해석하시오.

1 He <u>tried to find</u> his lost bag.

→ _____

2 Lisa <u>tried painting</u> the wall of her room blue.

→ _____

3 I <u>regret to say</u> that I cannot attend the meeting.

→ _____

4 My brother <u>forgot putting</u> the key in the drawer.

→ _____

5 When I went into the room, he <u>stopped talking</u> on the phone.

→ _____

C 주어진 단어를 알맞은 형태로 고쳐 쓰시오.

1 It is no use _____ things that happened in the past. (regret)

2 I think that this book is worth _____. (read)

3 I cannot imagine _____ without computers. (live)

4 He decided _____ a cartoonist in the future. (be)

5 She spent most of her time _____ TV. (watch)

D 밑줄 친 부분을 바르게 고쳐 문장을 다시 쓰시오.

1 She is busy <u>prepare</u> dinner.

→ _____

2 We are looking forward <u>to go</u> to your wedding.

→ _____

3 All the students agreed <u>accepting</u> the offer.

→ _____

4 It seemed that he did not want to spend any money <u>fix</u> his laptop.

→ _____

E 우리말과 같은 뜻이 되도록 괄호 안의 말을 바르게 배열하시오.

1 나는 많은 짐을 한번에 옮기려고 노력했다. (at once, carry, I, tried, to, luggage, a lot of)

→ _____

2 제가 에어컨을 끄는 것을 꺼리시나요? (mind, turning off, you, my, the air conditioner, do)

→ _____

3 Paul은 어렸을 때 이탈리아로 여행 갔던 것을 기억했다. (Paul, he, traveling, Italy, to, remembered, young, when, was)

→ _____

F 괄호 안의 말을 이용하여 우리말을 영어로 쓰시오.

1 나는 오늘 쇼핑하러 가고 싶다. (feel like, go shopping)

→ _____

2 그는 혼자 영화 보러 가는 것이 익숙하다. (used, go to the movies, alone)

→ _____

3 그는 나가기 전에 창문을 닫는 것을 잊었다. (forget, close, go out)

→ _____

4 그녀는 친구에게 거짓말을 한 것을 후회한다. (regret, tell lies)

→ _____

UNIT 01

Functions of Participles
분사의 기능

A 괄호 안에서 알맞은 말을 고르시오.

1 That is an (exciting, excited) play. You should see it.

2 His behavior made me (embarrassing, embarrassed).

3 Nara always feels (boring, bored) in science class.

4 I got cut by a piece of (breaking, broken) glass.

5 Mr. Kim had his office (cleaning, cleaned) yesterday.

6 The woman (talking, talked) to Paul is my aunt.

7 The researcher announced an (amazing, amazed) discovery in biology.

B 밑줄 친 부분을 바르게 고쳐 쓰시오.

1 I heard him <u>played</u> the piano.   → _____

2 The girl <u>carried</u> the puppy is my sister.   → _____

3 You look <u>depressing</u> these days. What's wrong?   → _____

4 Working overtime for many days made me <u>tiring</u>.   → _____

5 Her speech left the audience <u>impressing</u>.   → _____

6 I saw Kyle <u>walked</u> along the beach this morning.   → _____

C 괄호 안에 주어진 단어를 알맞은 형태로 쓰시오.

1 The boy _____ on the stage is my brother. (dance)

2 I visited my friend _____ in an accident. (hurt)

3 Sumin had her eyes _____ at the hospital. (test)

4 The diamond _____ yesterday was found in a museum. (steal)

5 The reason for his absence was _____. (surprise)

6 The news article made the readers _____. (shock)

D 밑줄 친 부분을 바르게 고쳐 문장을 다시 쓰시오.

1 Did you see Teddy <u>played</u> baseball in the park?

→ _____

2 Too much homework made me <u>stressing out</u>.

→ _____

3 I could feel my dog <u>licked</u> my right arm.

→ _____

4 The water <u>flow</u> in this brook is from the mountain valley.

→ _____

E 우리말과 같은 뜻이 되도록 괄호 안의 말을 바르게 배열하시오.

1 보물은 동굴 안에 숨겨져 있었다. (was, in, hidden, the cave, the treasure)

→ _____

2 이 노트북 컴퓨터는 매우 혼란스러운 설명서를 가지고 있다. (laptop, a, very, has, confusing, computer, this, manual)

→ _____

3 그녀는 결과에 대해 꽤 만족하는 것처럼 보였다. (satisfied, she, with, quite, the results, seemed)

→ _____

4 어떤 사람들은 무서운 영화를 보는 것을 즐긴다. (movies, enjoy, some, watching, frightening, people)

→ _____

F 괄호 안의 말을 이용하여 우리말을 영어로 쓰시오.

1 더운 날씨는 나를 하루 종일 지치게 만들었다. (exhaust, all day long)

→ _____

2 나는 Jane Austin이 쓴 소설을 자주 읽는다. (novels, write, by)

→ _____

3 그 사진에서 내 옆에 서 있는 사람은 나의 선생님이다. (stand, next to, picture)

→ _____

Participle Clauses
분사구문

A 괄호 안에서 알맞은 말을 고르시오.

1 (Walk, Walking) along the river, I came across my old friend.

2 (Eaten, Eating) breakfast, she watched the news on TV.

3 (Listening, Be listening) to music, David jogged in the park.

4 (Taken, Taking) the class, you should concentrate during it.

5 You will never get lost (following, being followed) these directions.

6 Not (having taken, have taking) her advice seriously, he failed in business.

B 밑줄 친 부분에 유의하여 문장을 해석하시오.

1 <u>Watching the funny movie</u>, I tried to relax.

→ _____

2 <u>Being busy these days</u>, I do not have time to relax.

→ _____

3 <u>Finishing work on Friday</u>, he usually goes to bed early.

→ _____

4 <u>Helping me do the cleaning</u>, I will let you play video games.

→ _____

5 <u>Admitting that he is honest</u>, I still cannot hire him.

→ _____

C 괄호 안에 주어진 단어를 알맞은 형태로 쓰시오.

1 _____ the subway, you will not be late for work. (take)

2 _____ well at school, I visited the health center. (feel)

3 _____ him a few times before, I recognized him easily. (see)

4 _____ of glass, this vase can be easily broken. (make)

D 다음 문장을 분사구문으로 바꾸어 쓰시오.

1 As she has no car, she goes to work by bus.

→ _____

2 After they finished the job training, they went back to America.

→ _____

3 Although he had left Korea in his childhood, he still remembered Korean.

→ _____

E 우리말과 같은 뜻이 되도록 괄호 안의 말을 바르게 배열하시오.

1 나는 그 프로젝트에 많은 돈을 썼기 때문에 나는 긍정적인 결과를 기대했다. (a lot of, having, on the project, money, I, a positive outcome, spent, expected)

→ _____

2 그 책을 여러 번 읽었음에도 불구하고 나는 그것을 완전히 이해하지 못한다. (the book, read, times, I, several, it, fully understand, having, do not)

→ _____

3 작문에서 F를 받아서 그는 그 과목을 다시 수강해야 했다. (getting, again, had to, an F, in composition, the subject, take, he)

→ _____

F 괄호 안의 말과 분사구문을 이용하여 우리말을 영어로 쓰시오.

1 그들을 몰랐기 때문에 나는 조용히 있었다. (know, keep silent)

→ _____

2 차는 도난당한 이후로 아직 발견되지 않고 있다. (steal, find)

→ _____

3 그는 시험에 실패했지만 내년에 다시 시도하기로 결심했다. (fail, the exam, try)

→ _____

4 오래 전에 지어져서 이 집은 매우 낡았다. (long, ago, old)

→ _____

Various Participle Clauses
다양한 분사구문들

A 괄호 안에서 알맞은 말을 고르시오.

1 (Frankly speaking, Speaking of), I am allergic to carrots.

2 (Compared with, Talking of) other books, this one is short and easy to read.

3 (Judging from, Strictly speaking), it was not his fault.

4 (Judging from, Generally speaking) his tanned skin, he just got back from vacation.

5 (Strictly speaking, Considering) his background, he must have been born with musical talent.

B 밑줄 친 부분에 유의하여 문장을 해석하시오.

1 Jenny was sitting with her arms folded.

　→ _____

2 The volleyball player kept playing with his foot injured.

　→ _____

3 Diane fell asleep with the light turned on.

　→ _____

4 The actor appeared with lots of people shouting with joy.

　→ _____

C 밑줄 친 부분을 바르게 고쳐 쓰시오.

1 Being cloudy, she brought an umbrella with her.　　→ _____

2 Amy was listening to music with her eyes closing.　　→ _____

3 Speaking from Kate, she has lived in China for 7 years.　→ _____

4 All his belongings were lost, he contacted the lost-and-found center.

　　　　　　　　　　　　　　　　　　　　　　　　　→ _____

D 다음 문장을 분사구문으로 바꾸어 쓰시오.

1 When the singer came on the stage, people applauded.

→ _____

2 As there was no food in the refrigerator, I went out to buy some.

→ _____

3 As her dress was too long, she had it shortened.

→ _____

E 우리말과 같은 뜻이 되도록 괄호 안의 말을 바르게 배열하시오.

1 이 수프를 먹기 전에 소금을 좀 넣으세요. (eating, some salt, this soup, before, add)

→ _____

2 내일은 휴일이므로 모든 관공서가 문을 닫을 것이다. (a holiday, be, tomorrow, closed, will, all government offices, being)

→ _____

3 그녀는 머리카락을 바람에 휘날리며 나를 기다리고 있었다. (with, in the wind, she, for, waiting, blowing, her hair, was, me)

→ _____

4 그리스어와 비교하면 영어는 배우기 쉽다. (to, Greek, English, compared, easy, with, is, learn)

→ _____

F 괄호 안의 말과 분사구문을 이용하여 우리말을 영어로 쓰시오.

1 그녀의 가족이 멀리 있어서 그녀는 외로움을 느꼈다. (family, far away)

→ _____

2 그는 신발끈이 풀린 채로 달리고 있었다. (shoelaces, untie)

→ _____

3 그의 건강을 고려하면 그는 집에 머물러야 한다. (consider, should)

→ _____

4 인터넷상의 비평들로 판단하건대 그 영화는 지루함에 틀림없다. (judge, the reviews)

→ _____

UNIT
01

Comparisons Using the Positive Degree
원급을 이용한 비교

A 괄호 안에서 알맞은 말을 고르시오.

1 Hana can run as (fast, faster) as Robert.

2 My brother eats (two, twice) as much as I do.

3 He needs to get used to the new system as quickly (as, than) possible.

4 Writing a story is not as (easy, easier) as telling a story.

5 Was the novel as (interesting, more interesting) as his last one?

6 This conference room is three times (as big, so bigger) as that one.

7 The tennis coach is not as (popular, more popular) as the swimming coach.

B 밑줄 친 부분을 바르게 고쳐 쓰시오.

1 I cannot learn new things as <u>more easily</u> as I did before. → _____

2 Oranges are not as <u>sour than</u> lemons.   → _____

3 The black coat is <u>so expensive</u> as the ivory one.   → _____

4 I will help you <u>as many as</u> possible.   → _____

5 Billy's smartphone is twice as <u>more expensive</u> as mine. → _____

6 The new computer works three times <u>so faster</u> as the old one.

                                            → _____

C 빈칸에 알맞은 말을 골라 쓰시오. (단, 한 번씩만 쓰시오.)

as	not	soon	long

1 This bag is pretty, but it is twice _____ heavy as that one.

2 We will try to send a repairman as _____ as possible.

3 The hamburger is _____ as delicious as the hot dog.

4 The new battery will last twice as _____ as the previous one.

D 두 문장의 의미가 같도록 빈칸에 알맞은 말을 쓰시오.

1 The blue box is 20 kg. The red box is 40 kg.

→ The red box is _____ as the blue box.

2 I want to get out of this place as soon as I can.

→ I want to get out of this place _____ .

3 Andy can play tennis well. Brian can play tennis well.

→ Andy can play tennis _____ Brian.

4 Judy is 13 years old. Jessica is 14 years old.

→ Judy is not _____ Jessica.

E 우리말과 같은 뜻이 되도록 괄호 안의 말을 바르게 배열하시오.

1 그 영화는 만화만큼 웃기지 않았다. (the movie, the cartoon, not, as, funny, was, as)

→ _____

2 너는 가능한 한 많이 경험해야 한다. (should, possible, you, much, experience, as, as)

→ _____

3 그 바이러스는 우리가 생각했던 것보다 두 배 더 빨리 퍼지고 있다. (the virus, twice, as, is, spreading, thought, fast, we, as)

→ _____

F 괄호 안의 말을 이용하여 우리말을 영어로 쓰시오.

1 이 길은 저 길만큼 울퉁불퉁하다. (road, bumpy)

→ _____

2 가능한 한 빨리 결과를 알려주세요. (let, know, the results, soon, possible)

→ _____

3 대부분의 반려동물은 사람만큼 오래 살 수 없다. (pet, live, humans)

→ _____

4 내 컴퓨터의 다운로드 속도는 업로드 속도보다 세 배 빠르다. (download speed, fast, upload speed)

→ _____

Comparisons Using Comparatives

비교급을 이용한 비교

A 괄호 안에서 알맞은 말을 고르시오.

1   Women usually live (long, longer) than men.

2   The (warm, warmer) the weather gets, the better I feel.

3   My hands are (very, much) bigger than yours.

4   The wind was getting (strong, stronger) and stronger.

5   I think time is (valuabler, more valuable) than money.

6   The more you smile, (happier, the happier) you become.

7   The actor is less (popular, more popular) than the director.

B 괄호 안에 주어진 단어를 알맞은 형태로 쓰시오.

1   The situation is _____ than I thought. (bad)

2   Homemade food is _____ than fast food. (healthy)

3   The less you sleep, _____ you get tired. (easily)

4   Doing your best is _____ than winning. (important)

5   The spot on my face is getting _____ and larger. (large)

6   The subway fare is less _____ in Korea than in Japan. (expensive)

C 빈칸에 알맞은 말을 골라 쓰시오.

better	much	more	than

1   Gold is more expensive _____ silver.

2   You look _____ than your picture.

3   As night approached, he grew more and _____ nervous.

4   Watching movies is _____ more interesting than reading books.

D 밑줄 친 부분을 바르게 고쳐 문장을 다시 쓰시오.

1 The new program is superior than the old one.

→ _____

2 The results were much good than we had expected.

→ _____

3 The hot it gets, the more water people drink.

→ _____

4 The boy from a small town became more famous and famous.

→ _____

E 우리말과 같은 뜻이 되도록 괄호 안의 말을 바르게 배열하시오.

1 삶이 점점 더 복잡해지고 있다. (more, gets, life, and, complicated, more)

→ _____

2 Jason의 인기가 점점 더 올라가고 있다. (Jason's popularity, and, higher, getting, is, higher)

→ _____

3 Sue는 쇼핑보다 독서에 훨씬 더 관심이 있다. (Sue, much, interested, than, in reading, in shopping, is, more)

→ _____

4 커피를 마실수록 나는 더 잠이 깼다. (awake, the, drank, was, more, more, I, coffee, the, I)

→ _____

F 괄호 안의 말을 이용하여 우리말을 영어로 쓰시오.

1 지금 교통이 두 시간 전보다 훨씬 더 복잡하다. (traffic, much, heavy)

→ _____

2 그녀의 회화 실력이 점점 더 좋아지고 있다. (speaking skills, get, good)

→ _____

3 나라의 경제 상황이 네가 아는 것보다 더 심각하다. (economic condition, serious)

→ _____

UNIT 03

Comparisons Using Superlatives

최상급을 이용한 비교

A 괄호 안에서 알맞은 말을 고르시오.

1 I am the (younger, youngest) of four brothers.

2 Ice hockey is the (popularest, most popular) sport in Canada.

3 It is one of the tallest (building, buildings) in the world.

4 Chris is the (more intelligent, most intelligent) of the two.

5 This is the most exciting game I (ever play, have ever played).

B 괄호 안에 주어진 단어를 알맞은 형태로 쓰시오.

1 Eddie is the ＿＿＿＿＿＿＿ of all the boys. (tall)

2 Jejudo is the ＿＿＿＿＿＿＿ island in Korea. (large)

3 English is one of the most common ＿＿＿＿＿＿＿ in the world. (language)

4 I think Mozart is the ＿＿＿＿＿＿＿ musician in the world. (good)

5 James is the ＿＿＿＿＿＿＿ person that I have ever met. (attractive)

C 밑줄 친 부분을 바르게 고쳐 문장을 다시 쓰시오.

1 This jacket is <u>the most popular</u> of the two.

　→ ＿＿＿＿＿＿＿＿＿＿＿＿＿＿＿＿＿＿＿＿＿

2 No other teacher at our school is <u>the friendliest</u> than Ms. Gates.

　→ ＿＿＿＿＿＿＿＿＿＿＿＿＿＿＿＿＿＿＿＿＿

3 The Nile is one of <u>the most longest river</u> in the world.

　→ ＿＿＿＿＿＿＿＿＿＿＿＿＿＿＿＿＿＿＿＿＿

4 Camels are <u>most important</u> animals in the desert.

　→ ＿＿＿＿＿＿＿＿＿＿＿＿＿＿＿＿＿＿＿＿＿

D 주어진 문장과 의미가 같도록 빈칸에 알맞은 말을 쓰시오.

1 The Pacific Ocean is the largest ocean on the earth.

= The Pacific Ocean is _____ on the earth.

= _____ on the earth _____ than the Pacific Ocean.

= No other ocean on the earth _____ .

2 Math is the most difficult subject for me.

= Math is _____ than _____ for me.

= No other subject _____ than math for me.

= No other subject is as _____ for me.

E 우리말과 같은 뜻이 되도록 괄호 안의 말을 바르게 배열하시오.

1 아시아는 세계에서 가장 큰 대륙이다. (Asia, the, the world, in, biggest, is, continent)

→ _____

2 그는 역사상 가장 불운한 사람 중 한 명이었다. (he, in history, unfortunate, was, one, the, most, men, of)

→ _____

3 다른 어떤 것도 너의 건강만큼 중요한 것은 없다. (other, thing, as, health, your, no, is, important, as)

→ _____

F 괄호 안의 말을 이용하여 우리말을 영어로 쓰시오.

1 Tyler는 모든 학생들 중에서 가장 똑똑하다. (smart, of, all the students)

→ _____

2 몽트뢰는 스위스에서 가장 아름다운 도시 중 하나이다. (Montreux, beautiful, city, Switzerland)

→ _____

3 번지 점프는 내가 지금까지 해 본 것 중 가장 인상적인 경험이다. (bungee jumping, impressive, experience, ever)

→ _____

UNIT
01

Subordinating Conjunctions
종속접속사

A 괄호 안에서 알맞은 말을 고르시오.

1 Tear up the receipt (after, before) you throw it away.

2 (Though, Unless) the salesperson does not suggest this product, I will buy it.

3 She is sitting on the bench (so, while) he is jogging.

4 He will help me (in order that, once) he comes back.

5 She has been sick (as, although) she is working overtime continuously.

B 밑줄 친 부분에 유의하여 문장을 해석하시오.

1 <u>Since</u> he was interested in the topic, he listened carefully.

    → _____

2 <u>Even though</u> it was snowing heavily, she was not late for school.

    → _____

3 <u>Unless</u> you sit up straight, you can hurt your back.

    → _____

4 <u>As soon as</u> he retires, he will go on a trip with his wife.

    → _____

C 두 문장의 의미가 같도록 빈칸에 알맞은 말을 골라 쓰시오.

unless	since	although

1 I had not seen her for a long time, but I could recognize her.

    = _____ I had not seen her for a long time, I could recognize her.

2 If you do not get enough sleep, you will easily get tired.

    = _____ you get enough sleep, you will easily get tired.

3 The artist's paintings are great, so many people come to see them.

    = Many people come to see the artist's paintings _____ they are
    great.

D 두 문장을 괄호 안의 말을 이용하여 한 문장으로 쓰시오.

1 I have plans tomorrow. I have to do my homework today. (as)

→ _____

2 It rains. I will bring an umbrella. (in case)

→ _____

3 Wash your hands often. You can avoid catching a cold. (in order that)

→ _____

E 우리말과 같은 뜻이 되도록 괄호 안의 말을 바르게 배열하시오.

1 내 수업이 끝날 때까지 엄마는 그곳에 있을 것이다. (my mom, is, will, over, be, until, my class, there)

→ _____

2 사람들이 지나다닐 수 있도록 이 박스들을 치우세요. (these boxes, can, so that, people, remove, pass by)

→ _____

3 비록 너무 더웠지만 아이들은 야구를 하고 있었다. (playing, though, it, was, the children, were, very hot, baseball)

→ _____

F 괄호 안의 말을 이용하여 우리말을 영어로 쓰시오.

1 그녀는 건물을 드나들 때 엘리베이터를 타지 않는다. (enter and leave, take the elevator)

→ _____

2 그는 바빴기 때문에 약속을 지킬 수 없었다. (keep one's promise)

→ _____

3 만약 가격이 적당하다면 나는 이 신발을 사고 싶다. (the price, reasonable)

→ _____

4 비록 내 친구들은 외국에 살지만 우리는 서로 정기적으로 연락한다. (abroad, contact, regularly)

→ _____

UNIT
02

Correlative Conjunctions / Indirect Questions
상관접속사 / 간접의문문

A   괄호 안에서 알맞은 말을 고르시오.

1   I need to buy (either, both) a black or white dress.

2   Mr. Pitt is a poet (but also, as well as) a professor.

3   I'd like to know (who won, who she won) the prize.

4   He is (both, not only) a former athlete and a businessman.

5   I wonder (nor, whether) you have visited India or not.

6   Can you tell me when (he left, did he leave)?

7   He will (whether, neither) persuade the customer nor promote our product.

B   빈칸에 알맞은 말을 골라 쓰시오. (단, 한 번씩만 쓰시오.)

if	where	whether	who

1   I am not sure _____ the department store is located.

2   The problem is _____ will be responsible for that work.

3   _____ he earns a lot of money does not matter.

4   I wondered _____ he had brought his passport.

C   밑줄 친 부분을 바르게 고쳐 쓰시오.

1   <u>If</u> he speaks Chinese or not is very important.   → _____

2   <u>Either</u> you nor he is the main actor in this movie.   → _____

3   I wondered where <u>moved you</u>.   → _____

4   Both coffee and tea <u>is</u> sold at this shop.   → _____

5   He is not only handsome <u>as well as</u> friendly.   → _____

6   My friend as well as I <u>play</u> badminton well.   → _____

7   Either Tom <u>nor</u> Sue will be our class representative.   → _____

D 두 문장을 한 문장으로 바꿔 쓰시오.

1 Do you think? What does he want to be?

→ _____

2 I wonder. Why did she lie to her parents?

→ _____

3 She does not like the class schedule. He does not like the class schedule.

→ _____

4 Can you tell me? Did he arrive at the hotel?

→ _____

E 우리말과 같은 뜻이 되도록 괄호 안의 말을 바르게 배열하시오.

1 그는 종이도 캔도 재활용하지 않는다. (cans, neither, he, paper, recycles, nor)

→ _____

2 그녀는 마음이 따뜻하고 활기차다. (warm-hearted, energetic, both, and, is, she)

→ _____

3 나는 그녀가 왜 그와 사랑에 빠졌는지 잘 모르겠다. (fell in, him, I, why, am, love with, she, not sure)

→ _____

4 나는 이 문장이 옳은지 아닌지 모르겠다. (correct, know, this sentence, do not, I, is, whether)

→ _____

F 괄호 안의 말을 이용하여 우리말을 영어로 쓰시오.

1 나는 파스타나 피자 둘 중 하나를 만들 것이다. (make, some pasta, a pizza)

→ _____

2 나는 네가 은행을 찾을 수 있을지 모르겠다. (sure, find, a bank)

→ _____

3 나는 왜 그가 새로운 곳들을 탐험하는지 궁금하다. (curious, explore, place)

→ _____

4 Jeff는 자신이 말을 너무 많이 하고 있다는 것을 깨달았다. (realize, that, talk)

→ _____

Relative Pronouns
관계대명사

A 괄호 안에서 알맞은 말을 고르시오.

1 I want to have a friend to (whom, who) I can talk about anything.

2 The TV drama is about a woman (whose, whom) boyfriend is a vampire.

3 It is the most boring movie (which, that) I have ever seen.

4 I have to do (that, what) I have to do.

5 I need to find something (that, whom) can relieve my stress.

6 People (whose, who) have pets are less likely to suffer from depression.

B 밑줄 친 부분에 유의하여 문장을 해석하시오.

1 I was so nervous then that I could not express <u>what</u> I thought well.

→ _____

2 Sometimes your brother or sister is the person <u>with whom</u> you are angriest.

→ _____

3 I just saw a girl <u>whose</u> coat was exactly the same as yours.

→ _____

4 Look at the guy <u>who</u> is wearing sunglasses over there.

→ _____

C 문장에서 삭제되어야 하는 부분에 × 표시 하시오.

1 The tiger which it grew too big has been sent to a larger zoo.

2 Isn't that the woman who she lives across the street from you?

3 This is the postcard that my cousin sent me it.

4 I thought hard to figure out what I really wanted the thing.

5 Sally is my friend whom I often study with her.

D 괄호 안에 주어진 단어를 바르게 배열하시오.

1 That is _____ I go to taekwondo class.
(with, the boy, whom)

2 I found the wallet _____ for a week.
(had, lost, he, which)

3 There is a small _____ all painted pink.
(are, walls, whose, café)

4 _____ is not to lie to my parents.
(the best thing, have ever done, that, I)

E 밑줄 친 부분을 바르게 고쳐 문장을 다시 쓰시오.

1 The person <u>who he</u> came up with the idea was Hank.

→ _____

2 I know someone <u>who</u> older brother is a police officer.

→ _____

3 People <u>which doesn't</u> exercise at all tend to be less healthy.

→ _____

4 The chair on <u>that</u> he sat down suddenly broke.

→ _____

F 괄호 안의 말을 이용하여 우리말을 영어로 쓰시오.

1 Helen Keller는 귀가 먹고 눈이 먼 교육자였다. (educator, who, deaf and blind)

→ _____

2 네가 필요한 것을 말하면 내가 그것을 가져다줄게. (what, get, for)

→ _____

3 당신이 필요한 어떤 것이라도 있나요? (there, anything, that)

→ _____

4 그 기자는 홍수에 의해 집이 파손된 남자를 인터뷰하고 있다. (reporter, interview, whose, be damaged by the flood)

→ _____

Relative Adverbs

관계부사

A 괄호 안에서 알맞은 말을 고르시오.

1 I do not understand the reason (when, why) you are doing this.

2 The employees discussed (how, the way how) the service could be improved.

3 Put it back in the drawer (how, where) you took it from.

4 It was the year (when, where) we graduated from elementary school.

5 La Viva is the place (for which, at which) you can have the best Mexican meal.

6 I will never forget (the day, where) when my father took me to the baseball park.

B 밑줄 친 부분에 유의하여 문장을 해석하시오.

1 They do not remember the day <u>on which</u> he came.

→ _____

2 I am looking for a bookstore <u>at which</u> I can buy used books.

→ _____

3 We should check the time <u>when</u> our train leaves.

→ _____

4 This is <u>how</u> I memorize English words.

→ _____

5 The house <u>where</u> I used to live was near the river.

→ _____

C 밑줄 친 부분을 생략할 수 있으면 ○, 생략할 수 없으면 × 표시 하시오.

1 I like <u>the way</u> he talks.   → _____

2 This is the place <u>where</u> Monet got his inspiration.   → _____

3 The library is <u>where</u> you can also watch a lot of good movies.   → _____

4 The reason <u>why</u> she wants to learn boxing is interesting.   → _____

D 괄호 안에 주어진 단어를 바르게 배열하시오.

1 Big Billy _____ you can buy tools and hardware.
(where, the place, is)

2 _____ people's clothes become colorful.
(spring, the time, when, is)

3 _____ in Cambodia was very hot and humid.
(we, the day, which, on, arrived)

4 _____ their offer is a mystery.
(she, the reason, turned down, why)

E 밑줄 친 부분을 바르게 고쳐 문장을 다시 쓰시오.

1 This is the house <u>from</u> which Jeff lives.

→ _____

2 2016 was the year <u>in</u> when Christmas fell on a Sunday.

→ _____

3 Do you know <u>why the reason</u> Sera cried?

→ _____

4 Do you remember the park <u>why</u> we used to play together?

→ _____

F 괄호 안의 말을 이용하여 우리말을 영어로 쓰시오.

1 평창은 2018 동계 올림픽이 열린 도시이다. (Pyeongchang, in which, the 2018 Winter Olympics, be held)

→ _____

2 네가 이 컴퓨터를 끌 수 있는 방법을 내가 보여 줄게. (let me, how, shut down)

→ _____

3 수요일과 일요일이 내가 내 방을 청소하는 날이다. (the days, when, clean)

→ _____

4 나는 내가 저녁을 먹은 식당에 내 가방을 놔두고 왔다. (leave, where, have)

→ _____

UNIT
03

Nonrestrictive Relative Clauses

관계사절의 계속적 용법

A 괄호 안에서 알맞은 말을 고르시오.

1 The company has a new CEO, (who, that) is less than 30 years old.

2 The notebook is in my bag, (where, which) you can find near my bed.

3 That is the student cafeteria, (that, where) you can buy lunch.

4 She has a good sense of color, (as, that) is evident from her artwork.

B 밑줄 친 부분에 유의하여 문장을 해석하시오.

1 Mia asked me to deliver a secret letter, <u>which</u> I read immediately.

→ _____

2 I have had a lot of worries in my life, <u>most of which</u> never happened.

→ _____

3 There is no one <u>but</u> has dreams.

→ _____

4 He is planning to move to a small apartment, <u>where</u> many people believe a ghost lives.

→ _____

C 빈칸에 알맞은 말을 골라 쓰시오.

when	where	whose	which	whom

1 Cindy, _____ brother was allergic to cats, gave her cat to my family.

2 Amy and her friends, none of _____ spoke Chinese, went to China.

3 Todd got a perfect score on the test, _____ surprised everyone.

4 I have just come back from Chuncheon, _____ my grandparents live.

5 The year 2002, _____ I was born, is mostly remembered for the Korea-Japan World Cup.

D 두 문장의 의미가 같도록 빈칸에 알맞은 말을 쓰시오.

1 Jejudo has a lot of tourists, and many of them visit Hallasan.

= Jejudo has a lot of tourists, _____ .

2 The foreign singer sang a beautiful song, but I could not understand it.

= The foreign singer sang a beautiful song, _____ .

3 Ryan is in the photography club, and that is why I joined it.

= Ryan is in the photography club, _____ I joined it.

4 Tina did not finish the food on her plate, but that was very unusual.

= Tina did not finish the food on her plate, _____ .

5 I found some grapes in the refrigerator, but most of them were rotten.

= I found some grapes, _____ , in the refrigerator.

6 I entered the restroom, and I met April there.

= I entered the restroom, _____ .

7 Selina went to Paris last month, and at that time, she visited many art museums.

= Selina went to Paris last month, _____ many art museums.

E 괄호 안의 말을 이용하여 우리말을 영어로 쓰시오.

1 그녀는 독일에서 자랐는데 그것이 그녀가 독일어를 이해하는 이유이다. (grow up, Germany, which, why)

→ _____

2 내가 학교 체육관에서 만났던 Steve는 매우 재능 있는 배드민턴 선수이다. (at the school gym, talented, badminton)

→ Steve, _____ .

3 너는 필요한 것보다 많은 음식을 먹지 말아야 한다. (should not, more food, than, be needed)

→ _____

4 나는 양말 열 켤레를 샀는데 그 중 하나에 구멍이 있었다. (pair of, one of, which, a hole)

→ _____

UNIT

04

Compound Relatives

복합관계사

A 괄호 안에서 알맞은 말을 고르시오.

1 (What, Whatever) comes next, I cannot eat any more.

2 She gave her flyers to (whoever, however) came out of the gate.

3 (Wherever, Where) you go, tell your parents your location.

4 (Whatever, However) wealthy a person is, money doesn't guarantee happiness.

5 Choose (whichever, that) pair of pants suits you best.

6 (No matter when, Wherever) I come home, my dog welcomes me.

B 밑줄 친 부분에 유의하여 문장을 해석하시오.

1 <u>Whoever</u> leaves the classroom last should turn off the lights.

→ _____

2 He is busy <u>whenever</u> I want to talk to him.

→ _____

3 <u>However</u> small a task is, she tries to do it well.

→ _____

4 It seems that he disagrees with <u>whatever</u> I suggest.

→ _____

C 빈칸에 알맞은 말을 골라 쓰시오.

anything	whoever	whatever	wherever

1 You can sit _____ you want.

2 Give it to _____ asks for it first.

3 _____ he did, he does not deserve this.

4 _____ that Daniel cooks is delicious.

D 두 문장의 의미가 같도록 빈칸에 알맞은 말을 쓰시오.

1 I will take whoever wants to go.

= I will take anyone _____ .

2 You cannot buy true friendship however rich you are.

= You cannot buy true friendship no _____ .

3 Dennis will make a mess wherever he happens to be.

= Dennis will make a mess no _____ .

4 Whatever they may say, it does not affect my feelings for you.

= No _____ , it does not affect my feelings for you.

E 밑줄 친 부분을 바르게 고쳐 문장을 다시 쓰시오.

1 Wherever <u>go</u>, I will follow you.

→ _____

2 He will kindly give an answer to <u>who</u> asks him a question.

→ _____

3 However <u>she is hungry</u>, she does not eat fast food.

→ _____

4 Whatever you want <u>are</u> yours.

→ _____

F 괄호 안의 말을 이용하여 우리말을 영어로 쓰시오.

1 Smith 시장은 그가 어디를 가든지 환영받는다. (mayor, be welcome, wherever)

→ _____

2 나는 저 노래를 들을 때마다 그를 떠올린다. (think of, whenever, hear)

→ _____

3 네가 네 친구들과 무엇을 하든지 10시 전에 집에 돌아와라. (whatever, return home, before)

→ _____

UNIT
01

Subjunctives
가정법

A 괄호 안에서 알맞은 말을 고르시오.

1 If I (have, had) a friend to talk to, I would not be lonely.

2 You will be welcomed if you (come, came) to my house.

3 If I had asked her to invite me, she (would have, has) done so.

4 If I had won the lottery, I (were, would) not be working here now.

5 It would be good if you (stopped, stop) by and said hello to everyone.

6 If you see Melanie, (give, will give) her this magazine.

B 밑줄 친 부분을 바르게 고쳐 쓰시오.

1 If he <u>has not</u> work part time, he could come home early.　→ _____

2 If I meet Sarah, I <u>would</u> tell her the truth.　→ _____

3 If you had bought the bag, you <u>will have</u> regretted it.　→ _____

4 If he had liked the new teacher, he <u>will not</u> have done it.　→ _____

5 If you <u>are</u> me, what would you do in this situation?　→ _____

6 If the accident <u>was</u> avoided, he would not be in the hospital now.

→ _____

C 두 문장의 의미가 같도록 빈칸에 알맞은 말을 쓰시오.

1 If I _____ free time, I could go out to see a movie.

→ I do not have free time, so I _____ go out to see a movie.

2 If she had had enough money, she could have bought a dress.

→ She _____ enough money, so she _____ a dress.

3 If he _____ ill on the day of the test, he _____ successful.

→ He was ill on the day of the test, so he was not successful.

4 If they had not stayed up until late at night, they _____ sleepy.

→ They _____ until late at night, so they are sleepy now.

D 주어진 문장을 가정법 문장으로 바꾸어 쓰시오.

1 I do not have a house with a swimming pool, so I cannot swim every day.

→ _____

2 I am not a famous soccer player, so I am not rich.

→ _____

3 You were busy, so I did not ask you to help me.

→ _____

4 James did not ask me what happened that day, so I did not say anything.

→ _____

E 우리말과 같은 뜻이 되도록 괄호 안의 말을 바르게 배열하시오.

1 네가 공부를 열심히 했더라면 대학에 갈 수 있을 텐데. (hard, you, studied, if, could, the university, you, enter, had)

→ _____

2 비행기가 제시간에 착륙했더라면 우리는 그 행사에 늦지 않을 텐데. (had, the event, not, landed, if, we, would, the plane, on time, late for, be)

→ _____

3 내가 Amy의 주소를 기억했더라면 그녀에게 크리스마스카드를 보냈을 텐데. (if, would, had, sent, I, Amy's address, I, have, her, a Christmas card, remembered)

→ _____

F 괄호 안의 말을 이용하여 우리말을 영어로 쓰시오.

1 내가 그 감독이라면 그 여배우를 캐스팅하지 않을 텐데. (director, cast, actress)

→ _____

2 내가 그 책을 가지고 있었다면 너에게 빌려줬을 텐데. (lend)

→ _____

3 그가 그 캠핑 여행을 갔더라면 그는 지금 그곳에 그들과 함께 있을 텐데. (camping trip)

→ _____

UNIT

02

I wish/as if/It is time + Subjunctive

I wish/as if/It is time + 가정법

A 괄호 안에서 알맞은 말을 고르시오.

1 I wish I (am, were) a movie star.

2 She dressed herself as if she (was, were) a princess.

3 Cheryl acted as if she (had not met, didn't meet) me before.

4 It is high time we (clean, cleaned) the room.

5 When I was broke, I wished I (saved, had saved) some money.

B 밑줄 친 부분을 바르게 고쳐 쓰시오.

1 I wish I <u>have not eaten</u> that much last night. → _____

2 She talked as if she <u>cooked</u> all the dishes by herself. → _____

3 It is time you <u>make</u> plans to travel to Europe. → _____

4 We wish he <u>makes</u> a good decision for himself. → _____

5 It is high time everybody <u>prepares</u> for the exam. → _____

6 The people wished they <u>chose</u> a different leader. → _____

C 두 문장의 의미가 같도록 빈칸에 알맞은 말을 쓰시오.

1 She talks as if she knew very much about the writer.

 → In fact, she _____ very much about the writer.

2 The fans wished the British singer _____ a Korean song.

 → The fans were sorry the British singer did not sing a Korean song.

3 It is high time we _____ the discussion.

 → It is a little late. We had better finish the discussion.

4 I wish he _____ Robin about our secret.

 → I am sorry he told Robin about our secret.

5 The boy acts as if he _____ a genius.

 → In fact, he is not a genius.

D 우리말과 같은 뜻이 되도록 괄호 안의 말을 바르게 배열하시오.

1 그는 마치 Dick과 싸웠던 것처럼 말했다. (talked, had, he, as if, fought, Dick, with, he)

→ _____

2 나는 더 많은 사람들이 자선 사업에 관심이 있으면 좋겠다. (charity work, interested in, I, were, wish, more people)

→ _____

3 그녀가 공부하는 것 외에 실용적인 기술을 배워야 할 시간이다. (besides, she, learned, time, it, a practical skill, is, studying)

→ _____

4 그는 마치 그 패션모델을 직접 만났던 것처럼 말했다. (had, as if, he, in person, talked, he, met, the fashion model)

→ _____

5 나의 할머니가 돌아가시지 않았더라면 좋을 텐데. (I, my grandmother, had, passed away, wish, not)

→ _____

6 우리가 보고서 쓰기를 마쳐야 할 시간이다. (is, we, the report, time, writing, high, finished, it)

→ _____

E 괄호 안의 말을 이용하여 우리말을 영어로 쓰시오.

1 내가 Raina와 함께 밴드에 들었다면 좋을 텐데. (wish, join the band)

→ _____

2 Aiden은 그 도시를 방문했던 것처럼 묘사했다. (describe, town, visit)

→ _____

3 James가 나를 위해 피자를 조금 남겨 놓았더라면 좋았을 텐데. (wish, leave, some pizza)

→ _____

4 Alicia는 그 신문 기사를 읽은 것처럼 말한다. (talk, as if, the newspaper article)

→ _____

5 내가 시험 문제의 모든 답을 안다면 좋을 텐데. (answers to, test questions)

→ _____

Implied Subjunctive / Leaving Out *if*

if절 대용어구 / if의 생략

A 괄호 안에서 알맞은 말을 고르시오.

1 (Having, Had) no cellphone, the boy could not contact his friends.

2 (To see, Seen) him dance, you would realize why he is called a dancing machine.

3 My friends helped me to do my homework. (Otherwise, If), I could not have finished it.

4 (Had, Being) she had more time to study, she could have gotten a better score.

B 밑줄 친 부분을 바르게 고쳐 쓰시오.

1 <u>Work</u> hard, you will become an expert in this field. → _____

2 <u>I were</u> in your shoes, I would make friends with her. → _____

3 Without his success, his family <u>lives</u> in difficulty. → _____

4 <u>Having</u> it not been for his efforts, the company might have gone bankrupt.

→ _____

C 두 문장의 의미가 같도록 빈칸에 알맞은 말을 쓰시오.

1 _____ told the rumor, he would have gotten frustrated.

→ If he had been told the rumor, he _____ frustrated.

2 If it had _____ her care, the boy could not have achieved his goal.

→ But for her care, the boy _____ his goal.

3 To _____, you would see his talent.

→ If you saw him do magic, you _____ his talent.

4 A good player would do his best in every match.

→ If he _____ a good player, he would do his best in every match.

D 우리말과 같은 뜻이 되도록 괄호 안의 말을 바르게 배열하시오.

1 휴대 전화가 없었더라면 우리의 삶은 더 단순했을지도 모른다. (been, it, more simple, had, for, not, have been, cell phones, our lives, might)

→ _____

2 좋은 책은 정보뿐만 아니라 즐거움도 준다. (a good book, information, would, you, give, pleasure, as well as)

→ _____

3 그와 얘기해 보면 그가 유머 감각이 있다는 것을 알게 될 것이다. (realize, talk to, would, to, of humor, him, he, a good sense, has, you)

→ _____

4 나는 교통 체증에 걸렸다. 그렇지 않았더라면 여기에 더 일찍 도착했을 텐데. (caught, here, I, in a traffic jam, would, I, have arrived, earlier, got, otherwise)

→ _____

5 나의 선생님의 도움이 없다면 나는 그 프로젝트를 끝낼 수 없을 텐데. (for, it, not, finish, my teacher's help, the project, not, were, could, I)

→ _____

E 괄호 안의 말을 이용하여 우리말을 영어로 쓰시오.

1 새로운 정책에 대하여 공지를 받았더라면 우리는 혼란스럽지 않았을 것이다. (be informed of, policy, confuse)

→ _____

2 인터넷이 없다면 사람들은 정보를 찾는 데 어려움을 겪을 것이다. (but for, have difficulty, find)

→ _____

3 부모님의 격려가 없었더라면 나는 내 직업을 포기했을지도 모른다. (without, encouragement, might, give up on, career)

→ _____

4 Tom은 아침 식사로 샌드위치를 먹었다. 그렇지 않았더라면 수업 중에 배가 고팠을 것이다. (eat, otherwise, in class)

→ _____

UNIT

01

Number Agreement
수일치

A 괄호 안에서 알맞은 말을 고르시오.

1 Each product (have, has) a serial number printed on the back.

2 Both surfing and scuba-diving (require, requires) basic swimming skills.

3 Listening to others (is, are) a key to effective communication.

4 (Have, Has) anyone seen Gail today?

5 Nobody (is, are) volunteering to be the leader of the team.

6 The Netherlands (is, are) not the background of the novel *A Dog of Flanders*.

B 밑줄 친 부분에 유의하여 문장을 해석하시오.

1 <u>A number of</u> students failed to turn in their homework on the due date.

→ _____

2 According to the police report, the majority of <u>the dead</u> were British.

→ _____

3 Nearly <u>three-fourths of</u> the earth's surface is covered with water.

→ _____

4 Experts say <u>the number of</u> languages in the world will decrease in the future.

→ _____

C 괄호 안에 주어진 단어를 알맞은 형태로 쓰시오.

1 The actor and director _____ won his third Oscar nomination. (have)

2 No one _____ why he is laughing. (know)

3 All of us _____ surprised by the news yesterday. (be)

4 Mathematics and economics _____ his majors. (be)

D 밑줄 친 부분을 바르게 고쳐 문장을 다시 쓰시오.

1 Every <u>parents loves</u> his or her child.

→ _____

2 The writer and the environmentalist <u>is</u> planning a charity event.

→ _____

3 The number of <u>person who go</u> abroad on vacation is increasing.

→ _____

4 All the information <u>were analyzed</u> by the computer.

→ _____

5 Creating new products <u>take</u> a lot of time.

→ _____

6 Half a million dollars <u>were</u> donated to the homeless.

→ _____

7 Whether you spend your vacation with us <u>are</u> important to me.

→ _____

8 The young <u>tends</u> to have a preference for exciting activities.

→ _____

E 괄호 안의 말을 이용하여 우리말을 영어로 쓰시오.

1 홍역은 중세에는 심각한 병이었다. (measles, disease, in the Middle Ages)

→ _____

2 저 햄버거에 9달러는 너무 비싸다. (for that hamburger, too)

→ _____

3 나머지 페이지들은 작가의 삶에 대한 내용이다. (the rest of, the author's life)

→ _____

4 그 물의 일부는 키보드 위에 쏟아졌다. (some of, be spilled, the keyboard)

→ _____

5 커피를 마시는 것은 Anne이 일어나자마자 하는 것이다. (drink, what, get up)

→ _____

UNIT 02

Tense Agreement

시제 일치

A 괄호 안에서 알맞은 말을 고르시오.

1 This sign says the store (opens, opened) at 9 a.m. from Monday through Friday.

2 We all hope that the plan (will, would) work.

3 As Henry put on his coat, the telephone (rings, rang).

4 The nurse said Charlie still (wakes, has woken) up at 6 every morning.

5 She wants to show her friends the photos she (take, took) last week.

6 Dad bought me a hair clip when my hair (is, was) very short.

B 괄호 안에 주어진 단어를 알맞은 형태로 쓰시오.

1 They will soon find out that he _____ for Japan. (have already left)

2 Do you know who _____ the steam engine? (invent)

3 Roy felt somebody _____ watching him. (be)

4 My grandfather emphasized that the early bird _____ the worm. (get)

5 Victoria thought she _____ be able to win first prize. (will not)

6 Today's history class is about the French Revolution, which _____ in 1789. (break out)

C 주어진 문장을 과거시제로 바꾼 문장을 완성하시오.

1 The doctor examines a patient who is suffering from a bad cold.
   → The doctor examined a patient who _____ from a bad cold.

2 The girl insists that she has paid for the popcorn.
   → The girl insisted that she _____ for the popcorn.

3 The teacher is explaining that light travels faster than sound.
   → The teacher was explaining that light _____ faster than sound.

D 괄호 안에 주어진 단어를 바르게 배열하시오. (단, 괄호 안에서 한 단어는 필요 없음)

1 I was surprised by _____ after I took the medicine.

(well, how, I, feel, felt)

2 They will do _____.

(anything, was, necessary, is, that)

3 He looked into the mirror and _____.

(his hair, started, comb, start, to)

4 I am wondering where _____.

(I, put, had, my phone, have)

E 밑줄 친 부분을 바르게 고쳐 문장을 다시 쓰시오.

1 Yesterday, I rode my bike to school but <u>walk</u> home later.

→ _____

2 Bob <u>will cook</u> a meal for his mother and then did all the dishes.

→ _____

3 The scientist proved that the earth <u>was</u> round.

→ _____

4 The boys loved the tree house which they <u>has built</u> themselves.

→ _____

F 괄호 안의 말을 이용하여 우리말을 영어로 쓰시오.

1 그 기차가 왔지만 Anna는 그녀의 기차표를 찾을 수 없었다. (come, but, can)

→ _____

2 Benjamin Franklin은 정직이 최선의 방책이라고 믿었다. (honesty, the best policy)

→ _____

3 나는 Ethan이 자기 전에 언제나 TV로 뉴스를 본다고 들었다. (always watch, go to bed)

→ _____

4 우리는 한국 전쟁이 1953년에 끝났다는 것을 알고 있다. (the Korean War, be over)

→ _____

UNIT 03

Indirect Speech
간접화법

A 괄호 안에서 알맞은 말을 고르시오.

1 My friend (said, told) me he would move to another city.

2 Dongsu asked the waiter (what, if) he could have chopsticks instead of a fork.

3 My mother asked me (whether, to) I had attended the English class.

4 The doctor (asked me what, told me that) I ate that morning.

5 Sandra (told, said) that her brother had looked fine the night before.

6 The old man asked me (if, to) close the blinds.

B 밑줄 친 부분을 바르게 고쳐 쓰시오.

1 She asked if she <u>may</u> sit next to me.   → _____

2 Mom asked Dad <u>that</u> feed the dog before he left.   → _____

3 Ms. Smith <u>said to</u> us whether we were going back home.   → _____

4 Mr. Taylor <u>told</u> when I would finish using the computer. → _____

5 Dad <u>said to</u> that he would come later.   → _____

C 빈칸에 알맞은 말을 골라 쓰시오.

do you	are you	has	did you

1 My sister asked if anyone had seen her key.

→ My sister said, "_____ anyone seen my key?"

2 The reporter asked him why he had committed such a crime.

→ The reporter asked him, "Why _____ commit such a crime?"

3 Andy asked her whether she was free the following night.

→ Andy said to her, "_____ free tomorrow night?"

4 The doctor asked me when I got headaches.

→ The doctor said to me, "When _____ get headaches?"

D 주어진 문장을 간접화법으로 전환한 문장을 완성하시오.

1 He said to me, "You're sitting on my bag now."

→ He told me that I _____ .

2 The lecturer said, "World War II began in 1939."

→ The lecturer _____ .

3 Lucy said to him, "I checked your email this morning."

→ Lucy told him that she had _____ .

4 The boy next to her said, "A new teacher came yesterday."

→ The boy next to her said that a new teacher _____ .

5 The lady said to the waiter, "Where can I wash my hands?"

→ The lady _____ the waiter _____ .

6 The janitor said to us, "Don't throw trash here."

→ The janitor told us _____ .

7 Ms. Jackson concluded, "The earth's rotation causes the seasons."

→ Ms. Jackson concluded that _____ .

8 Mr. Kim said to his passengers, "Would you mind if I opened the window?"

→ Mr. Kim asked his passengers whether _____ .

E 괄호 안의 말을 이용하여 우리말을 영어로 쓰시오.

1 그 간호사는 내가 다음 날에 그곳에 갈 수 있는지 내게 물었다. (if, the next day)

→ _____

2 Holly는 그녀의 수프에 파리가 있다고 말했다. (a fly, soup)

→ _____

3 나의 어머니는 비가 오면 창문을 닫으라고 내게 말씀하셨다. (close, if, rain)

→ _____

4 그 소녀들 중 한 명이 그녀의 차례가 언제인지 내게 물었다. (one of, her turn)

→ _____

UNIT

01

Emphasis, Negation, & Parallel Structure

강조, 부정, 병렬 구조

A 괄호 안에서 알맞은 말을 고르시오.

1 It is in the pink box (whose, that) Diana keeps the letters she receives.

2 Neither skiing nor (to snowboard, snowboarding) interests me.

3 I am against child labor. (No, Not) child should be forced to work.

4 I (did, do) know the answer, but I hesitated to speak up.

5 Eva not only runs a restaurant but also (attending, attends) graduate school.

B 밑줄 친 부분에 유의하여 문장을 해석하시오.

1 <u>It was</u> from the ceiling <u>that</u> a strange sound came last night.

→ _____

2 I have <u>no</u> intention to fight with you.

→ _____

3 Nina's dance was <u>not only</u> elegant <u>but also</u> powerful.

→ _____

4 He <u>does</u> look like a different person without his glasses.

→ _____

5 <u>Not every</u> animal needs oxygen to survive.

→ _____

C 빈칸에 알맞은 말을 골라 쓰시오.

that	no	did	none

1 There is _____ food left in the refrigerator.

2 _____ of us could buy the ball because we had no money.

3 It was Ron _____ gave me the movie ticket.

4 He _____ read the book, but he did not remember any of its characters.

D 괄호 안에 주어진 단어를 바르게 배열하시오.

1 Daniel did _____ video games.
(played, and then, his homework, finish)

2 _____ has blond hair like their mother.
(them, of, neither)

3 You _____ electronic devices during the test.
(any, have, not, must)

4 I like Sue not because of her appearance _____.
(because, her personality, but, of)

E 밑줄 친 부분을 바르게 고쳐 문장을 다시 쓰시오.

1 Audrey Hepburn was a <u>kindly, beautifully</u>, and passionate person.

→ _____

2 Eating too much and not <u>to exercise</u> at all are harmful to your health.

→ _____

3 It <u>is I who</u> answered your call a while ago.

→ _____

4 <u>Not</u> of them has any complaints though they were in a difficult situation.

→ _____

F 괄호 안의 말을 이용하여 우리말을 영어로 쓰시오.

1 나의 아버지가 일을 일찍 마치시는 날은 바로 매주 금요일이다. (it, every Friday, that)

→ _____

2 우리 둘 중 누구도 먼저 사과하기를 원하지 않았다. (neither of, apologize)

→ _____

3 이 문법 규칙에 예외는 없다. (there, no exception to)

→ _____

4 나는 오후에 쇼핑을 가든지 아니면 삼촌을 방문할 것이다. (either, go, visit)

→ _____

Apposition, Inversion, & Ellipsis

동격, 도치, 생략

A 괄호 안에서 알맞은 말을 고르시오.

1 Please stay if you (can, stay can).

2 (Here comes, Comes here) our hero.

3 I heard the news (that, if) Scott would join the baseball team.

4 I could not bear the thought (that, of) losing you.

5 Not only did she lose her bike, but (she was, was she) also late for class.

B 밑줄 친 부분에 유의하여 문장을 해석하시오.

1 There is no hope <u>that</u> we will win the game.

→ _____

2 In the center of the garden <u>was a beautiful fountain</u>.

→ _____

3 To some, history is boring. <u>To others, fun.</u>

→ _____

4 Not a word <u>did he say</u> as he passed by me.

→ _____

C 빈칸에 알맞은 말을 골라 쓰시오.

be	did	is	were

1 Little _____ he expect that he would meet her again.

2 She has no desire to _____ a doctor like her father.

3 These days, my parents are busier than they _____ before.

4 Not until I got home _____ I realize that my shoes were untied.

5 George Washington, the first president of the USA, _____ called the father of the country.

D 괄호 안에 주어진 단어를 바르게 배열하시오.

1 She was sitting at the table _____.
                                    (eating, not, but)

2 Into the woods _____.
                      (the deer, disappeared)

3 She did not want any help, _____.
                                  (I, did, nor, offer, it)

4 _____ was sent to Ms. Carter, the English teacher.
      (of, appreciation, a letter)

E 밑줄 친 부분을 바르게 고쳐 문장을 다시 쓰시오.

1 Here are they!

→ _____

2 My mom told me to throw away my old toys, but I did not want to be.

→ _____

3 I am a member of the reading club, and neither is Barbara.

→ _____

4 The chances of be hit by lightning in your lifetime are one in 3,000.

→ _____

F 괄호 안의 말을 이용하여 우리말을 영어로 쓰시오.

1 나는 절대 같은 실수를 하지 않을 것이다. (make, the same)
→ Never _____.

2 샤워하고 있는 동안 노래를 흥얼거리는 것이 그의 습관이다. (to hum a song, while, taking)
→ _____

3 지붕 위에는 벌집이 있었다. (a beehive)
→ On _____.

4 페미니즘은 남자들과 여자들이 동등한 권리를 가져야 한다는 믿음이다. (feminism, the belief, that, should, equal rights)
→ _____

MEMO

HAVE A GOOD DAY

Time
FOR
GRAMMAR
Fourth Edition

EXPERT

Time FOR GRAMMAR

Fourth Edition

Time for Grammar is the unique English grammar practice book, helping students learn English grammar in easy and fast ways. This fourth edition of **Time for Grammar** focuses more on practicing English grammar. Students learn practical and usable English grammar with up-to-date, interesting English expressions.
Now it's time for grammar!

Time
FOR
GRAMMAR
Fourth Edition

Time for Grammar is the unique English grammar practice book, helping students learn English grammar in easy and fast ways. This fourth edition of ***Time for Grammar*** focuses more on practicing English grammar. Students learn practical and usable English grammar with up-to-date, interesting English expressions.
Now it's time for grammar!

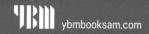

Time FOR GRAMMAR

Answers

EXPERT

Time

FOR

GRAMMAR

Fourth Edition

Answers

Sentence Patterns

UNIT 01 **S + V & S + V + C** p. 11

A 1 The car accident happened early in the morning.
      S   V   M

  2 My aunt lives across the street from my house.
      S   V   M

  3 The guy stood in the rain without an umbrella.
      S   V   M

  4 Jenny appeared at the party in her new red dress.
      S   V   M

B 1 silent   **2** tasted
  3 nervous   **4** sweet

C 1 became sick   **2** the light turns green
  3 The stew went bad
  4 Paul's face turned red

D 1 kept calm   **2** seemed nervous
  3 started with   **4** suddenly appeared

UNIT 02 **S + V + O & S + V + I.O. + D.O.** p. 13

A 1 David brought me a glass of water when I went
    into his house.   I.O.   D.O.

  2 My teacher told us the news about the field trip.
             I.O.   D.O.

  3 When should I show my dad his birthday present?
             I.O.   D.O.

  4 The doctor wrote her patient a prescription for
    her stomachache. I.O.   D.O.

B 1 to see   **2** making
  3 to save   **4** dicussed

C 1 to me   **2** for their children
  3 to her friend   **4** of her teacher

D 1 enter the hall
  2 me a piece of cake
  3 answer the phone
  4 passed a napkin to me

UNIT 03 **S + V + O + O.C.** p. 15

A 1 consider him a pop star
  2 make us better people
  3 appointed Mr. Smith the defense minister
  4 called the accident a miracle

B 1 happy   **2** interesting
  3 knocking   **4** washed

C 1 to get   **2** ask
  3 to change   **4** clean

D 1 saw many people swim (swimming)
  2 reminded Tim to wear
  3 found the final exam difficult
  4 had the children play

WRITING CONNECTION

p. 16

STEP 1   **Grammar Check-up**

A 1 ⓐ   **2** ⓐ   **3** ⓒ   **4** ⓓ   **5** ⓑ   **6** ⓒ

B 1 ⓐ, sweet   **2** ⓑ, resembles
  3 ⓐ, arrived   **4** ⓐ, to me
  5 ⓑ, use

A 1 1형식은 「주어 + 동사 + (수식어구)」로 이루어진다.
  2 2형식은 「주어 + 동사 + 주격 보어」로 이루어진다.
  3 3형식 문장에서 quit은 동명사를 목적어로 취한다.
  4 3형식 문장에서 expect는 to부정사를 목적어로 취한다.
  5 4형식 동사 ask를 3형식으로 쓸 때 전치사 of를 사용한다.
  6 5형식 문장에서 encourage는 목적격 보어로 to부정사를 취한다.

B 1 taste가 감각동사이므로 보어 자리에는 형용사가 온다.
  2 resemble은 3형식 동사이므로 전치사 없이 목적어를 취한다.
  3 arrive는 목적어를 취하지 않으므로 수동태로 쓸 수 없다.
  4 4형식 동사 offer를 3형식으로 쓸 때 간접목적어 앞에 전치사 to를 사용한다.
  5 사역동사 let은 목적격 보어로 원형부정사를 취한다.

p. 17

STEP 2   **Phrases to Sentences**

A 1 will occur   **2** seems kind
  3 prepared a room for him
  4 lend me the book (lend the book to me)
  5 saw Janice search (searching) for
  6 advised me to take

B 1 was occurred → A sandstorm occurred, so we could not see anything from the window.
  2 attend to → Andrew went to New York because he had to attend a seminar.
  3 my mistake to me → I apologized to Serena, and she forgave me my mistake.
  4 taking → We had our picture taken by the best photographer in town.
  5 of me → Nick sent some flowers to me when I was in the hospital.
  6 wrongly → She proved the information wrong by doing a search on the Internet.

A
1 1형식은 「주어 + 동사 + (수식어구)」로 이루어진다.
2 2형식은 「주어 + 동사 + 주격 보어」로 이루어진다.
3 4형식 동사 prepare를 3형식으로 쓸 때 간접목적어 앞에 전치사 for를 사용한다.
4 4형식: 「수여동사 + 간접목적어 + 직접목적어」 = 3형식: 「동사 + 목적어 + 전치사 + (대)명사」
5 지각동사 see는 목적격 보어로 원형부정사 또는 현재분사를 취한다.
6 advise는 목적격 보어로 to부정사를 취한다.

B
1 occur는 목적어를 취하지 않으므로 수동태로 쓸 수 없다.
2 attend는 3형식 동사이므로 전치사 없이 바로 뒤에 목적어가 온다.
3 forgive는 4형식에서 3형식으로 전환이 불가한 동사이다.
4 사역동사 have는 목적어와 목적격 보어가 수동의 관계일 때 목적격 보어로 과거분사를 취한다.
5 4형식 동사 send를 3형식으로 쓸 때 간접목적어 앞에 전치사 to를 사용한다.
6 prove는 목적격 보어로 형용사를 취한다.

STEP3 **Sentence Practice** p. 18

A
1 a. agreed to compete
   b. The interviewer agreed to meet me tomorrow.
2 a. taught me a lesson (taught a lesson to me)
   b. I owed him dinner (owed dinner to him) because of his help.
3 a. let me read
   b. Amy had me listen to her favorite singer's song.
4 a. makes her happy
   b. I think the movie will make Jenny sad.

B
1 You look mature because of the suit.
2 I want to turn off this machine, but I do not know how.
3 Before Tony went out, he left me a message on the table.
4 The students elected Joe the class president.

A
1 3형식 문장에서 agree는 to부정사를 목적어로 취한다.
2 4형식 문장은 「주어 + 수여동사 + 간접목적어 + 직접목적어」의 어순이다.
3 5형식 문장에서 사역동사는 목적격 보어로 원형부정사를 취한다.
4 5형식 문장의 목적격 보어로 형용사가 올 수 있다.

B
1 2형식 문장이며 look은 형용사를 보어로 취한다.
2 3형식 문장은 「주어 + 동사 + 목적어」의 어순이다.
3 4형식 문장은 「주어 + 수여동사 + 간접목적어 + 직접목적어」의 어순이다.
4 5형식 문장에서 elect는 목적격 보어로 명사(구)를 취한다.

ACTUAL TEST pp. 19-22

1 ② **2** ② **3** ① **4** ③ **5** ④ **6** ③ **7** ③
8 ④ **9** ② **10** ④ **11** ④ **12** ③ **13** ⑤ **14** ⑤
15 ③ **16** ④ **17** ① **18** ② **19** ① **20** ② **21** ②
22 to **23** their attention to the teacher
24 The nurse asked the age of the patient. (The nurse asked the patient the age.)
25 We decided to meet at the bus station (bus stop).
26 I made her wait
27 He persuaded me to go to the library with him.
28 As my computer did not work, it cost me a lot of money.

CHALLENGE!
01 [예시 답] My parents advise me to experience many things at school.
02 [예시 답] I made my sister some chicken soup on her birthday.

1 감각동사 taste는 형용사를 주격 보어로 취한다.
2 ask는 목적격 보어로 to부정사를 취한다.
3 happen은 목적어나 보어를 취하지 않는다.
4 enjoy는 목적어로 동명사를 취한다.
5 ① happen은 수동태로 쓸 수 없으며 ② remain은 형용사를 보어로 취하고 ③ 명사를 보어로 취하는 것은 '~처럼 보이다'라는 의미의 look like이며 ⑤ seem은 형용사를 보어로 취한다.
6 discuss, marry, resemble, obey는 전치사와 함께 쓰지 않는다.
7 4형식 문장을 3형식 문장으로 바꿀 때 get은 간접목적어 앞에 전치사 for를 쓴다.
8 ④ 4형식 문장을 3형식 문장으로 전환할 때 offer는 간접목적어 앞에 전치사 to를 쓴다.
9 ②는 「주어 + 동사 + 간접목적어 + 직접목적어」인 4형식 문장이고, 나머지는 「주어 + 동사 + 목적어 + 목적격 보어」인 5형식 문장이다.
10 ④는 「주어 + 동사 + 목적어」로 이루어진 3형식 문장이고, 나머지는 「주어 + 동사 + 주격 보어」로 이루어진 2형식 문장이다.
11 ④ quit은 동명사를 목적어로 취한다.
12 ③은 3형식이고 나머지는 1형식이다.
13 ⑤는 4형식이고 나머지는 5형식이다.
14 지각동사 뒤의 목적어와 목적격 보어가 수동 관계이므로 목적격 보어는 과거분사가 되어야 한다.
15 get이 사역동사처럼 쓰일 때 목적격 보어로 to부정사를 취한다.
16 지각동사 see는 목적격 보어로 현재분사를 취할 수 있다.
17 buy는 3형식으로 쓰일 때 간접목적어 앞에 전치사 for를 쓰며 expect는 목적격 보어로 to부정사를 취한다.
18 want는 목적격 보어로 to부정사를 취하며 attend는 전치사와 함께 쓰이지 않는다.
19 지각동사는 목적격 보어로 현재분사나 원형부정사를 취한다.

20 seem은 보어로 형용사를 취한다.

21 occur는 수동태로 쓸 수 없는 동사이며 appear는 주격 보어로 형용사를 취하고 encourage는 목적격 보어로 to부정사를 취한다.

22 get이 사역동사로 쓰일 때 목적격 보어로 to부정사를 취하며 show는 4형식을 3형식으로 바꿀 때 간접목적어 앞에 전치사 to를 쓴다.

23 give는 4형식을 3형식으로 바꿀 때 간접목적어 앞에 전치사 to를 쓴다.

24 ask는 4형식을 3형식으로 바꿀 때 간접목적어 앞에 전치사 of를 쓴다.

[25-26] 해석

내 친구 Sarah와 나는 주말에 놀이공원에 가기로 계획했다. 우리는 버스 정류장에서 만나기로 결정했다. 하지만 나는 늦게 일어났다. 나는 그녀를 오랫동안 기다리게 했다. 나는 미안했고 사과했다.

25 decide는 to부정사를 목적어로 취한다.

26 사역동사 make는 목적격 보어로 원형부정사를 취한다.

27 persuade는 목적격 보어 자리에 to부정사를 취한다.

28 4형식 문장은 「주어 + 동사 + 간접목적어 + 직접목적어」로 이루어진다.

CHALLENGE!

01 advise는 목적격 보어로 to부정사를 취한다.

02 4형식 문장은 「주어 + 동사 + 간접목적어 + 직접목적어」로 이루어진다.

CHAPTER

02 Perfect Aspect

UNIT 01 Present Perfect p. 25

A 1 bought 2 have been 3 has gone
4 has just finished 5 have visited
6 have been staying

B 1 have, been 2 have, seen 3 has gone

C 1 have been waiting 2 has been running
3 has been snowing

D 1 have already repaired 2 has lost
3 have never eaten [have not eaten]
4 has been traveling [has traveled]

UNIT 02 Past Perfect / Future Perfect p. 27

A 1 will have 2 had
3 will have 4 had

B 1 will have finished
2 will have been sleeping
3 had been standing 4 had not been able

C 1 had gone 2 have finished
3 had started 4 had been studying
5 have been talking

D 1 had been getting along well [had gotten along well]
2 had not attended
3 will have finished
4 will have been working [will have worked]

WRITING CONNECTION

STEP 1 Grammar Check-up p. 28

A 1 ⓑ 2 ⓒ 3 ⓒ 4 ⓑ 5 ⓐ 6 ⓑ
B 1 ⓐ, had already seen
2 ⓐ, had worked [had been working]
3 ⓐ, was 4 ⓑ, have changed
5 ⓐ, have been married 6 ⓐ, has been

A 1 현재완료진행 의문문이며 현재완료진행은 「have been v-ing」로 쓴다.
2 Sue가 도착한 과거보다 더 이전의 일을 나타내고 있으므로 과거완료 「had + p.p.」를 쓴다.
3 이 영화를 이미 본 것 같다는 의미이므로 현재완료 「have + p.p.」를 쓴다.

4 시계를 잃어버린 것보다 소유하고 있던 것이 더 이전의 일이므로 과거완료 「had + p.p.」로 쓴다.

5 미래의 어느 시점 쯤이면 일이 끝날 것을 나타내므로 미래완료 「will have + p.p.」로 쓴다.

6 현재를 나타내는 so far가 있으므로 과거부터 현재까지 계속되었다는 것을 나타내기 위해 현재완료 「have + p.p.」를 쓴다.

B **1** 내가 추천한 것보다 그녀가 그 영화를 본 것이 더 이전의 일이므로 과거완료를 쓴다.

2 대학에서 일했던 것이 더 과거의 일이므로 과거완료 혹은 과거완료진행을 쓴다.

3 과거의 '그때'를 나타내는 부사 then이 있으므로 단순 과거를 쓴다.

4 미래의 어느 시점에 완료되는 일이므로 미래완료를 쓴다.

5 50년 전부터 지금까지 결혼 상태를 유지해 온 것이므로 현재완료를 쓴다.

6 오늘 의사를 만날 것이라고 했으므로 아직까지 아픈 것을 알 수 있기에 현재완료를 쓴다.

B **1** 현재까지 다섯 권의 소설을 쓴 것이므로 현재완료를 쓴다.

2 미래의 어느 시점에 완료될 일이므로 미래완료를 쓴다.

3 Sue가 친구들에게 이야기한 시점보다 학교를 그만둔 것이 더 이전의 일이므로 과거완료를 쓴다.

4 내가 도착했을 때 Mark가 이미 한 시간 동안 구덩이를 파던 중이었으므로 과거완료진행을 쓴다.

5 며칠간 눈이 계속 내리고 있으므로 현재완료 또는 현재완료진행을 쓴다.

6 언니가 대학에 입학한 이후 계속 스페인어를 공부하고 있으므로 현재완료 또는 현재완료진행을 쓴다.

---

p. 29
STEP 2 **Phrases to Sentences**

A **1** has gone
2 have been waiting (have waited)
3 had just finished **4** will have moved
5 has just stopped **6** will have found

B **1** writes → The author has written five novels so far.

2 has already left → He will have already left the house when his children get up tomorrow morning.

3 quit → Sue told her friends that she had quit school.

4 have been digging → Mark had been digging a hole for an hour when I came into the garden.

5 will have been snowing → It has snowed (has been snowing) hard for a few days.

6 studies → My sister has studied (has been studying) Spanish since she entered the university.

A **1** 엄마가 쇼핑을 가서 지금 집에 없는 것이므로 현재완료를 쓰며 결과의 용법이다.

2 과거부터 지금까지 계속 기다리고 있으므로 현재완료진행 또는 현재완료(계속)를 쓴다.

3 초인종이 울린 것보다 청소가 끝난 것이 더 과거의 일이므로 과거완료를 쓰며 완료의 용법이다.

4 미래의 어느 시점에 완료되는 일은 미래완료를 쓴다.

5 현재 시점에 완료된 일을 말하고 있으므로 현재완료를 쓴다.

6 십 년 후에 완료될 일을 말하고 있으므로 미래완료를 쓴다.

---

p. 30
STEP 3 **Sentence Practice**

A **1** a. have not finished
b. He has not finished his meal yet.

2 a. will have gone to bed
b. We will have finished dinner by the time the movie starts.

3 a. had been staying with
b. She had been working on the group project until yesterday.

4 a. have been climbing up
b. The plumber has been fixing the sink for two hours.

B **1** I have been living in the school dormitory for three months.

2 We will have known each other for ten years by next year.

3 Once I had cleaned my room, I took a nap.

4 When I got home, my sister had been watching TV.

A **1** 현재완료는 「have + p.p.」로 쓴다.

2 미래완료는 「will have + p.p.」로 쓴다.

3 과거완료진행은 「had been + v-ing」로 쓴다.

4 과거부터 현재까지 계속 진행되고 있는 동작은 현재완료진행으로 나타낸다.

B **1** 현재까지 계속 기숙사에 살고 있으므로 현재완료진행을 쓴다.

2 미래의 특정 시점까지 계속될 일이므로 미래완료를 쓴다.

3 내가 낮잠을 잔 것보다 방 청소를 한 것이 더 이전이므로 과거완료를 쓴다.

4 내가 귀가하기 이전에 여동생이 TV를 보고 있었으므로 과거완료진행을 쓴다.

1 ⑤   2 ③   3 ④   4 ④   5 ③   6 ③   7 ③

8 ④   9 ②, ⑤   10 ④   11 ②   12 ③   13 ①

14 ⑤   15 ③   16 ③   17 ①   18 ⑤   19 ③

20 ⑤   21 ②

22 had lost

23 I have not found it yet.

24 have been working (have worked)

25 Vicky thought her parents had first met in high school.

26 My brother has been cleaning from morning till now.

27 Since it had not rained for a month, the ground was dry.

28 I will have watched the movie five times if I see it one more time.

CHALLENGE!

01 [예시 답] Yes, I have traveled in Australia with my family before.

02 [예시 답] I will have been studying English for 7 years next year.

---

1 전화기를 잃어버려서 현재까지도 없는 것이므로 현재완료를 써야 하며 결과 용법에 해당한다.

2 숙제를 하는 것이 현재 벌써 끝난 상태인지를 묻는 것이므로 현재완료를 쓴다.

3 그녀가 이웃을 공원에서 마주치기 전에 과거의 일정 기간 동안 계속하고 있던 일을 나타내는 것이 적절하므로 과거완료진행을 쓴다.

4 ④ 내가 공항에 도착했던 과거의 일보다 더 이전의 일이므로 과거완료가 적절하다.

5 ③ since는 계속의 의미를 나타내는 현재완료와 함께 쓰일 수 있다.

6 ① has been raining (has rained) ② moved
④ has been working (has worked) ⑤ had already escaped

7 ① had been ② taught
④ has been sleeping (has slept) ⑤ have not seen

8 부사구 last month는 명백한 과거를 나타내므로 현재완료와 함께 쓰일 수 없다.

9 현재완료는 명백한 과거를 나타내는 ①, ③, ④와는 함께 쓰일 수 없다.

10 지난 6월부터 지금까지 여행을 하고 있는 것이므로 현재완료진행이 적절하다.

11 아빠가 집에 온 것이 더 과거의 일이므로 과거완료가 알맞다.

12 주어진 문장과 ③은 경험을 나타내는 현재완료이다. ① 계속 ② 결과 ④ 결과 ⑤ 완료

13 작년부터 지금까지 모든 경기를 이기고 있는 것이므로 현재완료를 쓴다.

14 과거의 어느 시점까지 계속된 일을 나타내므로 과거완료진행을 쓴다.

15 (A) 그녀를 알아본 것보다 만난 것이 더 이전이므로 과거완료
(B) 작년 이후로 계속 일을 하고 있으므로 현재완료 또는 현재완료진행

16 (A) 그가 친구에게 말한 것보다 노트북을 산 것이 더 이전의 일이므로 과거완료가 적절하며 (B) 과거의 어느 시점까지 계속된 일을 나타내므로 과거완료진행을 쓴다.

17 '막 ~했다'라는 의미로 완료를 나타내는 현재완료를 쓴다.

18 미래의 어느 시점의 일을 말하고 있으므로 미래완료를 쓴다.

19 과거에 잃어버린 안경을 지금도 찾지 못하고 있으므로 현재완료로 나타내는 것이 적절하다.

20 ⑤ 결과를 의미하는 현재완료이므로 '파리에 가서 현재 여기 없다'는 의미의 해석이 적절하다.

21 ⓐ 미래의 어느 시점에 현재의 행동이 계속될 것임을 나타내므로 미래완료/미래완료진행이 적절 ⓒ 과거를 나타내는 부사구 last week가 있으므로 현재완료를 쓸 수 없고 ⓕ 삼십 분 동안 기다리고 있으므로 현재완료/현재완료진행

[22-23] **해석**

파리로의 여행은 나의 오랜 꿈이었다. 나는 수년 동안 돈을 절약했고, 지난달 마침내 비행기 표를 샀다. 나는 에펠 탑 보기를 학수고대했었다. 탑에서 줄을 서서 기다리는 동안, 나는 지갑을 잃어버렸다는 것을 깨달았다! 그 이후로 나는 아직 그것을 찾지 못하고 있다.

22 지갑을 잃어버린 것을 안 것보다 앞서 일어난 일이므로 과거완료를 쓴다.

23 과거에 지갑을 잃어버리고 현재까지 찾지 못한 것이므로 현재완료를 쓴다.

24 미래의 어느 시점에 현재의 행동이 계속될 것임을 나타내므로 미래완료진행 또는 미래완료가 알맞다.

25 부모님이 처음 만난 시점이 Vicky가 생각을 한 것보다 더 이전이므로 과거완료를 쓰는 것이 적절하다.

26 아침부터 지금까지 계속되고 있으므로 현재완료진행을 쓴다.

27 땅이 말라있던 과거의 시점보다 비가 오지 않은 것이 더 과거의 일이므로 과거완료를 쓴다.

28 미래의 어느 시점에 완료될 일을 말하고 있으므로 미래완료로 나타낼 수 있다.

CHALLENGE!

01 경험을 나타내는 현재완료

02 미래완료진행 「will have been + v-ing」

03 Modals

UNIT 01 can, may, must, should p. 37

A 1 could   2 May
    3 must   4 should not

B 1 need not buy (do not need to buy)
    2 has to go   3 not able to complete

C 1 don't have to   2 should
    3 be able to   4 could

D 1 may (might) be at the bank
    2 cannot be an international lawyer
    3 had to pay the bill
    4 ought to be delivered by tomorrow

UNIT 02 Other Expressions with Modals p. 39

A 1 leave   2 would rather   3 did not
    4 had better not   5 go

B 1 may as well   2 would rather
    3 used to   4 had better

C 1 너는 이 날씨에는 더 따뜻한 옷을 입는 게 좋을 것이다.
    2 선생님이 부모께 나의 성적에 관해 말했음에 틀림없다.
    3 그 오래된 건물은 전시회를 위한 장소이었다.
    4 나는 빨래를 하느니 (차라리) 설거지를 하겠다.

D 1 used to be late
    2 may have seen the movie
    3 would rather surf
    4 should have checked the schedule

WRITING CONNECTION

STEP 1 Grammar Check-up p. 40

A 1 ⓑ   2 ⓒ   3 ⓓ   4 ⓑ   5 ⓐ   6 ⓓ

B 1 ⓐ, may as well   2 ⓐ, had better not
    3 ⓑ, must arrive   4 ⓐ, walk
    5 ⓐ, have to   6 ⓐ, ought not to

A 1 '~일 리가 없다'는 cannot be로 나타낼 수 있다.
    2 과거의 능력을 나타내는 조동사는 could이다.
    3 과거의 상태는 used to로 나타낼 수 있다.
    4 약한 의무를 나타내는 조동사는 ought to이다.
    5 had better: ~하는 게 좋을 것이다
    6 may as well: ~하는 게 낫겠다

B 1 '~하는 게 낫겠다'는 may as well로 나타낸다.
    2 had better의 부정은 had better not이다.
    3 조동사 must 다음에는 동사원형이 와야 한다.
    4 과거의 습관을 나타내는 used to 다음에는 동사원형이 와야 한다.
    5 don't have to는 '~할 필요가 없다'라는 의미로, did not 다음에는 동사원형이 와야 한다.
    6 ought to의 부정은 ought not to이다.

STEP 2 Phrases to Sentences p. 41

A 1 had better start   2 should learn
    3 would rather watch   4 should not cross
    5 may be a reason
    6 may have stayed up

B 1 He must have lost his phone in the library yesterday.
    2 I may have left my umbrella at school.
    3 You should have come earlier. The bus has already left.
    4 Alice used to take a walk during her lunch break every day.
    5 You should have come to the party. Then you would have had a great time with us.
    6 I may as well finish cleaning my room before going out.

A 1 '~하는 게 좋을 것이다'는 had better로 나타낼 수 있다.
    2 '~해야 한다'는 should로 나타낼 수 있다.
    3 '(차라리) ~하겠다'는 would rather로 나타낼 수 있다.
    4 should는 약한 의무를 나타내며 부정은 should 뒤에 not을 쓴다.
    5 '~일지도 모른다'는 may로 나타낼 수 있다.
    6 '~했을지도 모른다'는 may have p.p.로 나타낼 수 있다.

B 1 '~했음에 틀림없다'는 must have p.p.로 나타낼 수 있다.
    2 '~했을지도 모른다'는 may have p.p.로 나타낼 수 있다.
    3 '~했어야 했는데'는 should have p.p.로 나타낼 수 있다.
    4 used to 다음에는 동사원형이 와야 한다.
    5 '~했어야 했는데'는 should have p.p.로 나타낼 수 있다.
    6 '~하는 게 낫겠다'는 may as well로 나타낼 수 있다.

p. 42

STEP3 Sentence Practice

A 1 a. should help
　　b. You should often water the pot.
　2 a. cannot have been real
　　b. The rumor cannot have been true.
　3 a. had better not be
　　b. You had better not study late at night.
　4 a. must have eaten
　　b. Joe was absent for school. He must have been sick.

B 1 Your bag might be in the living room.
　2 You can do a survey on the Internet.
　3 You may as well ask for your teacher's advice.
　4 You must not throw the garbage on the street.

A 1 약한 의무는 should로 나타낼 수 있다.
　2 '~이었을 리가 없다'는 cannot have p.p.로 나타낼 수 있다.
　3 '~하지 않는 게 좋을 것이다'라는 경고성 조언은 had better not으로 나타낼 수 있다.
　4 '~했음에 틀림없다'는 must have p.p.로 나타낼 수 있다.

B 1 '~일지도 모른다'라는 추측은 might로 나타낼 수 있다.
　2 '~할 수 있다'는 can으로 나타낼 수 있다.
　3 '~하는 게 낫겠다'는 may as well로 나타낼 수 있다.
　4 '~해서는 안 된다'는 must not으로 나타낼 수 있다.

ACTUAL TEST

pp. 43-46

1 ④　2 ③　3 ③　4 ②　5 ②　6 ④　7 ①
8 ②　9 ③　10 ④　11 ②　12 ④　13 ②　14 ③
15 ③　16 ②　17 ②　18 ⑤　19 ③　20 ②　21 ⑤
22 should
23 When you come to my home, you don't have to [need not/don't need to] bring anything.
24 may have been
25 cannot have eaten
26 Kate used to have long hair, but she had it cut off.
27 You had better apologize to your teacher.
28 You ought not to run down the stairs.

CHALLENGE!

01 [예시 답] I should have studied harder last year.
02 [예시 답] I used to watch a comedy show the most when I was in elementary school.

1 '~하는 게 좋을 것이다'는 had better로 나타낼 수 있다.
2 '~했을지도 모른다'는 may have p.p.로 나타낼 수 있다.
3 '~했어야 했는데'는 should have p.p.로 나타낼 수 있다.
4 '차라리 ~하는 게 좋다'는 would rather로 나타낸다.
5 과거의 습관이나 상태는 used to로 나타낼 수 있다.
6 과거의 능력을 나타낼 때는 could를 쓴다.
7 '~했음에 틀림없다'라는 과거의 확신은 must have p.p.로 나타낸다.
8 '~하는 게 낫겠다'라는 내용이 적절하므로 may as well로 나타낸다.
9 ③ 약한 의무를 나타내는 말은 ought to이다.
10 ④ '(차라리) ~하는 게 좋다'는 would rather로 나타낸다.
11 조동사의 부정은 조동사 다음에 not을 쓴다.
12 cannot have p.p.는 '~이었을 리가 없다'는 의미로 부정의 확신을 나타낸다.
13 ② may가 허가의 의미로 쓰였으며 나머지는 약한 추측의 의미로 쓰였다.
14 ③ can이 능력의 의미로 쓰였으며 나머지는 허가의 의미로 쓰였다.
15 don't have to는 '~할 필요가 없다'라는 의미이나 must는 의무 또는 강한 추측을 나타내므로 의미가 같지 않다.
16 주어진 문장과 ②는 과거의 습관을 나타내는 used to이며, ① be used to v-ing는 '~에 익숙하다'라는 의미이고, 나머지는 use의 수동태로 '~하는 데 사용되다'라는 의미이다.
17 허가의 의미를 나타내는 조동사는 can과 may이며 '~하는 게 좋을 것이다'는 had better로 나타낼 수 있다.
18 의무를 나타내는 조동사는 must와 should, ought to이며 '~했음에 틀림없다'는 must have p.p.로 나타낼 수 있다.
19 may as well은 '~하는 게 낫겠다'라는 의미이다.
20 must have p.p.는 '~했음에 틀림없다'라는 의미이다.
21 ⑤ 과거 사실에 대한 후회를 나타내므로 should have p.p.를 써야 한다.

22 [해석]
　　나는 다른 사람의 물건을 훔치는 사람들을 이해할 수 없다. 나는 자전거를 타고 지하철역에 갔고 자전거 거치대에 그것을 잠가 두었다. 내가 돌아왔을 때, 그것이 사라졌다! 나는 거기에 내 자전거를 두지 말았어야 했는데!
　　should not have p.p.: ~하지 않았어야 했는데

23 '~할 필요가 없다'는 don't have to 또는 need not, don't need to로 쓴다.
24 may have been: ~이었을지도 모른다
25 '~이었을 리가 없다'는 cannot have p.p.로 나타낼 수 있다.
26 과거의 상태는 used to로 나타낼 수 있다.
27 '~하는 게 좋을 것이다'라는 뜻의 경고성 충고는 had better로 나타낼 수 있다.
28 '~해서는 안 된다'는 ought not to로 나타낼 수 있다.

CHALLENGE!

01 should have p.p.: ~했어야 했는데
02 과거의 습관이나 상태는 used to로 나타낼 수 있다.

04 Passives

UNIT 01 Passive Voice p. 49

A 1 happened 2 was changed
3 not sung 4 announced
5 post 6 should be washed

B 1 has been stolen 2 are being repaired
3 was damaged by 4 will be given

C 1 was being flown
2 am going to be paid weekly
3 was written by the writer
4 the Christmas tree had been decorated by Dad

D 1 will be finished 2 were asked
3 is being built 4 have been sold

UNIT 02 Passives of S+V+I.O.+D.O./S+V+O+O.C. p. 51

A 1 of 2 for 3 to 4 for 5 to

B 1 was given a bunch of flowers, were given to me
2 was asked her name, was asked of the girl
3 were made for me

C 1 to take (taking) 2 to help 3 to leave
4 popular 5 one

D 1 was made happy 2 was given to us
3 was made to wash the dishes
4 was seen to play (playing)

UNIT 03 Other Passive Forms p. 53

A 1 at 2 in 3 with 4 with 5 about 6 with

B 1 looked after by 2 turned off by
3 be picked up 4 is known that

C 1 is filled with 2 are worried about
3 was looked up 4 is said to be

D 1 were pleased with 2 is not put up with
3 is composed of 4 It is believed that

WRITING CONNECTION

STEP 1 Grammar Check-up p. 54

A 1 ⓓ 2 ⓑ 3 ⓑ 4 ⓐ 5 ⓒ 6 ⓒ

B 1 ⓐ, had 2 ⓑ, was won
3 ⓑ, to take (taking) 4 ⓐ, known to
5 ⓐ, bought for

A 1 목적어가 that절인 문장의 수동태: 「It + be + p.p. + that . . .」
2 수동태의 형태는 「be + p.p.」이다.
3 조동사가 있는 문장의 부정 수동태: 「조동사 + not + be + p.p.」
4 수동태의 의문문은 be동사가 문장 맨 앞에 위치한다.
5 be filled with: ~로 가득하다
6 4형식 문장을 수동태로 쓸 때 show는 간접목적어 앞에 to를 쓴다.

B 1 소유를 나타내는 동사 have는 수동태로 쓸 수 없다.
2 목적어가 없고 뒤에 행위자를 나타내는 by Tom이 있으므로 과거 수동태를 쓴다.
3 지각동사의 수동태는 「be + p.p. + to부정사/현재분사」의 형태로 쓴다.
4 be known to: ~에게 알려지다
5 4형식 문장을 수동태로 쓸 때 buy는 간접목적어 앞에 전치사 for를 쓴다.

STEP 2 Phrases to Sentences p. 55

A 1 is being fixed by 2 were taken by
3 will be delivered 4 was believed to
5 being blocked 6 will be given to you

B 1 a new invention was created by Andrew
2 was looked at by the doctor
3 is made to solve the problem alone by the parents
4 were shown to Wendy by me
5 was cooked for his family by Michael
6 Ben is considered the smartest student at school by all of the students.

A 1 현재진행 수동태는 「be + being + p.p.」로 쓴다.
2 과거시제 수동태
3 미래시제 수동태
4 that절을 목적어로 하는 수동태에서 that절의 주어를 수동태 문장의 주어로 쓰면 that절의 동사를 to부정사로 바꾼다.
5 현재진행 수동태가 의문문에서 쓰였기에 be being p.p.에서 be동사 is를 문장 맨 앞에 쓴다.
6 4형식 문장을 수동태로 바꿀 때 give의 직접목적어를 주어로 할 경우 간접목적어 앞에 전치사 to를 써야 하며, 미래의 일을 말하고 있으므로 미래시제 수동태로 쓴다.

B 1 수동태 문장으로 전환하기 위해 문장의 목적어인 a new invention을 주어 자리에 쓰고 동사를 be p.p.로 바꾼다.
2 동사구 look at은 수동태로 바꿔 쓸 때 덩어리째 움직인다.
3 수동태 문장에서 사역동사의 목적격 보어인 동사원형은 to부정사로 바뀐다.
4 4형식 문장에서 직접목적어를 주어로 하는 수동태로 바꿀 때 show는 간접목적어 앞에 to를 쓴다.
5 4형식 문장에서 직접목적어를 주어로 하는 수동태로 바꿀 때 cook은 간접목적어 앞에 for를 쓴다.
6 5형식 문장의 수동태는 목적어를 주어 자리에 쓰고 동사를 수동태로 바꾼 다음 목적격 보어를 「be + p.p.」 뒤에 쓴다.

p. 56

STEP 3 Sentence Practice

A 1 a. is visited by
   b. The mountain is climbed by one million tourists a year.
   2 a. Are, being watered
   b. Are the puppies being taken care of by her?
   3 a. is interested in
   b. The students are interested in taking pictures.
   4 a. were asked of
   b. The letter was sent to me by Ron.

B 1 Jenny will be elected team leader.
   2 My bike is being repaired now.
   3 It is said that Alex left the country months ago.
   4 The event should be canceled because of the bad weather.

A 1 수동태는 「be + p.p. + by 행위자」로 쓴다.
   2 현재진행 수동태의 의문문
   3 be interested in: ~에 관심이 있다
   4 4형식 문장을 수동태로 바꿀 때 직접목적어를 주어로 할 경우 ask는 간접목적어 앞에 전치사 of를, send는 전치사 to를 쓴다.

B 1 5형식인 「elect A B」를 미래시제 수동태로 쓰면 「A will be elected B」가 된다.
   2 현재진행 수동태는 「be + being + p.p.」로 쓴다.
   3 목적어가 that절인 문장의 수동태: 「It + be + p.p. + that . . .」
   4 조동사가 있는 문장의 수동태는 「조동사 + be + p.p.」로 쓴다.

ACTUAL TEST

pp. 57-60

1 ⑤ 2 ③ 3 ① 4 ② 5 ① 6 ① 7 ④
8 ⑤ 9 ① 10 ④ 11 ④ 12 ⑤ 13 ③ 14 ③
15 ⑤ 16 ③ 17 ③ 18 ③ 19 ⑤ 20 ② 21 ④
22 (A) were built (B) was placed
23 Nowadays, dolmens can be seen in Ireland, Wales, and Scotland.
24 Tricky questions have been asked of me by the reporter.
25 A huge poster will be hung outside the building by us.
26 is thought to
27 He was seen to come out of the school by his friends.
28 She was made to tell her parents everything.

CHALLENGE!

01 [예시 답] I was taught English by Ms. Park last year.
02 [예시 답] I was given a new bicycle by my dad last Christmas.

1 주어가 동작의 영향을 받는 대상이고 과거를 나타내는 부사 yesterday가 있으므로 수동태 were bought가 알맞다.
2 4형식 문장을 수동태로 바꿀 때 직접목적어를 주어로 쓸 경우 ask는 간접목적어 앞에 전치사 of를 쓴다.
3 4형식 문장을 수동태로 바꿀 때 직접목적어를 주어로 쓸 경우 give는 간접목적어 앞에 전치사 to를 쓴다.
4 목적어가 없고 주어와 동사가 수동의 관계이므로 수동태로 쓴다.
5 과거시제가 사용된 능동의 문장을 수동태로 바꾸는 것이므로 be동사는 과거형이 되어야 한다.
6 ① '~으로 가득하다'는 be filled with로 나타낼 수 있다.
7 be married to: ~와 결혼하다
  be worried about: ~에 대해 걱정하다
8 4형식 동사인 offer는 직접목적어를 주어로 하여 수동태로 쓸 경우 간접목적어 앞에 전치사 to를 쓰며 주어진 우리말의 시제가 미래이므로 「will + be + p.p.」로 쓴다.
9 5형식 문장을 수동태로 바꿀 때 목적어를 주어로 하고 동사를 수동태로 바꾼 다음, 목적격 보어는 「be + p.p.」 뒤에 그대로 쓴다.
10 목적어가 that절인 문장의 수동태: 「that절의 주어 + be + p.p. + to부정사」
11 조동사가 포함된 수동태는 「조동사 + be + p.p.」로 쓴다.
12 ⑤ 동사 buy는 수동태의 주어로 간접목적어를 쓰지 않는다.
13 동사구를 수동태로 전환할 때는 동사를 「be + p.p.」로 바꾸고 나머지 부분은 그대로 쓴다.
14 being을 넣으면 모두 현재진행 수동태가 되는데 ③은 조동사 will이 있으므로 동사원형 be가 들어가야 한다.
15 ⑤ '~에 대해 걱정하다'는 'be worried about'으로 쓰며 나머지는 모두 전치사 with가 쓰이는 표현이다.
16 '~에 놀라다'는 be surprised at으로 쓰며 나머지에는 모두 of가 들어가야 한다.
17 (A) 주어 This sweater와 동사 make가 수동의 관계이므로 수동태 (B) 주어 The neon sign과 동사 see가 수동의 관계이며, 조동사 can이 있으므로 조동사의 수동태
18 (A) 주어 Dolphins가 동사 consider의 대상이므로 수동태로 써야 하며 (B) 수동태의 부정은 be동사 뒤에 not을 붙인다.
19 consist, arrive, fall, resemble, lack은 수동태로 쓸 수 없는 동사이다.
20 ⓓ 수동태 진행형은 「be + being + p.p.」이며 ⓔ 조동사가 있는 문장의 수동태는 「조동사 + be + p.p.」이다.
21 ①, ③은 목적어를 취하지 않는 자동사라서 수동태로 전환이 불가하고 ②, ⑤는 소유를 나타내는 동사이므로 수동태로 쓸 수 없다.

[22-23] 해석
  고인돌은 고대의 무덤이다. 그것들은 약 6,000년 전에 지어졌다. 고대의 사람들은 무덤을 만들기 위해 큰 돌들을 세웠다. 그 벽들은

선돌들로 구성되었다. 또 다른 큰 돌은 그 다른 돌들의 위에 놓여졌다. 요즘에 고인돌은 아일랜드, 웨일스, 스코틀랜드에서 목격될 수 있다.

22 주어와 동사의 관계가 수동이며 글의 시제가 과거이므로 (A), (B) 모두 과거 수동태로 써야 한다.

23 조동사가 있는 문장의 수동태는 「조동사 + be + p.p.」이다.

24 4형식 문장의 직접목적어를 주어로 하여 수동태로 바꿀 때 ask는 간접목적어 앞에 전치사 of를 쓴다.

25 미래 수동태: will be p.p.

26 목적어가 that절인 문장에서 that절의 주어를 수동태 주어로 쓸 때 that절 동사는 to부정사로 쓴다.

27 지각동사의 목적격 보어는 수동태에서 to부정사나 현재분사로 쓴다.

28 사역동사의 수동태는 「be + p.p. + to부정사」로 쓴다.

CHALLENGE!

01 과거시제 수동
02 과거시제 수동

To-infinitives

UNIT 01 Substantive To-infinitives p. 63

A 1 To meet 　 2 to go 　 3 It
　 4 to read 　 5 to make

B 1 easy to become a vegetarian
　 2 good for your throat to drink lots of warm water
　 3 it difficult to live in a new country
　 4 it unhealthy to eat late at night

C 1 what to do 　　 2 where to go
　 3 how to send 　　 4 whom to call

D 1 to go jogging 　　 2 how to use
　 3 I found it useful to
　 4 Her advice was to write

UNIT 02 Adjective & Adverbial To-infinitives p. 65

A 1 to open 　 2 to do 　 3 to live in
　 4 to work with 　 5 with

B 1 are to marry 　 2 to catch 　 3 to win
　 4 is to be taken 　 5 are to succeed

C 1 너는 교통 법규를 준수해야 한다.
　 2 어둠에서는 아무것도 보이지가 않는다.
　 3 이 문제를 풀다니 Andy는 천재임에 틀림없다.
　 4 나는 건강을 유지하기 위해 일주일에 세 번 체육관에 간다.
　 5 모든 사람이 자라서 유명한 음악가가 되는 것은 아니다.

D 1 lucky to have a friend
　 2 are to begin our trip
　 3 someone to talk to
　 4 to study Spanish

UNIT 03 Subject, Tense, and Voices of To-infinitives p. 67

A 1 of you 　 2 for us 　 3 of him
　 4 of you 　 5 for me

B 1 to travel 　 2 to have caught
　 3 to have had 　 4 seem to like

C 1 It was rude of him to say that to his parents.
　 2 Sam is believed to speak five different languages.
　 3 These shirts are to be washed by tomorrow.

D 1 to know the fact 　　 2 of you to advise me
　 3 for Tom to pass 　　 4 to have written

UNIT 04 Infinitives as Object Complements p. 69

A 1 to come 2 to leave 3 to turn
   4 to exercise 5 remember

B 1 come (coming) 2 to fix 3 go
   4 close 5 tremble (trembling)

C 1 touch (touching) 2 go
   3 carry (carrying) 4 study
   5 walk (walking)

D 1 allow you to wear
   2 saw a helicopter land (landing)
   3 heard someone shout (shouting)
   4 wants me to stop

UNIT 05 Common Structures of Infinitives p. 71

A 1 to explain 2 for me to eat
   3 warm enough 4 enough time

B 1 so stubborn that he cannot change his mind
   2 short enough for me to read in a day
   3 too big to fit under the seat
   4 smart enough to overcome his difficulties

C 1 솔직히 말하면, 음식이 형편없었다.
   2 사실대로 말하면, 수학 수업은 지루하다.
   3 이상하게 들리겠지만, 침대가 너무 편안했지만 나는 잠을 푹 잘 수 없었다.
   4 그들은 숲에서 길을 잃었다. 설상가상으로, 비가 내리기 시작했다.

D 1 light enough to carry 2 too tired to finish
   3 old enough to stay
   4 To be honest with you

WRITING CONNECTION

STEP 1 Grammar Check-up p. 72

A 1 ⓐ 2 ⓒ 3 ⓒ 4 ⓑ 5 ⓐ 6 ⓓ

B 1 ⓑ, to sit on 2 ⓑ, stay out
   3 ⓐ, her sing (singing) 4 ⓑ, to read
   5 ⓐ, to hurt 6 ⓑ, break (breaking)

A 1 to부정사가 부사적 용법 중 '목적(~하기 위해서)'의 의미로 쓰이면 in order to 또는 so as to로 바꿔 쓸 수 있다.
   2 '~하는 방법'은 「how + to부정사」로 쓴다.
   3 「be + to부정사」로 가능의 의미를 나타낸다.
   4 사람의 성격을 나타내는 형용사 impolite가 있으므로 to부정사의 의미상의 주어는 「of + 목적격」으로 쓴다.
   5 사역동사 have는 목적격 보어로 원형부정사를 취한다.
   6 '너무 ~해서 …할 수 없는'은 「too + 형용사/부사 + to부정사」로 나타낼 수 있다.

B 1 a chair를 수식하는 to부정사구이며 의자 위에 앉는 것이므로 전치사 on을 써야 한다.
   2 사역동사는 목적격 보어로 원형부정사를 취한다.
   3 지각동사는 목적격 보어로 원형부정사 또는 현재분사를 취한다.
   4 want는 목적격 보어로 to부정사를 취한다.
   5 It은 가주어, to부정사구는 진주어이다.
   6 지각동사는 목적격 보어로 원형부정사 또는 현재분사를 취한다.

STEP 2 Phrases to Sentences p. 73

A 1 smart enough to 2 To begin with
   3 too difficult for me to
   4 to be the leader
   5 for Chris to finish the project
   6 how to make a good impression

B 1 difficult it → He found it difficult to drive on the left side of the road.
   2 seeing → The inside of the tunnel is too dark to see anything.
   3 of you → It is important for you to make the right decision.
   4 fixing → Thank you so much for helping me fix (to fix) my bike.
   5 to capture → The police are known to have captured the suspect last year.
   6 for → It was very nice of him to apologize to me first.

A 1 형용사 + enough + to부정사: …할 만큼 충분히 ~하다
   2 to begin with: 우선
   3 too + 형용사/부사 + to부정사: 너무 ~해서 …할 수 없는
   4 want는 목적격 보어로 to부정사를 취한다.
   5 to부정사의 의미상의 주어는 「for + 목적격」으로 쓴다.
   6 '~하는 방법'은 「how + to부정사」로 쓴다.

B 1 가목적어 (it) . . . 진목적어 (to부정사) 구조이다.
   2 too . . . to부정사: 너무 ~해서 …할 수 없는
   3 important는 사람의 성격을 나타내는 형용사가 아니므로 의미상의 주어로 「for + 목적격」을 써야 한다.
   4 help는 목적격 보어로 원형부정사 또는 to부정사를 취한다.
   5 경찰이 범인을 잡은 것이 과거의 일이므로 완료부정사를 써야 한다.
   6 사람의 성격을 나타내는 형용사 nice는 to부정사의 의미상의 주어로 「of + 목적격」을 쓴다.

STEP 3 Sentence Practice p. 74

A 1 a. too busy to spend
     b. I am too tired to cook dinner.
   2 a. to support
     b. He is an unkind man to ignore the lady who asked for directions.

3 a. relax (to relax)

 b. Drinking a cup of warm tea helps me sleep (to sleep) well.

4 a. it, to exercise

 b. I make it a rule to drink eight glasses of water a day.

B 1 We should take some water to drink while hiking.

2 My mother seemed to be disappointed with my behavior.

3 It is so kind of you to give your seat to the old lady.

4 Mr. Parker was hoping to be elected as the mayor.

A 1 too + 형용사/부사 + to부정사: 너무 ~해서 …할 수 없는

2 to부정사의 부사적 용법 중 '판단의 근거'이다.

3 help는 목적격 보어로 원형부정사 또는 to부정사를 취한다.

4 to부정사구가 목적어일 때 목적어 자리에 가목적어 it을 쓰고 to부정사를 뒤로 보낼 수 있다.

B 1 명사를 수식하는 to부정사의 형용사적 용법이다.

2 주절의 시제와 to부정사의 시제가 같으므로 단순부정사를 쓴다.

3 사람의 성격을 나타내는 형용사가 나오면 to부정사의 의미상의 주어로 「of + 목적격」을 쓴다.

4 to부정사와 그 주어가 수동의 관계이므로 수동형 to부정사를 써야 한다.

ACTUAL TEST pp. 75-78

1 ⑤ 2 ③ 3 ② 4 ④ 5 ① 6 ② 7 ④
8 ① 9 ② 10 ② 11 ②, ③ 12 ④ 13 ⑤
14 ② 15 ⑤ 16 ⑤ 17 ② 18 ② 19 ⑤
20 ④ 21 ①
22 to have recovered
23 strong enough to carry
24 It is not easy to live with many family members.
25 It was polite of them to write a thank-you letter to my grandma.
26 The picture is too heavy for me to hang on the wall.
27 The bear does not seem to be afraid of humans.
28 They were so poor that they could not buy Christmas presents for each other.

CHALLENGE!

01 [예시 답] I eat healthy food and exercise regularly to stay healthy.

02 [예시 답] It is difficult for me to get up early in the morning.

1 ⑤ suggest는 동명사를 목적어로 취하며 나머지는 모두 to부정사를 목적어로 취한다.

2 ③ get은 사역동사처럼 쓰일 때 to부정사를 목적격 보어로 취하지만 나머지 사역동사는 목적격 보어로 원형부정사를 취한다.

3 ② 사람의 성격을 나타내는 형용사 polite는 to부정사의 의미상 주어로 「of + 목적격」을 취한다.

4 ④ force는 to부정사를 목적격 보어로 취한다.

5 ① 지각동사 see는 목적격 보어로 원형부정사 또는 현재분사를 취한다.

6 주어진 문장과 ②는 to부정사의 부사적 용법 중 '감정의 원인' ① 부사적 용법(형용사 수식) ③ 명사적 용법 ④, ⑤ 부사적 용법(목적)

7 주어진 문장과 ④의 「be + to부정사」는 '예정'
① 가능 ② 운명 ③ 의무 ⑤ 의도

8 「not . . . enough + to부정사」 = 「too + 형용사/부사 + to부정사」

9 가주어/가목적어 (it) . . . 진주어/진목적어 (to부정사) 구조이다.

10 ② 주절과 that절의 시제가 일치하므로 단순부정사를 써야 한다.

11 「의문사 + to부정사」는 문장에서 명사의 역할을 할 수 있다. 「why + to부정사」는 쓰이지 않는다.

12 사람의 성질을 나타내지 않는 형용사의 경우 to부정사의 의미상의 주어는 「for + 목적격」으로 나타낸다.

13 문맥상 '설상가상으로'라는 말이 적절하므로 독립부정사 to make matters worse를 쓸 수 있다.

14 문맥상 너무 어려서 운전할 수 없다는 의미가 적절하며 '너무 ~해서 …할 수 없다'는 「too + 형용사 + to부정사」로 나타낼 수 있다.

15 ⑤ to부정사의 의미상의 주어가 of you이므로 집에 데려다 준 사람은 '그'이다.

16 to부정사의 의미상의 주어는 「for + 목적격」으로 나타내는데, 사람의 성격을 나타내는 형용사와 함께 쓸 때는 「of + 목적격」으로 쓴다.

17 사역동사는 목적격 보어로 원형부정사를 취하며 주절의 주어와 to부정사의 관계가 수동이므로 수동형 to부정사를 쓴다.

18 ②의 it은 비인칭주어이며 나머지는 to부정사를 진주어로 하는 가주어 it이다.

19 지각동사는 목적격 보어로 현재분사 또는 원형부정사를 취한다.

20 ④ It은 가주어, to부정사구가 진주어인 구문이 되어야 하므로 riding은 to ride가 되어야 한다.

21 주어와 to부정사구의 관계가 수동일 경우 수동형 to부정사를 쓴다.

22 to부정사의 시제가 주절의 시제보다 앞설 때 완료부정사를 쓴다.

23 「so + 형용사 + that + 주어 + can (could)」는 「형용사 + enough + to부정사」로 바꿔 쓸 수 있다.

24 가주어 It을 문두에 쓰고 to부정사구를 문장 뒤로 보낸다.

25 사람의 성질을 나타내는 형용사 polite는 to부정사의 의미상의 주어로 「of + 목적격」을 취한다.

26 「too + 형용사 + to부정사」는 '너무 ~해서 …할 수 없는'이라는 의미이며 to부정사의 의미상 주어는 「for + 목적격」으로 쓴다.

27 주절의 시제와 to부정사의 시제가 같을 때 단순부정사를 쓴다.

28 「too + 형용사 + to부정사」는 「so + 형용사 + that + 주어 + cannot (could not)」으로 바꿔 쓸 수 있다.

CHALLENGE!

01 to부정사의 부사적 용법 중 '목적(~하기 위해서)'

02 가주어 It, 진주어 to get up early in the morning

Gerunds

UNIT 01 Functions & Usage of Gerunds p. 81

A 1 drinking   2 my   3 closing
   4 Studying   5 teaching

B 1 not having studied   2 being invited
   3 having overcome
   4 my brother's (my brother) using

C 1 traveling   2 being touched
   3 being called   4 bothering

D 1 considered moving   2 being encouraged
   3 hate their (them) eating   4 having helped

UNIT 02 Gerunds vs. To-infinitives p. 83

A 1 doing   2 to be
   3 watching   4 to give

B 1 나는 친구에게 돈을 갚는 것을 잊어버렸다.
   2 민호는 승리할 기회를 놓친 것을 후회한다.
   3 나는 버스를 잡으려고 노력했지만, 충분히 빨리 달릴 수 없었다.
   4 그녀는 학교에 책을 가져온 것을 기억했지만, 그것을 찾을 수 없었다.

C 1 is worth watching
   2 It is no use turning on
   3 like having lunch   4 is busy fixing

D 1 difficulty taking down
   2 forget to lock the door
   3 stopped using   4 my (me) turning off

WRITING CONNECTION

STEP 1 Grammar Check-up   p. 84

A 1 ⓒ   2 ⓒ   3 ⓐ   4 ⓑ   5 ⓒ   6 ⓒ
B 1 ⓐ, preparing   2 ⓑ, postponing
   3 ⓑ, making   4 ⓑ, to turn off
   5 ⓑ, getting   6 ⓑ, falling down

A 1 동명사는 보어로 쓰일 수 있다.
   2 decide는 to부정사를 목적어로 취하는 동사이다.
   3 mind는 동명사를 목적어로 취하는 동사이며 동명사의 의미상 주어는 소유격 또는 목적격으로 나타낸다.
   4 avoid는 동명사를 목적어로 취하는 동사이다.
   5 spend time (money) + v-ing: ~하는 데 시간(돈)을 쓰다
   6 stop + v-ing: ~하는 것을 멈추다
     stop + to v: ~하기 위해 멈추다

B 1 be busy v-ing: ~하느라 바쁘다
   2 keep on v-ing: 계속해서 ~하다
   3 avoid는 동명사를 목적어로 취하는 동사이다.
   4 문맥상 '~할 것을 잊지 마라'라는 뜻이 되어야 하므로 「forget + to v」를 쓴다.
   5 feel like v-ing: ~하고 싶다
   6 전치사는 동명사를 목적어로 취하며 Mary가 넘어진 것은 능동이므로 능동형 동명사를 써야 한다.

STEP 2 Phrases to Sentences   p. 85

A 1 mind turning on   2 regret to say
   3 could not help eating   4 forget meeting
   5 prevented him from entering
   6 looking forward to going

B 1 to climb → Can you imagine climbing the highest mountain in the world?
   2 losing → I am really sorry for having lost your umbrella.
   3 heard → On hearing the news of the accident, he burst into tears.
   4 to be → I remember being taught how to ride a bicycle by my father when I was 6.
   5 bringing → Dan forgot to bring his wallet when he left his house.
   6 working → My father decided to work in a different industry.

A 1 mind는 동명사를 목적어로 취한다.
   2 regret + to v: ~하게 되어 유감이다
   3 cannot help v-ing: ~하지 않을 수 없다
   4 forget + v-ing: ~했던 것을 잊다 (과거)
   5 prevent . . . from v-ing: …가 ~하는 것을 막다
   6 look forward to v-ing: ~하기를 고대하다

B 1 imagine은 동명사를 목적어로 취한다.
   2 우산을 잃어버린 것이 더 이전의 일이므로 완료동명사 having p.p.로 쓴다.
   3 on v-ing: ~하자마자
   4 remember + v-ing: ~했던 것을 기억하다 (과거)
   5 forget + to v: ~할 것을 잊다 (미래)
   6 decide는 to부정사를 목적어로 취한다.

STEP 3 Sentence Practice   p. 86

A 1 a. regret not having read
     b. I regret not having apologized to you earlier.

2 a. no use worrying about

   b. It is no use regretting what you did in the past.

3 a. I tried eating Indian food

   b. Sam tried fixing his computer, but he failed.

4 a. forget to visit Grandma

   b. Do not forget to buy a pen on your way to school.

B **1** Running a marathon is worth trying.

   2 I lost my glasses, so I had difficulty reading a book.

   3 I am looking forward to traveling with you this year.

   4 We will hold a party to celebrate George's winning.

A **1** regret + v-ing: ~한 것을 후회하다. 책을 읽지 않은 것과 사과를 하지 않은 것은 더 이전의 일이므로 완료동명사 사용

   2 it is no use v-ing: ~해 봐야 소용없다

   3 try + v-ing: 시험 삼아 ~해 보다

   4 forget + to v: ~할 것을 잊다 (미래)

B **1** be worth v-ing: ~할 만한 가치가 있다

   2 have difficulty v-ing: ~하는 데 어려움이 있다

   3 look forward to v-ing: ~하기를 고대하다

   4 동명사의 의미상의 주어는 동명사 앞에 소유격으로 쓸 수 있다.

ACTUAL TEST
pp. 87-90

1 ⑤   **2** ④   **3** ②   **4** ③   **5** ④   **6** ③   **7** ⑤
8 ③   **9** ④   **10** ⑤   **11** ③   **12** ①   **13** ④   **14** ③
15 ⑤   **16** ④   **17** ②   **18** ④   **19** ④   **20** ③   **21** ②

22 (A) to turn off (B) turning off

23 hanging → to hang

24 has difficulty dealing with

25 like working out

26 He complained about being treated like a child by adults.

27 He was used to eating dinner alone.

28 There are different ways of protecting the environment.

CHALLENGE!

01 [예시 답] I regret not having had the courage to take part in a speech contest.

02 [예시 답] I wish to study abroad to learn a foreign language in the future.

1 mind는 동명사를 목적어로 취하는 동사이다.

2 promise는 to부정사를 목적어로 취하며 to부정사의 부정은 not을 to부정사 앞에 쓴다.

3 be worth v-ing: ~할 만한 가치가 있다

4 decide는 to부정사를 목적어로 취한다.

5 ④ have difficulty v-ing: ~하는 데 어려움이 있다

6 ③ 전치사는 동명사를 목적어로 취한다.

7 ⑤ keep . . . from v-ing: …가 ~하는 것을 막다

8 완료동명사는 having p.p.로 쓴다.

9 ① agree는 to부정사를, ③ delay, ⑤ mind는 동명사를 목적어로 취하는 동사이다. ② try + to v: ~하려고 노력하다

10 ① learn은 to부정사를 목적어로 취하며 ② 동명사의 의미상 주어는 소유격 또는 목적격을 쓰고 ③ recommend, ④ consider는 동명사를 목적어로 취한다.

11 '~한 것을 후회하다'는 regret + v-ing로 나타낼 수 있으며 문장의 동사보다 동명사가 더 앞선 시제이므로 완료동명사를 쓴다.

12 '~해 봐야 소용없다'는 it is no use v-ing를 써서 나타낼 수 있다.

13 postpone, enjoy, imagine, stop은 동명사를 목적어로 취하지만 promise는 to부정사를 목적어로 취한다.

14 remember + v-ing는 '~했던 것을 기억하다'라는 의미

15 동명사가 문장의 주어이고 동명사의 부정형은 동명사 앞에 not을 쓴다.

16 ⓑ 전치사는 목적어로 동명사를 취하며 ⓓ 동명사가 문장의 주어로 쓰일 때는 이어지는 동사는 단수형으로 쓴다.

17 be used to v-ing: ~하는 데 익숙하다   used to v: ~하곤 했다

18 (A) recommend는 동명사를 목적어로 취하며 문맥상 부정의 형태가 적절하고 (B) want는 to부정사를 목적어로 취한다.

19 expect와 wish는 to부정사를 목적어로 취한다.

20 동명사의 의미상 주어는 소유격이나 목적격으로 나타내며 decide는 to부정사를 목적어로 취한다.

21 ② look forward to v-ing: ~하기를 고대하다

[22-23] 해석

   때때로 우리 엄마는 건망증이 심하시다. 며칠 전에 그녀는 가스레인지를 잠그는 것을 잊으셨다. 그녀는 가스레인지 불을 켜둔 채 집을 나섰다. 몇 시간 뒤에 그녀는 집에 왔고 가스 냄새를 맡았다. 그녀는 무서웠다. 지금은 비록 그녀가 가스를 잠갔더라도 가스레인지를 체크하기 위해 항상 집에 오신다. 왜냐하면 그녀는 가스를 잠갔던 것을 기억하지 못하기 때문이다. 나는 '가스레인지 확인하기!'라는 메모를 대문에 걸어두기로 결심했다.

22 forget + to v: ~해야 하는 것을 잊다
remember + v-ing: ~했던 것을 기억하다

23 decide는 to부정사를 목적어로 취하는 동사이다.

24 have difficulty v-ing: ~하는 데 어려움이 있다

25 feel like v-ing: ~하고 싶다

26 동명사의 수동태는 being p.p. 형태로 쓴다.

27 be used to v-ing: ~하는 데 익숙하다

28 전치사는 동명사를 목적어로 취한다.

CHALLENGE!

01 완료동명사: having p.p.

02 wish는 to부정사를 목적어로 취한다.

TEXTBOOK

Participles

UNIT 01   Functions of Participles   p. 93

A 1 waiting   2 crying   3 stolen
   4 pleasing   5 depressed   6 broken

B 1 exhausted   2 boring
   3 disappointed 4 satisfied
   5 waiting   6 amazing

C 1 cry (crying) 2 finish (finishing)
   3 repaired   4 play (playing)
   5 wrapped   6 done

D 1 drunk man   2 broken window
   3 heard him leave (leaving)
   4 have, ironed

UNIT 02   Participle Clauses   p. 95

A 1 Sending   2 Cutting
   3 Having   4 Having

B 1 Because I did not have an umbrella
   2 When he intends to do a certain thing
   3 Although she was invited to his birthday party
   4 If we walk slowly

C 1 (Being) exhausted by a lack of sleep,
      → 수면 부족으로 인해 지쳤기 때문에
   2 (Being) given an opportunity,
      → 기회가 주어진다면
   3 (Having been) fired by his company,
      → 그의 회사에서 해고당했지만/해고당한 뒤
   4 (Having been) written many decades ago,
      → 수십 년 전에 쓰여졌지만

D 1 Speaking in front of people
   2 Having studied
   3 Knowing

UNIT 03   Various Participle Clauses   p. 97

A 1 Since (As, Because) it was cold
   2 If you do me a favor
   3 When she played the piano
   4 Although Taeho has lived in America for years

B 1 여행 말인데
   2 그의 피부색으로 판단하건대
   3 솔직히 말해서
   4 그가 어리다는 것을 고려하면

C 1 with a cool breeze blowing
   2 with their eyes closed tight
   3 With night falling
   4 with his mouth stuffed with pizza

D 1 The weather permitting
   2 Strictly speaking
   3 Compared with her sister
   4 with her fingers drumming

WRITING CONNECTION

STEP 1   Grammar Check-up   p. 98

A 1 ⓑ   2 ⓒ   3 ⓒ   4 ⓑ   5 ⓐ   6 ⓑ

B 1 ⓑ bored   2 ⓑ exhausted
   3 ⓐ Considering   4 ⓐ Putting
   5 ⓐ (Having been) Broadcasted
      ((Being) Broadcasted)

A 1 '당황하게 하는 순간'이므로 능동의 의미인 현재분사
   2 '포장된 점심'이므로 수동의 의미인 과거분사
   3 '모아진 미술 작품'이므로 수동의 의미인 과거분사
   4 '도난당한 보물'이므로 수동의 의미인 과거분사
   5 '흥분하게 하는 뉴스'이므로 능동의 의미인 현재분사
   6 '깨진 유리'이므로 수동의 의미인 과거분사

B 1 심심해진 것이므로 수동의 의미인 과거분사
   2 신데렐라가 지치게 된 것이므로 수동의 의미인 과거분사
   3 Considering '~을 고려하면'
   4 그가 옷을 입었다는 능동의 의미인 현재분사
   5 뉴스가 방송된 것이므로 수동 분사구문

STEP 2   Phrases to Sentences   p. 99

A 1 fallen popcorn   2 watching the match
   3 The rain starting
   4 Having completed the work
   5 His head (being) stuck
   6 Walking down the beach

B 1 Finished → Having finished cleaning the bathroom, she sat on the sofa to rest.
   2 Judged → Judging from the dark circles on his face, he must be under lots of stress.
   3 being arrived → Her mom arriving, she looked happy and cheerful.
   4 Having nominated → (Having been) Nominated for the award, the actor did not show up.
   5 watch → I could not focus on the test with the teacher watching over my shoulder.

> **6** Having held → Holding the flashlight steadily, Jennifer slowly entered the building.

A **1** '떨어진 팝콘'이므로 수동의 의미인 과거분사

2 '경기를 보면서'이므로 현재분사

3 주절의 주어와 부사절의 주어가 다르므로 분사구문의 주어를 생략하지 않는다.

4 식사를 하러 나가기 이전에 일을 완료한 것이므로 완료형 분사구문으로 쓴다.

5 분사구문의 주어는 his head이고, 주절의 주어는 he이므로 분사구문에서 주어를 생략하지 않는다.

6 분사구문과 주절의 주어가 같으므로 분사구문의 주어를 생략할 수 있다.

B **1** 소파에 앉기 전에 욕실 청소를 마쳤으므로 주절보다 한 시제 앞서는 완료형 분사구문

2 Judging from '~로 판단하건대'

3 도착하는 것은 능동이므로 being arrived를 arriving으로 바꿈

4 후보로 지명된 것이므로 수동 분사구문

5 「with + 명사 + 분사」 형태로 명사와 분사가 능동 관계이므로 분사 자리에 현재분사

6 분사구문의 내용이 주절의 내용보다 이전에 일어난 일이 아니므로 완료형 분사구문을 쓰지 않는다.

STEP 3 Sentence Practice
p. 100

A **1** a. The boring speech

b. The tiring night shift made the nurses exhausted.

2 a. Frankly speaking

b. Strictly speaking, his report was not that great.

3 a. (Having been) Rescued, the wounded man

b. (Having been) Treated, the boy was taken to his parents.

4 a. (Being) Discouraged by the low pay

b. (Being) Encouraged by cheers, the team did their best in the finals.

B **1** Loving his boxing gloves, Paul wore them even in bed.

2 Having been published in Korea in 751 A.D., the document is extremely valuable.

3 Almost everyone in the stadium stood cheering for the players.

4 Lost in thought, Daniel did not hear Kelly calling him.

A **1** '지루한 연설, 힘든 야간 근무'는 능동의 의미인 현재분사, 간호사가 지치는 것이므로 수동의 의미인 과거분사

2 Frankly speaking '솔직히 말해서' Strictly speaking '엄격히 말하면'

---

3 수동 분사구문 Having been p.p.에서 Having been을 생략할 수 있다.

4 수동 분사구문 Being p.p.에서 Being은 생략할 수 있다.

B **1** 이유의 분사구문

2 그 문서가 출판된 것은 가치가 있는 지금보다 이전에 일어난 일이므로 완료형 분사구문

3 동시동작의 분사구문

4 수동 분사구문으로 Being이 생략되었다.

ACTUAL TEST
pp. 101-104

1 ③ **2** ② **3** ⑤ **4** ③ **5** ① **6** ③ **7** ②
8 ④ **9** ② **10** ④ **11** ③ **12** ② **13** ①, ②
14 ① **15** ② **16** ①, ⑤ **17** ② **18** ⑤ **19** ②
20 ③ **21** ②

22 The tail (being) held horizontally, the dog is alert.

23 (A) tucked (B) wagging

24 (Having been) Interrupted several times, he was annoyed.

25 Cathy having lived in Korea for 10 years, her Korean is very natural.

26 We were terrified by the haunted house.

27 Not having slept for two days, she was not able to concentrate.

28 Strictly speaking, tomatoes are not fruits but vegetables.

CHALLENGE!

01 [예시 답] P.E. class is exciting to me. [I am bored in math class.]

02 [예시 답] While studying, I usually listen to music.

---

1 '만들어진 상품'이므로 수동의 의미인 과거분사가 알맞다.

2 '울고 있는 아기'이므로 능동의 의미인 현재분사가 알맞다.

3 「with + 명사 + 분사」이며, '숙제를 집에 남겨둔 채'라는 뜻으로 명사와 분사가 수동 관계이므로 과거분사를 쓴다.

4 완료형 분사구문으로 ③ saw는 seen이 되어야 한다.

5 분사구문에서 부사절의 주어가 주절의 주어와 같을 때 생략한다.

6 분사구문을 만들 때 접속사와 주어를 생략(주절의 주어와 같을 때)하고 동사를 현재분사로 만든다.

7 접속사와 주어를 생략하고 부사절의 내용이 주절의 내용보다 이전에 일어난 일이므로 완료형 분사구문으로 만든다.

8 분사가 명사를 수식할 때 명사와의 관계가 수동이면 과거분사로, 능동이면 현재분사로 쓴다.

9 (A) '사건을 조사하고 있는 경찰'이므로 능동의 의미인 현재분사
(B) '사용된 차'이므로 수동의 의미인 과거분사

10 (A) 독립분사구문으로 All things (being) considered
(B) 이유를 나타내는 분사구문

11 그녀의 노래를 듣고 사람들이 전율을 느끼게 된 것이므로 수동의 의미인 과거분사 thrilled가 보어로 와야 한다.

12 '눈이 감겨진 채로'이므로 수동의 의미인 과거분사 closed가 와야 한다.

13 Judging from '~로 판단하건대' Considering '~을 고려하면'

14 ①은 face를 꾸며 주는 형용사로서의 분사이고 나머지는 목적격 보어로 쓰인 분사이다.

15 수식을 하는 명사나 분사구문의 주어와 수동의 관계인 경우 과거분사 written을 써야 한다. ② 주절의 주어인 Brian이 분사구문의 주어이므로 Writing 또는 Having written으로 써야 한다.

16 부사절의 시제가 주절보다 앞서므로 완료형 수동 분사구문 「Having been + p.p.」를 사용하며 Having been은 생략 가능하다.

17 두 개의 절을 연결할 때에는 접속사, 분사구문, 전치사구를 쓸 수 있다.

18 Packing her things는 While she was packing her things 또는 When she was packing her things의 의미로 이해할 수 있다.

19 「leave + 목적어 + 분사」에서 분사는 목적어와 수동의 관계이므로 unattending은 unattended가 되어야 한다.

20 부사절의 내용이 주절의 내용보다 이전에 일어난 일일 때 완료형 분사구문을 쓰며, confuse는 주어가 사람일 때 과거분사로 써야 하므로 Having confused는 Having been confused가 되어야 한다.

21 주절의 주어와 부사절의 주어가 다를 때는 분사구문의 주어를 생략할 수 없으므로 Being a cloudy night는 It (being) a cloudy night가 되어야 한다.

[22-23] 해석
　　개의 꼬리 위치는 사회적인 신호이다. 다시 말하면, 그것은 일종의 감정 측정기로 여겨질 수 있다. 수직으로 세워진 꼬리는 경고로, '내가 여기 대장이야. 물러서!'를 의미한다. 중간 높이는 개가 긴장을 풀고 있다는 것을 보여 준다. 만약 꼬리가 수평으로 머물러 있으면 개가 경계 상태라는 것이다. 꼬리 위치가 더 낮아질수록 이것은 개가 불안해지고 있다는 신호이다. 몸 아래로 접혀져 있는 꼬리는 '제발 나를 해치지 마세요.'라는 의미의 두려움의 표시이다. 꼬리를 흔드는 개가 항상 행복하고 다정한 것은 아니라는 것을 기억하라.

22 주어가 다르므로 접속사만 생략하고 is를 being으로 바꾼다. being은 생략될 수 있다.

23 (A) '몸 아래로 접힌 꼬리'이므로 수동의 의미인 과거분사
(B) '꼬리를 흔드는 개'이므로 능동의 의미인 현재분사

24 부사절의 시제가 주절의 시제보다 앞서므로 완료형 분사구문으로 쓴다.

25 주절의 주어와 부사절의 주어가 다를 때는 분사구문의 주어를 생략할 수 없다.

26 겁에 질리게 된 것이므로 수동의 의미인 과거분사 terrified를 사용했고, haunted house는 '귀신이 나오는 집'이라는 뜻의 표현이다.

27 완료형 분사구문의 부정은 Not having p.p.

28 '엄격히 말하면'은 Strictly speaking이다.

CHALLENGE!

01 감정을 느끼게 만드는 것은 현재분사로, 사람이 느끼는 감정은 과거분사로 나타낸다.

02 분사구문의 뜻을 명확하게 하기 위해 접속사를 분사 앞에 남겨두기도 한다.

CHAPTER
08 Comparisons

UNIT 01 **Comparisons Using the Positive Degree** p. 107

A 1 thick　2 as　3 hard　4 as　5 not as

B 1 twice as old as [two times older than]
2 three times as fast as
3 three times as much as [three times more than]
4 as fast as possible
5 as soon as possible

C 1 as soon as possible　　2 as old as
3 three times as long　　4 as expensive as

D 1 as busy as　　2 did not play as well as
3 warm water as often as possible
4 has three times as many books

UNIT 02 **Comparisons Using Comparatives** p. 109

A 1 heavier　　2 than　　3 less difficult
4 much　　5 to　　6 more popular

B 1 네가 더 바쁠수록 시간이 더 빨리 간다.
2 네가 더 친절할수록 사람들은 더 행복하다.
3 날씨가 더 추워질수록 놀이터에 아이들이 더 적다.

C 1 worse and worse
2 more and more flexible
3 louder and louder
4 more and more nervous

D 1 was easier than
2 more and more active
3 The more, the better
4 much friendlier than

UNIT 03 **Comparisons Using Superlatives** p. 111

A 1 latest　　2 prettier　　3 most difficult
4 best　　5 by far

B 1 one of the richest men
2 one of the most beautiful women
3 one of the most impressive documentary films
4 One of the best ways

C 1 = any other pizza
= No, better
= No, good
2 = luckier than any other student
= No, luckier than
= No, as, as

D 1 one of the ugliest dogs
  2 No other student, as fast as [faster than]
  3 the most memorable scene (that) I have ever seen

WRITING CONNECTION

p. 112

STEP 1 Grammar Check-up

A 1 ⓐ 2 ⓑ 3 ⓑ 4 ⓒ 5 ⓐ 6 ⓒ
B 1 ⓐ as   2 ⓑ comedians
  3 ⓑ more generous   4 ⓑ fast
  5 ⓑ than   6 ⓐ quieter

A 1 not as + 원급 + as: ···만큼 ~하지 않은
  2 빈칸 뒤에 than이 있으므로 빈칸에는 friendly의 비교급이 들어 가야 한다.
  3 빈칸 앞에 the가 있으므로 「the + 최상급」
  4 good의 비교급은 better, 최상급은 best이다. 빈칸 뒤에 than이 있으므로 빈칸에는 비교급이 들어가야 한다.
  5 비교급을 강조하는 표현은 much이다.
  6 the + 최상급 + 단수명사 + I have ever p.p.: 내가 ···한 것 중에서 가장 ~한

B 1 as soon as possible: 가능한 한 빨리
  2 one of the + 최상급 + 복수명사: 가장 ~한 ··· 중의 하나
  3 the + 비교급, the + 비교급: ···하면 할수록 더 ~한
  4 not as + 원급 + as: ···만큼 ~하지 않은
  5 배수사 + 비교급 + than: ···보다 몇 배 더 ~한
  6 비교급을 강조할 때 「비교급 + than ever」를 쓴다.

p. 113

STEP 2 Phrases to Sentences

A 1 than any other person
  2 as efficient as
  3 No other baby is cuter than [as cute as]
  4 much more relaxed
  5 one of the politest people
  6 longer, the more bored

B 1 most happy → Today is the happiest day of my life.
  2 least → The less you spend, the more you save.
  3 than → My brother is superior to me in many ways.
  4 those → The climate of this region is hotter than that of the southern region.
  5 hardly → Andy worked twice as hard as others.
  6 or → Online learning is getting more and more popular around the world.

A 1 비교급 + than any other + 단수명사: 다른 어떤 ···보다 더 ~한
  2 not as + 원급 + as: ···만큼 ~하지 않은
  3 부정주어 + 동사 + 비교급 + than, 부정주어 + 동사 + as + 원급 + as: 다른 어떤 것도 ···보다 ~하지 않다
  4 relaxed의 비교급은 more relaxed이고, 비교급을 강조하는 부사 much는 비교급 앞에 쓴다.
  5 one of the + 최상급 + 복수명사: 가장 ~한 ··· 중의 하나
  6 the + 비교급, the + 비교급: ···하면 할수록 더 ~한

B 1 happy의 최상급은 happiest이다.
  2 the + 비교급, the + 비교급: ···하면 할수록 더 ~한
  3 superior to: ~보다 나은
  4 비교 대상이 the climate of this region과 the climate of the southern region이므로 the climate를 대신할 수 있는 대명사는 단수형 that이다.
  5 부사 hardly는 '거의 ~하지 않는'이라는 뜻으로, 여기에서는 worked를 수식하는 '열심히'라는 뜻의 부사 hard를 써야 한다.
  6 get + 비교급 and 비교급: 점점 더 ~하게 되다

p. 114

STEP 3 Sentence Practice

A 1 a. much bigger than
    b. Toronto is much colder than Seoul.
  2 a. as long as
    b. The journey to Paris was not as boring as before.
  3 a. The higher, the colder
    b. The harder you study, the more you will learn.
  4 a. the most expensive
    b. This is one of the newest cell phones in the store.

B 1 My ticket did not cost as much as yours.
  2 The game became more and more exciting.
  3 The planet is three times as big as the sun.
  4 This is one of the best movies I have ever seen.

A 1 much + 비교급 + than: ···보다 훨씬 더 ~한
  2 not as + 원급 + as: ···만큼 ~하지 않은
  3 the + 비교급, the + 비교급: ···하면 할수록 더 ~한
  4 one of the + 최상급 + 복수명사: 가장 ~한 ··· 중의 하나

B 1 not as + 원급 + as: ···만큼 ~하지 않은
  2 비교급 and 비교급: 점점 더 ~한
  3 배수사 + as + 원급 + as: ···보다 몇 배 더 ~한
  4 one of the + 최상급 + 복수명사: 가장 ~한 ··· 중의 하나

1 ④ 2 ⑤ 3 ④ 4 ② 5 ③ 6 ④ 7 ④
8 ① 9 ② 10 ⑤ 11 ④ 12 ③ 13 ③ 14 ①
15 ③ 16 ① 17 ⑤ 18 ③ 19 ④ 20 ⑤ 21 ②

22 Ron is one of the luckiest boys
23 (A) best (B) better
24 English will become more and more important.
25 These jeans are twice as expensive as those ones.
26 The dish that the chef recommended is not as delicious as the other dishes.
27 The darker it got, the colder it got.
28 more important

CHALLENGE!

01 [예시 답] The school sports day was the most exciting event.
02 [예시 답] I play soccer better than any other student in my class. 〔No one plays soccer better than I do in my class.〕

1 빈칸 뒤에 than이 있으므로 비교급이 들어가야 한다.
2 very는 비교급을 강조할 수 없다.
3 bravest가 최상급이므로 most가 필요 없다.
4 코끼리가 가장 무겁다는 최상급의 의미인데, ②는 다른 동물들은 코끼리만큼 무겁다는 의미이다.
5 the + 최상급 + of all: 모든 것 중에서 가장 ~한
6 No (other) + 단수명사 + 동사 + 비교급 + than: 어떤 것도 …보다 ~하지 않다
7 ④ play as well as Manchester United F.C. 또는 play better than Manchester United F.C.로 써야 한다.
8 ① junior to 또는 younger than으로 써야 한다.
9 not as + 원급 + as = less + 원급 + than
10 ⑤ 「as + 원급 + as + possible」이므로 more는 much가 되어야 한다.
11 ④ 「one of the + 최상급 + 복수명사」이므로 place는 places가 되어야 한다.
12 ③은 Jina는 Patty만큼 나이가 많지 않다는 뜻이므로 'Patty is not as old as Jina.'가 되어야 한다.
13 than 대신 to를 쓰는 비교급 문장인데, ③은 to부정사의 의미상의 주어인 「for + 목적격」이므로 빈칸에 전치사 for가 들어가야 한다.
14 「as + 형용사/부사의 원급 + as」를 포함한 문장인데, ①은 비교급이 있으므로 빈칸에 than이 들어가야 한다.
15 빈칸에 the가 들어가야 하는데, ③은 비교급 more가 있으므로 빈칸에 than이 들어가야 한다.
16 as + 원급 + as possible
   = as + 원급 + as + 주어 + can 〔could〕
17 비교급 + than any other + 단수명사

18 become + 비교급 and 비교급: 점점 더 ~하게 되다
19 (A) not as + 원급 + as
   (B) as + 원급 + as
20 (A) 비교급 + than
   (B) as + 원급 + as possible
21 「배수사 + as + 원급 + as」는 「배수사 + 비교급 + than」과 의미가 같으므로 less는 more로 써야 한다.

[22-23] 해석

나는 Ron이 세상에서 가장 운이 좋은 소년들 중의 하나라고 생각한다. 비록 그의 가족은 부유하지는 않지만 그는 훌륭한 부모님, 애정 어린 조부모님, 귀여운 여동생 그리고 든든한 형이 있다. 그의 아버지는 내가 아는 최고의 요리사이고, 그의 형은 마을의 어떤 음악가보다 기타를 잘 친다.

22 one of the + 최상급 + 복수명사
23 (A) the + 최상급 + 주어 + have ever p.p.
   (B) 비교급 + than any other + 단수명사
24 비교급 and 비교급: 점점 더 ~한
25 배수사 + as + 원급 + as: …보다 몇 배 더 ~한
26 not as + 원급 + as: …만큼 ~하지 않은
27 the + 비교급, the + 비교급: …하면 할수록 더 ~한
28 최상급은 「부정주어 + 동사 + 비교급 + than」으로 바꿔 쓸 수 있다.

CHALLENGE!

01 the + 최상급
02 비교급 + than any other + 단수명사
   = No (other) + 단수명사 + 단수동사 + 비교급 + than

CHAPTER

09 Conjunctions

TEXTBOOK

UNIT 01 Subordinating Conjunctions p. 121

A 1 As soon as   2 Even though
   3 when   4 before   5 although

B 1 If   2 so that
   3 in case   4 Since

C 1 even though (although, though)
   2 If, do not   3 Because (As, Since)

D 1 since I woke up
   2 so that (in order that) we can make a good decision
   3 once you get to know
   4 Even though my uncle lives near me

UNIT 02 Correlative Conjunctions / Indirect Questions p. 123

A 1 either   2 has   3 and   4 nor   5 but

B 1 why he was crying
   2 what time the bank opens
   3 whether (if) your parents are joining us
   4 Whether you have a dream or not

C 1 what you bought
   2 how he got in shape
   3 whether (if) he had been there before
   4 whether (if) I had my passport with me

D 1 who will become the next president
   2 Neither Sam nor Tom complained about
   3 whether (if) a room is available
   4 not only swimming but also camping instruction

WRITING CONNECTION

STEP 1 Grammar Check-up p. 124

A 1 ⓑ   2 ⓓ   3 ⓓ   4 ⓒ   5 ⓐ   6 ⓓ

B 1 ⓑ so (in order)
   2 ⓐ Though (Although, Even though)
   3 ⓐ not only   4 ⓐ because (as, since)
   5 ⓑ whether (if)   6 ⓐ Whether

A 1 even though: 비록 ~이지만
   2 when: ~할 때
   3 의문사가 있는 간접의문문의 어순: 의문사 + 주어 + 동사

4 unless: ~하지 않는다면
5 neither A nor B: A도 B도 아닌
6 both A and B: A와 B 둘 다

B 1 so that, in order that: ~하기 위해서
   2 though, although, even though: 비록 ~이지만
   3 not only A but also B: A뿐만 아니라 B도
   4 자명종이 울리지 않은 것이 늦게 일어난 이유이므로, 결과를 나타내는 so가 아니라 이유의 접속사를 써야 한다.
   5 의문사가 없는 간접의문문의 어순: whether (if) + 주어 + 동사
   6 if절은 목적어절로만 쓰이므로 If는 Whether가 되어야 한다.

STEP 2 Phrases to Sentences p. 125

A 1 whether (if) she remembers her childhood (or not)
   2 not only mathematics but also art (art as well as mathematics)
   3 because (as, since) my back hurts
   4 Once she graduates from school
   5 have dinner either before or after the show
   6 how many people would attend the meeting

B 1 during → It began to rain while they were playing soccer.
   2 if → My mom was only sixteen when she met my father.
   3 such that → She practiced hard so that (in order that) she could perform well in the competition.
   4 that → The librarian asked the students whether (if) they could be quiet or not.
   5 Despite → Although (Though, Even though) my best friend moved to a different city, we still keep in touch.
   6 were → Neither you nor I was responsible for the matter.

A 1 whether (if) . . . or not: ~인지 아닌지
   2 not only A but also B, B as well as A: A뿐만 아니라 B도
   3 because, as, since: ~ 때문에
   4 Once: 일단 ~하면
   5 either A or B : A와 B 둘 중 하나
   6 의문사가 있는 간접의문문: 의문사 + 주어 + 동사, 「how + 형용사」는 '얼마 ~한'이란 뜻으로 하나의 의문사처럼 사용된다.

B 1 ~ 동안에: during + 명사(구), while + 주어 + 동사
   2 when: ~할 때
   3 so that, in order that: ~하기 위해서
   4 whether (if) . . . or not: ~인지 아닌지
   5 비록 ~이지만: despite + 명사(구), although + 주어 + 동사
   6 neither A nor B에서는 B에 동사의 수를 일치시킨다.

p. 126

STEP3 Sentence Practice

A 1 a. Though (Although, Even though), heights
    b. Though (Although, Even though) I am afraid of the dark, I went home alone at night.
  2 a. either, or watch
    b. She will either join the drama club or make a new club.
  3 a. Since, good
    b. Since my father's car is more than 15 years old, it is not in good condition.
  4 a. why, arrived
    b. Do you know why she changed her job recently?

B 1 Because I was too tired, I could not do my homework. (I could not do my homework because I was too tired.)
  2 While he was in the hospital, both the teacher and his classmates visited him. (Both the teacher and his classmates visited him while he was in the hospital.)
  3 Take either the bus or the subway to get there.
  4 She wants to know how I made the cake.

A 1 though, although, even though: 비록 ~이지만
  2 either A or B: A와 B 둘 중 하나
  3 since: ~ 때문에
  4 의문사가 있는 간접의문문의 어순: 의문사 + 주어 + 동사

B 1 because: ~ 때문에
  2 while: ~ 동안에, both A and B: A와 B 둘 다
  3 either A or B: A와 B 둘 중 하나
  4 의문사가 있는 간접의문문의 어순: 의문사 + 주어 + 동사

ACTUAL TEST
pp. 127-130

1 ② 2 ③ 3 ④ 4 ⑤ 5 ③ 6 ③ 7 ④
8 ④ 9 ③ 10 ① 11 ⑤ 12 ④ 13 ② 14 ③
15 ② 16 ④ 17 ⑤ 18 ⑤ 19 ④ 20 ② 21 ③
22 so, that   23 not only, but also
24 I would like to know whether (if) each room has a separate bathroom.
25 What do you think the importance of learning languages is?
26 I will not buy the goods though the price is reasonable. (Though the price is reasonable, I will not buy the goods.)
27 Helen told me where Michael had gone.
28 Do you know who took my shoes?

CHALLENGE!
01 [예시 답] I think I am both generous and outgoing.
02 [예시 답] I am good at not only drawing but also writing.

1 부모님이 엄격하시지만 네가 같이 가면 캠핑 가는 것을 허락해 주실 거라는 의미로 Although와 if가 알맞다.
2 그녀는 잘못된 방향으로 가고 있었기 때문에 은행이 어디에 있는지 찾을 수 없었다라는 의미로 Because와 where가 알맞다.
3 as가 이유의 접속사로 쓰였으므로 since와 바꿔 쓸 수 있다.
4 의문사가 없는 의문문을 간접의문문으로 만들 때 if나 whether를 사용한다.
5 ③ 'Rebecca가 사과하지 않으면'이라는 의미가 되어야 하므로 If는 Unless가 되어야 한다.
6 ③ 동사의 수를 Jisub에 일치시켜야 하므로 like는 likes가 되어야 한다.
7 ④ 의문사가 있는 간접의문문의 어순은 「의문사 + 주어 + 동사」이므로 when Olivia's birthday is가 되어야 한다.
8 not either A or B는 neither A nor B와 같다.
9 so that: ~하기 위해서
10 with age: 나이가 듦에 따라, as: ~하면서
11 ~ 동안에: during + 명사(구), while + 주어 + 동사
12 as: ~ 때문에 (이유), ~할 때 (시간)
13 while: ~하는 동안, ~인 반면에
14 so that, in order that: ~하기 위해서 (목적)
15 unless는 if . . . not과 바꿔 쓸 수 있다.
16 ④ as는 '~대로'라는 의미로 쓰였고, 나머지는 시간(~하면서, ~할 때)의 의미를 나타낸다.
17 ⑤ since는 '~ 때문에'라는 의미로 쓰였고, 나머지는 시간(~이래로, ~이후로)의 의미를 나타낸다.
18 ⑤는 '만약 ~라면'이라는 뜻의 조건의 접속사이고, 나머지는 '~인지 아닌지'라는 뜻의 명사절을 이끄는 접속사이다.
19 의문사가 없는 간접의문문의 어순: 「whether (if) + 주어 + 동사」
20 의문사가 있는 간접의문문의 어순: 의문사 + 주어 + 동사
21 neither A nor B: A도 B도 아닌
22 in order that, so that: ~하기 위해
23 B as well as A는 not only A but also B로 바꿔 쓸 수 있다.
24 종속절이 '각 방에 분리된 화장실이 있는지'라는 의미이므로 that을 whether나 if로 써야 한다.
25 동사가 think인 의문문에서 의문사절이 목적어절일 때 의문사는 문장 맨 앞으로 이동한다.
26 though: 비록 ~이지만
27 의문사가 있는 간접의문문의 어순: 의문사 + 주어 + 동사
28 의문사가 주어인 간접의문문의 어순: 의문사 + 동사

CHALLENGE!
01 both A and B: A와 B 둘 다
02 not only A but also B: A뿐만 아니라 B도

CHAPTER 10 Relatives

UNIT 01 Relative Pronouns p. 133

A 1 who   2 whose   3 whom
   4 that   5 that

B 1 which   2 who   3 that
   4 that   5 what   6 whose

C 1 who (that)   2 that (which)
   3 whose   4 which   5 whom

D 1 who (that) was wearing
   2 The pants which my mother bought
   3 People that I talked to
   4 subject that he is interested in

UNIT 02 Relative Adverbs p. 135

A 1 where   2 when
   3 why   4 the way

B 1 some reasons why
   2 how
   3 The day when
   4 this house where

C 1 where   2 reason
   3 when   4 which (that)
   5 at which (where)

D 1 The day when we arrived
   2 the city in which
   3 the reason why I do not
   4 how (the way) you solved

UNIT 03 Nonrestrictive Relative Clauses p. 137

A 1 who   2 which
   3 than   4 as

B 1 where   2 which   3 whose
   4 who   5 who(m)

C 1 when   2 where
   3 which   4 whom

D 1 grandfather, who is 70
   2 which I found impossible
   3 most of which
   4 He was born in 1989, when

UNIT 04 Compound Relatives p. 139

A 1 Whoever   2 whatever

   3 Whichever   4 Whoever
   5 whatever

B 1 matter who   2 anyone
   3 No matter which   4 No matter what

C 1 Whenever   2 However
   3 wherever   4 where
   5 how

D 1 Whoever has the most experience
   2 Whichever path you take
   3 However hungry he is

WRITING CONNECTION

STEP 1 Grammar Check-up p. 140

A 1 ⓒ   2 ⓐ   3 ⓑ   4 ⓐ   5 ⓒ   6 ⓐ

B 1 ⓑ which   2 ⓐ whose
   3 ⓑ it 삭제   4 ⓑ you
   5 ⓑ which

A 1 선행사가 사람일 때의 주격 관계대명사가 들어가야 한다.
   2 장소의 선행사 다음 관계부사 where가 쓰인다.
   3 선행사 book에 대한 추가적인 정보를 제공하는 계속적 용법의 관계대명사가 알맞다.
   4 시간의 선행사가 있으므로 관계부사 when이 들어가야 한다.
   5 이유의 선행사가 있으므로 관계부사 why가 들어가야 한다.
   6 선행사가 사람이고 빈칸 이하의 관계사절에서 목적어가 필요하므로 목적격 관계대명사 whom이 들어가야 한다.

B 1 전치사의 목적어로 관계대명사 that은 쓰이지 못한다.
   2 선행사 a boy의 소유물인 bike를 나타낼 수 있는 소유격 관계대명사가 알맞다.
   3 목적격 관계대명사가 쓰였으므로 이어지는 절의 목적어는 삭제된다.
   4 「복합관계부사 + 주어 + 동사」 어순이 되어야 한다.
   5 앞 절의 내용 전체 또는 일부를 받는 계속적 용법의 관계대명사는 which이다.

STEP 2 Phrases to Sentences p. 141

A 1 the person who (that) is in charge
   2 The book which (that) you lent
   3 whose father is an actor
   4 Whoever borrowed this ball
   5 where I can read alone
   6 when everything went smoothly

B 1 whose → James still remembers the days when there were no personal computers.

2 which → I cannot remember the person (who(m)) I asked to keep an eye on my bag.

3 that → Let's discuss what will happen next in this story.

4 have → The heavy rain, which is unusual in this city, has destroyed my flowers.

5 whatever → David keeps on telling the same story to whoever will listen.

6 which → The company where my dad works is making a lot of profits these days.

Ⓐ **1** 사람이 선행사일 때 주격으로 쓰일 수 있는 관계대명사 who 또는 that을 쓴다.

2 선행사가 사물이므로 목적격 관계대명사 which 또는 that을 쓴다.

3 하나의 아버지가 배우이므로 소유격 관계대명사 whose를 쓴다.

4 '~한 사람이 누구든'이라는 뜻을 표현하기 위해 복합관계대명사 whoever를 이용한다.

5 장소를 수식하는 관계사절이 되도록 관계부사 where를 쓴다.

6 선행사가 yesterday이므로 관계부사 when을 쓴다.

Ⓑ **1** 시간의 선행사 뒤에 관계부사 when이 오는 것이 알맞다.

2 사람 선행사 뒤에 올 수 있는 목적격 관계대명사가 필요하다. 목적격 관계대명사는 생략될 수 있다.

3 관계대명사 앞에 선행사가 없기 때문에 선행사를 포함한 관계대명사 what이 들어가야 한다.

4 which가 이끄는 관계사절이 삽입되어 있으므로, 동사는 문장의 주어인 The heavy rain과 수가 일치하도록 has로 써야 한다.

5 전치사 to의 목적어로 쓰인 복합관계사절에 주어가 없으므로 '누가 듣더라도'의 의미가 되도록 복합관계대명사 whoever를 써야 한다.

6 선행사가 장소이고 이어지는 절이 구성 성분을 모두 갖춘 완전한 절이므로 관계부사 where를 써야 한다.

STEP 3 **Sentence Practice** p. 142

Ⓐ **1** a. which I was born in

b. This is the house in which the great scholar was born. [This is the house which (that) the great scholar was born in.]

2 a. what you have

b. Take out what you have in your bags and put everything on the desk.

3 a. who lives next door

b. who lives in China, teaches computer science

4 a. where my parents like to have dinner

b. This is the dessert shop where I buy some pies on Sundays.

Ⓑ **1** The man whom you met yesterday is my uncle.

---

2 I cannot figure out how I should open this bottle.

3 She ended up coming in second place, which was very disappointing to her.

4 I want to move to a place where nobody recognizes me.

Ⓐ **1** 관계대명사가 전치사의 목적어일 때 전치사는 관계사절 끝에 오거나 관계대명사 앞에 올 수 있다.

2 what은 선행사를 포함한 관계대명사이다.

3 계속적 용법으로 관계대명사 앞에 콤마(,)를 써서 선행사에 대한 추가 정보를 제공한다.

4 선행사가 장소인 경우 관계부사 where를 쓴다.

Ⓑ **1** 선행사가 사람이고 목적격 관계대명사인 경우 whom을 쓴다.

2 선행사가 방법인 경우 관계부사 how를 쓴다.

3 which가 앞 절의 내용 전체를 받는다.

4 선행사가 장소인 경우 관계부사 where를 쓴다.

ACTUAL TEST pp. 143-146

1 ② **2** ④ **3** ③ **4** ⑤ **5** ① **6** ③ **7** ④
8 ① **9** ④ **10** ③ **11** ② **12** ① **13** ⑤ **14** ④
15 ③ **16** ④ **17** ④ **18** ③ **19** ⑤ **20** ② **21** ③

22 who did not have a cell phone

23 my passport, which was very annoying

24 I don't like films which (that) have sad endings.

25 Whenever you open that website, you will see an ad pop up first.

26 The house where they have lived for 20 years needs repairs.

27 My friend Yuna, whose mother is Japanese, went to Japan to see her grandparents.

28 Nobody knew the reason why he left the village.

CHALLENGE!

01 [예시 답] I want to have friends who are willing to listen to me whenever I want to talk.

02 [예시 답] March 2, when Jiho and I became best friends, is a special day.

1 선행사가 사람일 때 주격 관계대명사는 who이다.

2 문맥상 선행사 a family가 소유한 집을 나타내야 하므로 소유격 관계대명사를 쓴다.

3 동물이 선행사일 때 전치사의 목적어로 쓰일 수 있는 관계대명사는 which이다.

4 선행사가 사람이고 이어지는 절에 주어가 없으므로 주격 관계대명사 who가 알맞다.

5 what은 the thing that〔which〕으로 바꿔 쓸 수 있다.

6 no matter where는 wherever로 바꿔 쓸 수 있다.

7 관계부사 how와 선행사 the way는 함께 쓰일 수 없으므로 둘 중 하나를 쓴다.

8 ①은 접속사 that이며, 나머지는 모두 선행사를 꾸며 주는 형용사절을 이끄는 관계대명사 that이다.

9 ④는 선행사를 포함한 관계대명사이고 나머지는 의문사 what이다. 의문사 what은 직접 또는 간접의문문에 쓰인다.

10 장소 선행사 a place 뒤에 관계부사 where 또는 in which가, 사람 선행사 children 뒤에 주격 관계대명사 who가 필요하다.

11 선행사 the dog의 뒤에 주격 관계대명사 that 또는 which가, 장소 선행사 a clinic 뒤에 계속적 용법의 관계부사 where가 필요하다.

12 '그가 나를 볼 때마다'라는 의미이므로 whenever가, '내가 무엇을 하든'이라는 의미이므로 Whatever가 알맞다.

13 관계부사 where는 선행사가 place와 같이 일반적인 의미일 경우 생략할 수 있고, 목적격 관계대명사도 생략 가능하지만 주격 관계대명사는 생략할 수 없다.

14 관계부사 why는 선행사가 reason과 같이 일반적인 의미일 경우 생략할 수 있고, 목적격 관계대명사도 생략 가능하지만 소유격 관계대명사는 생략할 수 없다.

15 주어진 문장의 that은 관계대명사이다.

16 주어진 문장의 that은 명사절을 이끄는 접속사 that이다.

17 ④ who를 소유격 관계대명사 whose로 고쳐야 한다.

18 ③ 관계대명사가 전치사의 목적어일 때 전치사는 관계사절 끝에 오거나 관계대명사의 앞에 올 수 있으므로 which 앞의 in이나 ourselves 다음의 in 중 하나를 삭제해야 한다.

19 '내가 그에게 언제 전화를 하더라도'라는 의미로, Whenever는 No matter when으로 바꿔 쓸 수 있다.

20 유사관계대명사 but은 「that . . . not」과 같은 의미를 나타낸다.

21 유사관계대명사 as는 관계대명사 which처럼 쓰인다.

22 선행사가 사람일 때 계속적 용법에 쓰이는 주격 관계대명사 who를 사용한다.

23 앞의 내용 전체를 가리키는 관계대명사의 계속적 용법에 알맞은 which를 쓴다.

24 선행사가 사물이므로 관계대명사 which 또는 that을 써야 하며 선행사 films가 복수이므로 관계사절에 복수동사를 써야 한다.

25 No matter when은 복합관계대명사 whenever로 나타낼 수 있다.

26 「장소 선행사 + where + 주어 + 동사」 어순에 유의한다.

27 선행사가 사람일 때 소유격을 나타내는 관계대명사 whose가 계속적 용법으로 쓰여 선행사에 대한 추가 정보를 제공한다.

28 「the reason + why + 주어 + 동사」 어순에 유의한다.

CHALLENGE!

01 선행사가 사람일 때 who는 주격 관계대명사, whom은 목적격 관계대명사이다.

02 선행사가 시간인 경우 관계부사 when을 사용한다.

CHAPTER

11

Subjunctive Mood

UNIT 01 Subjunctives p. 149

A **1** would **2** were **3** had had
4 could **5** had not

B **1** had known **2** would keep
3 had not moved **4** could have shared
5 were not

C **1** had not died **2** had ignored
3 would enjoy **4** could buy

D **1** If I were you, would not go out
2 had told, would have been put
3 had not rained, play soccer
4 had hurried, would not have missed

UNIT 02 I wish/as if/It is time + Subjunctive p. 151

A **1** were **2** had worked
3 had been **4** had not said
5 had read

B **1** knew **2** had lived
3 had done **4** saw

C **1** were **2** had
3 take **4** stopped
5 think

D **1** were my real brother
2 had not argued with
3 as if he found
4 It is high time you went to school

UNIT 03 Implied Subjunctive / Leaving Out *if* p. 153

A **1** would **2** Without **3** To see
4 be **5** would be

B **1** Were I you
2 Had I not moved
3 Had I a mentor
4 Should it cost

C **1** it were not for his help
2 it had not been for your advice
3 it were not for your help
4 it had not been for his support

D **1** Otherwise, I would have hit
2 it not for water
3 How would life be

WRITING CONNECTION

p. 154

STEP 1 Grammar Check-up

Ⓐ 1 ⓒ   2 ⓓ   3 ⓓ   4 ⓐ   5 ⓑ

Ⓑ 1 ⓑ said   2 ⓑ will go
  3 ⓑ have   4 ⓑ went
  5 ⓐ made   6 ⓐ had bought

Ⓐ 1 단순 조건절이므로 주절에 조동사 will을 사용한다.
  2 혼합 가정법으로 '내가 캐나다에서 태어났더라면'은 과거 사실에 반대되는 가정이므로 「If + 주어 + had p.p.」로 나타낸다.
  3 주절의 시제를 보아 가정법 과거완료이므로 if절은 「had + p.p.」로 나타낸다.
  4 현재 많은 돈이 없는 것의 아쉬움을 나타내므로 「I wish + 주어 + 과거동사」를 사용한다.
  5 주절의 시제로 보아 가정법 과거 문장이므로 「If + 주어 + 과거동사」로 나타낸다. if절의 동사가 be동사일 경우 were를 사용한다.

Ⓑ 1 현재 일에 대한 아쉬움을 나타내므로 「I wish + 주어 + 과거동사」를 사용한다.
  2 단순 조건절이므로 주절은 「will + 동사원형」으로 나타낸다.
  3 혼합 가정법으로 주절에는 「주어 + would + 동사원형」이 와야 한다.
  4 「It is time + 주어 + 과거동사」이므로 goes가 went가 되어야 한다.
  5 현재 사실의 반대이므로 가정법 과거를 사용한다.
  6 가정법 과거완료이므로 「If + 주어 + had p.p.」로 나타낸다.

p. 155

STEP 2 Phrases to Sentences

Ⓐ 1 If she had kept
  2 If he had been more serious
  3 were good at making speeches
  4 would visit, knew
  5 as if it were
  6 Otherwise, have gotten injured

Ⓑ 1 will → If I spoke English fluently, I would not worry about the interview.
  2 knows → Mina talks as if she knew lots of celebrities, but she does not.
  3 did not fight → Jessica would come to the party if she had not fought with you yesterday.
  4 Not had it been → Had it not been for the map, we would not have found our way home.
  5 were born → If he had been born in better circumstances, he would be pursuing his dream now.

6 of → If it were not for an elbow injury, she would play basketball.

Ⓐ 1 가정법 과거완료이므로 if절에 had p.p., 주절에 would have p.p.를 사용한다.
  2 가정법 과거완료이므로 if절에 had p.p., 주절에 would have p.p.를 사용한다.
  3 현재 사실에 대한 유감을 나타내므로 「I wish + 주어 + 과거동사」를 사용한다.
  4 가정법 과거이므로 주절에 「would + 동사원형」, if절에 과거동사를 사용한다.
  5 「as if + 가정법 과거」는 현재 사실의 반대를 표현한다.
  6 Otherwise는 '그러지 않았더라면'이라는 의미로 if절 대용어구로 사용된다.

Ⓑ 1 가정법 과거이므로 if절에 과거동사, 주절에 「would + 동사원형」을 사용한다.
  2 현재 사실의 반대를 가정하고 있으므로 「as if + 주어 + 과거동사」를 사용한다.
  3 혼합 가정법으로 주절에는 「would + 동사원형」, if절에는 had p.p.가 와야 한다.
  4 if절에서 if를 생략하고 had와 주어를 도치한 형태이다.
  5 혼합 가정법으로 if절에는 had p.p.가 와야 한다.
  6 '~이 없다면'은 「If it were not for + 명사」로 나타낸다.

p. 156

STEP 3 Sentence Practice

Ⓐ 1 a. wish he thought
     b. I wish he were diligent
  2 a. had not been, would have bought
     b. If the price of the dress had been reasonable, I would have bought it.
  3 a. as if he understood English
     b. The dog looked at me as if it understood my words.

Ⓑ 1 If I had not broken my leg, I would go skiing with you.
  2 If I were John, I would choose baseball rather than studying.
  3 If I had learned to swim, I might be enjoying myself in the pool now.
  4 Medical treatment would help you heal better.
  5 Being left alone, Michael would play computer games all day.

Ⓐ 1 「I wish + 주어 + 과거동사」 '~라면 좋을 텐데'
  2 과거 사실에 반대되는 가정을 하고 있으므로 가정법 과거완료 「if + 주어 + had p.p., 주어 + would + have + p.p.」
  3 「as if + 주어 + 과거동사」 '마치 ~인 것처럼'

B **1** 혼합 가정법 「If + 주어 + had p.p., 주어 + would + 동사원형」
2 가정법 과거 「If + 주어 + 과거동사, 주어 + would + 동사원형」
3 혼합 가정법 「If + 주어 + had p.p., 주어 + might + 동사원형」
4 명사구 Medical treatment가 if절의 의미를 대신한다.
5 분사구문이 if절의 의미를 대신한다.

ACTUAL TEST
pp. 157-160

1 ⑤ **2** ④ **3** ② **4** ① **5** ③ **6** ② **7** ④
8 ④ **9** ② **10** ④ **11** ④ **12** ③ **13** ④ **14** ⑤
15 ④ **16** ④ **17** ④ **18** ① **19** ② **20** ⑤ **21** ②
22 I wish I had not eaten
23 It is high time that
24 If Mina did not forget her bus card, she would not be late for school.
25 If I had taken my parents' advice, I would be happier now.
26 Alex eats fast as if he had something urgent to do.
27 If it had not been for his advice, I would not have started the business.
28 I wish you were more polite to others.

CHALLENGE!

01 [예시 답] If I had a billion won, I would donate most of the money to charity.
02 [예시 답] I wish I had studied harder when I was in elementary school.

1 가정법 문장으로 가정법에는 접속사 if가 사용된다.
2 가정법 과거완료의 if절에는 had p.p.가 온다.
3 현재의 일에 대한 아쉬움을 나타낼 때는 「I wish + 주어 + 과거동사」이므로 빈칸에는 had가 알맞다.
4 (A) 가정법 과거이므로 if절에 과거동사를 쓴다.
(B) 주장, 제안, 요구의 동사의 목적절에 「should + 동사원형」을 쓰며, 이때 should는 보통 생략한다.
5 (A) 단순 조건절이므로 if절에 현재시제를 쓴다.
(B) 혼합 가정법이므로 「If + 주어 + had p.p., 주어 + would/could/might + 동사원형」으로 쓴다.
6 ② 가정법 과거의 주절은 「주어 + would/could/might + 동사원형」이다.
7 ④ 주절이 과거완료인 것으로 보아 가정법 과거완료 문장이므로 밑줄 친 부분은 had not been이 되어야 한다.
8 과거 사실의 반대를 가정하고 있으므로 가정법 과거완료로 if절에 had p.p., 주절에 would have p.p.를 쓴다.
9 「It is (high) time (+ that) + 주어 + 과거동사」의 형태로 주절의 시제가 is로 현재시제이지만 that절의 동사는 가정법 과거에 맞게 써야 한다.

10 혼합 가정법 「If + 가정법 과거완료, 가정법 과거」 형태에서 if가 생략되어 주어와 동사가 도치되었다.
11 명사구가 if절을 대신하는 경우이다.
12 '여행이 좀 더 길었더라면 너를 방문했을 텐데'라는 의미로, 과거 사실의 반대를 나타내는 가정법 과거완료를 쓴다.
13 「I wish + 주어 + 과거동사」 '~라면 좋을 텐데'
14 모두 가정법 과거인데 ⑤는 가정법 과거완료로 의미상으로 한 시제 앞선다.
15 Otherwise는 '그러지 않았더라면'이라는 의미로 if절 대용어구로 사용되며 과거 사실의 반대이므로 주절에서는 would 다음에 동사원형이 와야 한다.
16 가정법 과거완료로 빈칸에 모두 had done이 들어가지만 ④는 가정법 과거이므로 did가 들어간다.
17 과거 일에 대한 유감을 표현하는 구문으로 빈칸에 모두 had given이 들어가지만 ④는 미래의 바람을 말하고 있으므로 would give가 들어간다.
18 「as if + 주어 + 과거동사」는 현재 사실의 반대를 가정한다.
19 주장, 제안, 요구의 동사의 목적절에는 「should + 동사원형」을 쓴다.
20 ⑤는 부정사구가 if절의 의미를 대신하고 있다. 가정법 문장은 현재의 반대를 나타내므로 그는 외국인이 아니다.
21 ②는 가정법 과거완료 문장에서 if가 생략되면서 주어와 동사가 도치된 경우이므로 if절은 If he had been at school이 되어야 한다.
22 과거 사실에 대한 유감, 아쉬움을 나타내므로 「I wish + 주어 + had p.p.」를 사용한다.
23 「It is (high) time + 주어 + 과거동사」 '~해야 할 시간이다'
24 가정법 과거이므로 if절에 과거동사를 사용한다.
25 혼합 가정법으로 과거에 부모님의 충고를 받아들이지 않은 것이 현재 영향을 미치는 것이므로 had been은 be가 되어야 한다.
26 「as if + 주어 + 과거동사」는 현재 사실의 반대를 가정한다.
27 「If it had not been for + 명사」 '~이 없었다면'
28 「I wish + 주어 + 과거동사」 '~라면 좋을 텐데'

CHALLENGE!

01 가정법 과거: 「If + 주어 + 과거동사, 주어 + would/could/might + 동사원형」
02 「I wish + 주어 + had p.p.」 '~했더라면 좋을 텐데'

Agreement & Narration

UNIT 01 Number Agreement p. 163

A 1 has 2 is 3 is
4 is 5 were

B 1 has 2 were 3 has
4 are 5 was

C 1 have 2 is 3 was
4 is 5 have

D 1 A number of students take part in
2 composer is going to
3 one-fifth of the pizza has
4 Most of the students know

UNIT 02 Tense Agreement p. 165

A 1 was 2 came 3 have to
4 had had 5 wonder 6 had met

B 1 was taking 2 would be waiting
3 had received 4 must protect

C 1 began 2 borders 3 helps
4 takes a walk 5 makes

D 1 would not be late again 2 he had studied
3 there are more than

UNIT 03 Indirect Speech p. 167

A 1 that, was 2 had been, before
3 told, should 4 lived, then

B 1 what my name was
2 how old her sister was
3 where his parents were

C 1 if (whether) it was 2 I would
3 to buy 4 not to

D 1 why he was so late 2 had already left for
3 if (whether) he could speak English
4 My mother advised me not to waste my time.

WRITING CONNECTION

STEP 1 Grammar Check-up p. 168

A 1 ⓐ 2 ⓑ 3 ⓐ 4 ⓓ 5 ⓒ 6 ⓑ

B 1 ⓐ growl 2 ⓑ hobbies
3 ⓑ weighs 4 ⓐ is
5 ⓑ was 6 ⓑ told

A 1 now로 보아 현재시제이며 금액 표현은 단수 취급한다.
2 「the + 형용사」는 '…한 사람들'이라는 뜻으로 복수 취급한다.
3 간접화법에서도 시제 일치 규칙이 적용되어, 주절의 시제가 과거일 때 종속절의 시제는 과거나 과거완료가 된다.
4 주절의 시제가 과거이므로 종속절의 시제도 과거로 맞춘다.
5 주절의 시제가 과거이므로 목적절의 시제도 과거로 맞춘다.
6 주절의 시제가 과거이므로 종속절의 시제도 과거로 맞춘다.

B 1 주어가 복수명사 The dogs이므로 복수동사를 쓴다.
2 주어가 서핑과 암벽 등반 등 두 가지로 복수이므로 복수명사로 지칭해야 한다.
3 each 다음의 명사와 동사는 단수형이어야 한다.
4 「관사 + 명사 and 명사」는 한 사람을 나타내므로 단수 취급한다.
5 「the number of + 복수명사」는 단수 취급한다.
6 주절의 시제가 과거이므로 종속절의 시제도 과거로 써야 한다.

STEP 2 Phrases to Sentences p. 169

A 1 Half (of) the cake has
2 who spoke English
3 A number of people come
4 Two years seems like a long time
5 Each student is
6 what the fight was about

B 1 will → I heard you would leave for Canada soon.
2 were → Some of the money was spent to buy clothes.
3 becomes → They learned that Korea became independent from Japan in 1945.
4 are → Measles is a highly contagious disease caused by a virus.
5 have excited → The arrival of new spring fashions has excited young shoppers.
6 was → Dad couldn't make it to dinner because his office is usually busy on Mondays.

A 1 「half + (of)」 뒤에 오는 명사의 수에 동사를 일치시킨다.
2 주절의 시제가 과거이므로 종속절의 시제도 이에 맞춘다.
3 a number of는 many의 의미로 뒤에 복수명사가 오며, 복수동사를 취한다.
4 시간 표현은 단수 취급한다.
5 each 다음의 명사와 동사는 단수형이어야 한다.
6 의문사가 있는 의문의 간접화법은 「의문사 + 주어 + 동사」의 순서로 쓴다. 동사는 the fight에 맞춰 단수형으로 써야 하며 주절이 과거이므로 종속절도 과거로 써야 한다.

B 1 주절이 과거시제이므로 종속절의 will은 would가 되어야 한다.
2 some of 뒤에 오는 명사의 수에 동사를 일치시킨다. money는 셀 수 없는 명사이므로 단수 취급한다.

3 역사적 사실은 과거시제로 쓴다.

4 -s로 끝나는 병명은 단수 취급한다.

5 주어부는 The arrival of new spring fashions로, the arrival에 맞춰 동사를 단수형으로 고쳐야 한다.

6 because 이하의 종속절에서 usually를 사용해 일상적이고 습관적인 사실을 말하고 있으므로 현재시제로 써야 한다.

STEP3 Sentence Practice p. 170

A 1 a. what we were doing
  b. She asked me what I was doing in her room.
 2 a. have been friends
  b. The actor and the actress are rivals in this film.
 3 a. thought, was killed
  b. Everyone thought she would major in piano in college.
 4 a. advised me to save
  b. The parents advised the little boy to behave properly in the restaurant.

B 1 If someone is using my personal information, what should I do?
 2 The nurse asked him whether he had eaten breakfast.
 3 Watching action movies is the way I relieve my stress.

A 1 의문사가 있는 의문문의 간접화법은 「의문사 + 주어 + 동사」의 순서로 쓴다.
 2 「관사 + 명사 + and + 관사 + 명사」는 두 사람을 나타내므로 복수 취급한다.
 3 주절의 시제가 과거이므로 종속절의 시제도 이에 맞춘다.
 4 명령문을 간접화법으로 전환할 때는 to부정사를 이용한다.

B 1 -one은 단수 취급한다.
 2 간접화법에서 전달문의 시제가 과거이고, 피전달문이 그보다 이전에 일어난 일이므로 과거완료로 표현한다.
 3 동명사구가 주어인 경우 단수 취급한다.

ACTUAL TEST pp. 171-174

1 ③ 2 ③ 3 ② 4 ④ 5 ② 6 ⑤ 7 ④
8 ③ 9 ④ 10 ④ 11 ① 12 ④ 13 ① 14 ②
15 ⑤ 16 ② 17 ③ 18 ⑤ 19 ④ 20 ⑤ 21 ③

22 (A) are (B) remains
23 Both my brother and I are well aware
24 Susan asked me where I would be on Christmas.
25 Mr. Smith told us (that) practice makes perfect.
26 Every man and every woman is given two towels in the sauna.
27 Fifteen kilometers is too far to walk.
28 The nurse told me to lie down on the bed.

CHALLENGE!

01 [예시 답] Both Sangmin and I have a good sense of humor.
02 [예시 답] About one-third of my classmates are girls.

1 수리적 사실은 현재시제로 쓰고 거리 단위는 단수 취급한다.
2 국명은 형태가 복수일지라도 단수 취급한다.
3 명사절이 주어인 경우 단수 취급하고 주절의 시제가 과거이므로 was가 알맞다.
4 almost는 부사로 뒤에 of를 쓰지 않는다.
5 「half + of」 뒤에 오는 명사의 수에 동사를 일치시킨다. 이때 명사가 셀 수 없는 것이면 단수 취급한다.
6 ⑤ -s로 끝나더라도 과목명은 단수 취급한다.
7 ④ each는 각각의 것을 나타내므로 단수 취급한다.
8 ③ 주절의 동사 knew에 맞게 의문사절의 동사가 과거형 was가 되어야 한다.
9 주절의 시제가 과거이므로 인용 부호 안에 있던 현재완료는 간접화법에서 과거완료가 되어야 한다.
10 의문사가 없는 의문문은 화법 전환 시 if나 whether를 사용하여 간접의문문으로 만든다.
11 의문사가 있는 의문문을 간접화법으로 전환 시 어순은 간접의문문의 어순 「의문사 + 주어 + 동사」를 따른다. 또한 주절의 시제가 과거이므로 종속절의 동사 leave도 과거형이 되어야 한다.
12 평서문과 명령문의 간접화법 전환 시 said to는 told로 바뀌어야 한다.
13 주절의 동사가 과거형인 thought이므로 이에 맞게 종속절에는 과거완료가 와야 한다. 따라서 have는 had가 되어야 한다.
14 콤마 사이의 부분은 삽입구이므로 문장의 주어인 The politician에 맞추어 동사 are는 is가 되어야 한다.
15 (A) 과학적 사실은 현재시제로 나타내므로 is가 와야 한다.
   (B) half of 다음에 나오는 명사가 복수형이므로 동사도 복수형이 되어야 하고 시제가 현재이므로 do not이 와야 한다.
16 주절이 과거일 때 종속절의 시제는 과거 또는 과거완료가 되어야 하므로 ②의 has moved는 moved 또는 had moved가 되어야 한다.
17 모두 is가 들어가야 하는데, ③은 both가 쓰였으므로 are가 들어가야 한다.

18 모두 has가 들어가야 하는데, ⑤는 주어가 복수형이므로 have가 들어가야 한다.

19 모두 과거형 did가 들어가야 하는데, ④는 John의 일반적인 성향을 나타내므로 현재형 does가 들어가야 한다.

20 명령문을 간접화법으로 전환 시에는 to부정사를 이용하므로, ⑤는 "The wife begged her husband not to take any risks."가 되어야 알맞다.

21 "Did you submit the papers in time?"이라는 의문문을 간접화법으로 전환한 것이므로, 의문사가 없는 의문문의 간접화법 전환 시 필요한 if 또는 whether가 들어가야 한다.

[22-23] 해석

　　나의 부모님이 미국으로 온 주요 이유 중 하나는 우리에게 좋은 교육적, 경제적 기회를 제공하고픈 바람이었다. 나의 형과 나 둘 다 그들이 우리를 위해 정말 열심히 일하고 계신다는 것을 잘 알고 있다. 우리 부모님의 노력과 희생은 우리가 최선을 다하게 하는 동기 부여의 원천이다. 대부분의 이민자 아이들처럼, 우리는 우리의 부모님을 부양해야 한다는 강한 의무감을 느낀다. 나는 우리가 가족에 두는 가치가 대부분의 다른 미국 아이들보다 높게 남아 있다고 생각한다.

22 (A) 주어가 복수명사이므로 are를 쓴다.

　　(B) 셀 수 없는 명사 the value가 주어이므로 단수동사를 쓴다.

23 종속절의 시제에 맞게 주절의 동사를 현재시제로 맞춰야 하고, 「both A and B」는 복수 취급하므로 복수동사로 고친다.

24 의문사가 있는 의문문의 간접화법 전환이다. said to는 asked로, will은 would로 바꾸고 「의문사 + 주어 + 동사」의 순서로 인용 부호 안의 내용을 정리한다.

25 평서문의 간접화법 전환이다. said to는 told로 바꾸고, 인용 부호를 없애고 that을 쓴다. 이때 that은 생략 가능하다. 인용 부호 안의 내용이 속담이므로 현재시제로 쓴다.

26 「every + 명사 + and + every + 명사」는 단수 취급한다.

27 거리 표현은 단수 취급한다.

28 명령문의 간접화법 전환은 to부정사를 이용한다.

CHALLENGE!

01 「both A and B」는 복수 취급한다.

02 「분수 + of」 다음에 나온 명사의 수에 동사를 일치시킨다.

CHAPTER

13

Sentence Arrangement

UNIT **01**　Emphasis, Negation, & Parallel Structure　p. 177

A　**1** do　　　　**2** finish　　　　**3** did
　　4 It　　　　**5** that

B　**1** No　　　　**2** no one　　　　**3** either
　　4 anything　　**5** any / no 삭제
　　6 Not all　　　**7** not always

C　**1** riding　　　**2** accurately
　　3 kindness　　**4** playing

D　**1** not only money but also fame
　　2 Not every boy likes
　　3 It is in this drawer that
　　4 do appreciate your help

UNIT **02**　Apposition, Inversion, & Ellipsis　p. 179

A　**1** Robin, a hot-tempered soccer player
　　2 Mrs. Robinson, one of my neighbors
　　3 The fact that he is the son of a rich man
　　4 the odds of winning the lottery

B　**1** walked the teacher　　**2** do I sleep
　　3 came the rain　　　　**4** did I know
　　5 is Sam

C　**1** He was, and (he) will remain, the greatest basketball player.
　　2 I will have to go this way, and you (will have to go) that way.
　　3 My mom enjoys reading books while (she is) drinking coffee on Sunday.
　　4 I ate much more food at the buffet than he (did).
　　5 Did Kate return the books (that) she borrowed last week?
　　6 I wish I had known (that) James moved to another school.

D　**1** comes love, comes marriage
　　2 Thomas, the brightest student in our class
　　3 will I go back

WRITING CONNECTION

p. 180

STEP 1 Grammar Check-up

A 1 ⓒ 2 ⓓ 3 ⓒ 4 ⓐ 5 ⓑ

B 1 ⓑ did 2 ⓑ did he
3 ⓐ to become 4 ⓑ that
5 ⓑ will I 6 ⓐ that

A 1 과거시제 문장에서 동사를 강조하는 조동사 did가 쓰였다.
2 조동사 did가 있고 주어와 도치된 것으로 보아 부정어가 문두에 온다.
3 「시간의 접속사 + (주어 + be동사) + 현재 분사」 형태이다.
4 동격의 that절이 쓰여 선행 명사(The fact)의 의미를 보충하는 경우이다.
5 부사구를 강조하기 위해 문두에 오면 주어와 조동사가 도치된다.

B 1 과거시제 절에서 동사를 강조할 때 did를 쓴다.
2 부정어 nor가 절 앞으로 나오면 주어와 조동사가 도치된다.
3 동격의 to부정사가 선행 명사 His desire의 의미를 보충하는 경우이다.
4 「It is〔was〕... that」 강조 구문이다.
5 문두에 부정 부사구가 오면 주어와 조동사가 도치된다.
6 동격은 that으로 나타낸다.

p. 181

STEP 2 Phrases to Sentences

A 1 Neal, a math genius
2 It is, that makes
3 did we see
4 live dozens of homeless
5 Neither of them
6 did, so did

B 1 come → Here comes the rain!
2 Not → Neither 〔None〕 of these shirts fits me perfectly.
3 open → She packed her suitcase, opened the door, and ran down the stairs.
4 to surrender → He would rather die than surrender to the enemy.
5 precise → Students were asked to do their assignments accurately and precisely.
6 thought she → Little did she think that Jake would call her again.

A 1 두 명사가 콤마로 이어져, 하나의 명사가 다른 하나의 의미를 보충하는 동격 구문이다.
2 「It is〔was〕... that」 강조 구문이다. that절의 동사의 수를 this awful weather에 맞춤에 유의한다.
3 「nor + 조동사 (did) + 주어 +동사원형」의 순서가 된다.
4 부사구가 문두에 오면 주어와 동사가 도치된다.

5 neither를 사용하여 '아무도 …하지 않다'라는 전체부정의 의미를 나타낸다.
6 과거시제 절에서 동사를 강조할 때 did를 쓴다.
「so V + S」: …도 그렇다

B 1 부사 here가 문두에 옴으로써 주어와 동사가 도치되었다. 다만 주어가 the rain이므로 수일치를 위해서 동사는 comes가 된다.
2 「of + 복수명사」와 함께 쓰이는 부정어는 neither나 none이다.
3 등위접속사로 연결된 두 개 이상의 구나 절은 같은 문법 형태여야 하는데, packed와 ran은 과거형이나 open만 현재형이므로 opened로 고친다.
4 'B하느니 A하겠다'는 뜻의 「would rather A than B」 형태이다. die와 surrender가 병렬 구조를 이뤄야하므로 to surrender에서 to를 삭제한다.
5 등위접속사로 연결된 두 개 이상의 단어, 구, 절은 문법적으로 형태가 같아야 하므로 precise는 precisely가 되어야 한다.
6 일반동사가 쓰인 문장에서 부정어 little이 문두에 왔으므로 do를 이용하여 주어와 동사가 도치되어야 한다.

p. 182

STEP 3 Sentence Practice

A 1 a. eats, watches
b. He takes a shower, has breakfast, and rides his bike
2 a. It was Jake who made
b. It was Ashley who 〔that〕 kicked the ball
3 a. did ask her, be more careful
b. I did ask him to help me.
4 a. did I expect to overcome
b. a finger did he move

B 1 You can either take the number 5 bus or walk to the theater.
2 It was at her aunt's wedding that Emma sang the song.
3 We did have a good time at Jimmy's birthday party.

A 1 등위접속사로 연결된 두 개 이상의 단어, 구, 절은 문법적으로 형태가 같아야 한다.
2 「It is〔was〕... that」 강조 구문에서 강조하는 것이 사람일 경우 that 대신 who를 쓸 수 있다.
3 과거시제 문장에서 동사를 강조할 때 did를 쓴다.
4 부정어가 문두에 오면 주어와 동사가 도치되며, 조동사가 없는 일반동사 문장에서는 do가 조동사 대신 쓰인다. 시제가 과거이므로 did를 사용한다.

B 1 「either A or B」에서 A와 B는 병렬 구조를 이루어 문법적으로 같은 형태가 와야 한다.
2 「It is〔was〕... that」 강조 구문에서 강조하는 말은 It과 that 사이에 쓴다.
3 일반동사를 강조하기 위해서는 조동사 do를 동사 앞에 쓴다. 시제가 과거이므로 did를 사용한다.

1 ⑤ **2** ④ **3** ① **4** ⑤ **5** ③ **6** ① **7** ⑤

8 ④ **9** ⑤ **10** ② **11** ② **12** ③ **13** ② **14** ①

15 ③ **16** ④ **17** ④ **18** ⑤ **19** ④ **20** ③ **21** ③

22 Sally likes neither watching movies nor listening to music.

23 It was at that moment that I achieved my goal of being a curator.

24 not always

25 Not until 2 o'clock did the shop open.

26 My parents are going to the concert, and so am I.

27 David heard the news that the meeting had been postponed while on vacation.

28 have I seen such a rude waiter

CHALLENGE!

01 [예시 답] After I woke up, I took a shower, put on my school uniform, ate breakfast, and then took the bus to school.

02 [예시 답] It is pursuing my dreams that makes my life meaningful.

---

1 상관접속사 「neither A nor B」에서 A와 B는 병렬을 이루므로, smokes에 맞춰 빈칸에는 3인칭 단수의 현재형 동사가 들어가야 한다.

2 빈칸 다음에 동사원형이 온 것으로 보아 빈칸에는 동사를 강조하는 조동사가 들어가는 것이 알맞다. 또한 과거를 나타내는 부사 yesterday가 있으므로 조동사의 과거형이 들어가야 함을 알 수 있다.

3 「It is〔was〕. . . that」강조 구문이다.

4 두 가지를 동시에 부정하려면 'A와 B 둘 다 …아니다'라는 의미의 「neither A nor B」를 쓴다.

5 '…도 마찬가지로 아니다'라는 부정 동의는 「neither + (조)동사 + 주어」 형태로 쓴다.

6 '…도 마찬가지이다'라는 긍정 동의는 「so + (조)동사 + 주어」 형태로 쓴다.

7 강조의 조동사 do 다음에는 동사원형이 오므로 I did saw는 I did see가 되어야 한다.

8 부정어가 문두에 올 경우 주어와 동사가 도치되므로 ④ Little I knew는 Little did I know가 되어야 한다.

9 등위접속사 and로 이어지고 있으므로 「how to + 동사원형」이 병렬 구조로 쓰여야 한다.

10 문두에 부정어가 오고 동사가 완료형일 경우 어순은 「부정어 + have〔had〕 + 주어 + p.p.」가 된다.

11 동사가 부정된 상태에서 전체 부정어 neither가 쓰이면 부정의 의미가 중복되므로 neither는 either가 되어야 한다.

12 that day로 보아 시제가 과거이므로 빈칸에는 과거시제 문장에서 동사를 강조하는 did가 알맞다.

13 부정어가 문두에 오면 주어와 조동사가 도치되며 우리말 해석이 '본

적이 없었다'이므로 시제는 과거완료를 사용한다.

14 부사구가 강조되느라 문두에 오면 주어와 동사가 도치된다.

15 동사 아닌 다른 문장 요소를 강조할 때는 「It is〔was〕 + 강조 내용 + that」을 쓴다. 시제가 과거이므로 was를 사용한다.

16 일반동사를 강조할 때는 동사 앞에 조동사 do를 쓰고 일반동사는 원형으로 쓴다. 주어진 문장이 현재시제이고 주어가 3인칭 단수이므로 does를 사용한다.

17 ① . . . and Ashley (has sun allergies), too. ② . . . if (it is) possible. ③ . . . but I'd rather not (tell him about his mistakes). ⑤ Everything (that) James said . . . .

18 부사가 강조되느라 문두에 오더라도 주어가 대명사인 경우 주어와 동사는 도치되지 않는다.

19 neither A nor B는 '둘 다 …아니다'라는 의미로, 두 가지를 모두 부정한다.

20 the difficulty of 뒤에 이어지는 부분은 the difficulty와 동격을 이루며 그 내용을 보충 설명하므로 ③은 '새로운 동료들과 어울리는 어려움을 극복하는 데 용기가 필요하다.'라는 의미이다.

21 부사절에서 접속사 뒤의 「주어 + be동사」가 생략 가능하나 ③의 saw는 일반동사이므로 I saw는 생략할 수 없다.

22 「neither A nor B」 형태이므로 병렬 구조가 되도록 nor 뒤의 동사구를 동명사구로 고친다.

23 '큐레이터가 되는 목표'라는 뜻을 표현하기 위해 동격 구조를 쓴다. that도 동격에 쓰일 수 있지만, that은 주어와 동사를 가진 절을 이끌기에 이 문장에서는 「명사 + of + (동)명사」 형태의 동격을 이용한다.

24 '항상 …한 것은 아니다'는 not always로 나타낸다.

25 부정어 not until 2 o'clock을 문두로 이동하고 주어와 동사를 도치시킨다.

26 '…도 마찬가지다'는 「so + 동사 + 주어」로 쓴다.

27 the news와 that절이 동격을 이루고, 시간의 접속사 while이 이끄는 절에서 주어와 be동사가 생략되어 있다.

28 부정어 Never가 문두에 있으므로 현재완료는 have와 주어를 도치하여 have I seen으로 써야 한다.

CHALLENGE!

01 등위접속사로 연결된 두 개 이상의 단어, 구, 절은 문법적으로 형태가 같아야 한다.

02 「It is . . . that」 강조 구문에서 강조하는 말은 It과 that 사이에 쓴다.

CHAPTER 01 Sentence Patterns

UNIT 01 S + V & S + V+ C — pp. 2-3

A 1 occurred 2 looks 3 appeared
4 sea 5 sweet

B 1 arrived 2 sick 3 strong
4 happened 5 felt

C 1 turned 2 terrific
3 grew up 4 weird

D 1 Some people believe that UFOs <u>are appeared</u> around the world.
→ Some people believe that UFOs appear around the world.
2 If there is no one at the station, the train will <u>leave at</u> earlier than usual.
→ If there is no one at the station, the train will leave earlier than usual.
3 The sky suddenly got <u>darken</u>, and heavy rain started to pour.
→ The sky suddenly got dark, and heavy rain started to pour.
4 The instructions that my teacher gave to me seem <u>easily</u> to follow.
→ The instructions that my teacher gave to me seem easy to follow.

E 1 His plan seemed unrealistic at first. (At first, his plan seemed unrealistic.)
2 Some cheese smells disgusting to me, but my sister disagrees.
3 Walking her dog every morning became her daily routine.

F 1 became a bestseller
2 The audience stayed silent
3 I felt happy
4 Ted looked pleased

UNIT 02 S + V + O & S + V + I.O. + D.O. — pp. 4-5

A 1 the building 2 explain 3 practicing
4 to 5 resemble

B 1 to listen 2 calling 3 spending
4 of 5 discuss

C 1 a suit for him 2 the job to him
3 had prepared a cozy room for us
4 another song for them

D 1 Nick fell in love with Suzy at first sight and <u>married with</u> her last year.
→ Nick fell in love with Suzy at first sight and married her last year.
2 If you avoid <u>to go</u> to the dentist, your toothache will get worse in no time.
→ If you avoid going to the dentist, your toothache will get worse in no time.
3 The pharaohs of Egypt built pyramids <u>to</u> themselves for religious purposes.
→ The pharaohs of Egypt built pyramids for themselves for religious purposes.

E 1 He showed us some photos of his puppy.
2 He often attends the book fair to meet new authors.
3 When I visited his house, he cooked meatballs for me.
4 Why don't you teach me how to play the guitar?

F 1 left me his favorite watch
2 want to put the new bed
3 envied their captain his shooting skills
4 stopped doing yoga

UNIT 03 S + V + O + O.C. — pp. 6-7

A 1 her 2 waiting 3 feel
4 the hero 5 to advance

B 1 to watch 2 howl (howling) 3 come
4 innocent 5 take (taking)

C 1 crash (crashing) 2 solve
3 to open 4 painted

D 1 They appointed Mr. Parker the new manager.
2 Jim had his cell phone checked by the repairman because it would not turn on.
3 He encouraged the man to make a speech in front of the crowd.

E 1 She considers her teacher a role model in her life.
2 The P.E. teacher allowed the students to practice soccer until 4 p.m.
3 They asked me to accept the offer.
4 If we cancel the game on Saturday, everyone will think us weak.

F 1 reminded Peter to film
2 watched the pigeons peck (pecking)
3 made me wait

CHAPTER 02 Perfect Aspect

UNIT 01 Present Perfect — pp. 8-9

A 1 made 2 finished 3 has been
4 have been 5 visited 6 got

B 1 have been looking for 2 have been making
3 has been eating 4 has been studying
5 have, been living

C 1 working 2 have 3 dreamed
4 visited 5 been dating 6 have lost
7 has fought

D 1 It has been snowing
2 My brother has been playing the game
3 Jake has been doing a part-time job

E 1 She has been watching the drama since last week.
2 I have eaten Indian food a few times.
3 Minsu has gone to Brazil to see his relatives.
4 The fans have been waiting to see his concert for two hours.

F 1 The students have been taking their final exams for two days.
2 They have finally completed the group project.
3 A puppy has been sitting under the tree since I saw him.
4 We have had a good relationship for several years.

UNIT 02 Past Perfect / Future Perfect — pp. 10-11

A 1 had known 2 will have been finished
3 had been 4 will have painted
5 will have used 6 had gone

B 1 had been running
2 will have been working
3 had been sleeping
4 will have been teaching
5 had been learning

C 1 will have lived 2 had gone
3 have taken 4 had been
5 will have been 6 had been
7 had you been

D 1 I will have finished baking a chocolate cake
2 Ellen had been doing her homework
3 Jane will have been studying Korean

E 1 The tourists will have arrived at the airport by then.
2 The dance group will have performed three times by this summer.
3 When she got home, her son had gone out to meet his friends.
4 When I stopped by my aunt's house, she had been baking cookies.

F 1 Jim will have started a new career by the end of this year.
2 Jina will have been doing her homework for two hours by 5.
3 He was very tired because he had been working outside for a long time.

CHAPTER 03 Modals

UNIT 01 can, may, must, should — pp. 12-13

A 1 May 2 ought not to
3 cannot 4 be able to
5 must 6 should 7 can

B 1 cannot 2 May
3 was able to 4 must not
5 don't have to

C 1 must be 2 don't have to bring
3 will be able to finish

D 1 can 2 have to
3 were able to

E 1 You must take some medicine and get some rest.
2 Her rude attitude cannot be accepted.
3 You should not spit on the street.
4 May I use your pencil?

F 1 He will be able to participate in the competition.
2 Can you print my report?
3 She may (might) not agree with her daughter's opinion.
4 The students have to be on time for class.

UNIT 02 Other Expressions with Modals — pp. 14-15

A 1 rather 2 to be
3 should 4 had better not
5 may as well 6 must

B 1 had better take   2 must have been
  3 used to go   4 may as well make

C 1 그는 그의 소중한 자동차를 팔았음에 틀림없다.
  2 너는 밖에 나가기 전에 선크림을 바르는 게 낫겠다.
  3 그들은 변경된 계획을 알았어야 했는데.
  4 그 교수가 그의 이론을 입증했을 리가 없다.
  5 그는 프랑스에서 식당에서 일하곤 했다.

D 1 may as well   2 used to
  3 would rather

E 1 You had better talk about your interests with your
    parents.
  2 I used to play the piano when I felt down.
  3 I would rather buy a magazine online.
  4 The dogs must have lost track of him.

F 1 You may as well eat something before taking
    medicine.
  2 The doctor cannot have lied to his patient.
  3 You should have told the police about what you
    saw.
  4 He may have been a famous actor before.

CHAPTER 04 Passives

UNIT 01 Passive Voice   pp. 16-17

A 1 was injured   2 appeared
  3 is being written   4 consists of
  5 has been ignored   6 are planted
  7 was being cleaned

B 1 is held   2 washed
  3 arrive   4 has been built
  5 cook   6 was broken

C 1 will stay   2 resembles
  3 was delivered   4 was booked
  5 were taken   6 can be found

D 1 These machines are repaired by Brian.
  2 The black dress is worn by her on special days.
  3 The flowers are being watered by Mom.
  4 The postcards are going to be sent to my parents
    by me.

E 1 I am being examined by the doctor.
  2 Are you invited to the wedding?
  3 His paintings are going to be exhibited soon.

F 1 This cell phone has been used since last month.
  2 The political news is reported by Jessica every
    morning.
  3 This book was revised in 2018.
  4 The café will be closed next Monday.

UNIT 02 Passives of S+V+I.O.+D.O./S+V+O+O.C.   pp. 18-19

A 1 to stretch   2 taught
  3 president   4 was shown
  5 to   6 for   7 to

B 1 told to help   2 made for
  3 heard to talk (talking) 4 built for
  5 made to finish

C 1 was asked   2 was made very upset
  3 was given   4 were brought for

D 1 He was heard to shout (shouting) in a loud voice
    by me.
  2 Many questions are asked of me by him whenever
    we meet.
  3 New sneakers were bought for me by my parents.
  4 I was made to mop the kitchen floor by Mr.
    Jackson.

E 1 The students were made to write down their
    names.
  2 I was asked to send the package by her.
  3 He is considered one of the most powerful
    people in his country.

F 1 The Christmas cards will be sent to me by my
    friends.
  2 He was seen to take (taking) a bus by us.
  3 This mug was made for my grandma by my uncle.
  4 I am called Alex by my close friends.

UNIT 03 Other Passive Forms   pp. 20-21

A 1 with   2 run over by   3 with
  4 of   5 taken care of   6 put off
  7 looked down on by

B 1 at   2 to   3 of
  4 about   5 with

C 1 filled with   2 brought up
  3 known to   4 thought to be
  5 composed of   6 disappointed with

D 1 is said that the sports star is living in Paris
  2 was thought to be canceled
  3 was turned in by Cindy yesterday

E 1 The box is filled with many flavors of chocolate.

2 The food will be handed out to the homeless by the volunteers.

3 It is believed that he is one of the most honest people in town.

F 1 Is she interested in social issues?

  2 My computer was turned off by John.

  3 The street is crowded with a lot of visitors.

  4 He is always surrounded with (by) many friends.

CHAPTER 05 To-infinitives

UNIT 01 **Substantive To-infinitives** pp. 22-23

A 1 To spread   **2** to go   **3** to join

  4 It   **5** it   **6** to walk

B 1 나는 그 단어를 어떻게 발음해야 할지 모르겠다.

  2 그 아이는 누구를 믿어야 할지 확신하지 못했다.

  3 그는 나에게 오늘 무엇을 해야 할지 적으라고 조언했다.

  4 엄마는 나에게 그것을 어디에서 사야 할지 말씀해 주시지 않았다.

  5 언제 버튼을 눌러야 할지 말해 줄 수 있나요?

C 1 To eat   **2** to keep   **3** to use

  4 to read   **5** to listen

D 1 She was very angry and refused to speak to me.

  2 It is important to do your best.

  3 I hope to see you again.

  4 It is necessary to understand different cultures.

E 1 It is important to keep your promises.

  2 He decided to become a photographer.

  3 I think it rude to be noisy in the library.

F 1 My dream is to become a famous sports star.

  2 He found it difficult to forget the bad things.

  3 I am thinking about where to put the key.

  4 It will not be easy to finish this project by next week.

UNIT 02 **Adjective & Adverbial To-infinitives** pp. 24-25

A 1 to do   **2** to dance with

  3 are to   **4** to see

  5 to burn off   **6** to carry

B 1 Thomas는 내일 시드니에 도착할 예정이다.

  2 앉을 의자가 충분히 있다.

3 네 기분을 상하게 했어서 미안하다.

4 그는 비행기를 타기 위해서 일찍 일어났다.

C 1 to wash   **2** to see   **3** to watch

D 1 She grew up to be a nurse.

  2 I am so lucky to have a chance to participate in this festival.

  3 Do you have a piece of paper to write on?

  4 He must be nervous to bite his lips.

E 1 I need a knife to cut the watermelon with.

  2 They are never to meet again.

  3 I was shocked to witness the accident.

  4 She turned on the computer to read some news articles.

F 1 You must practice hard to win the match.

  2 Do you have an extra chair to sit on?

  3 You are to take out the garbage before playing outside.

  4 She must be sad to have failed the test.

UNIT 03 **Subject, Tense, and Voices of To-infinitives** pp. 26-27

A 1 of her   **2** for him   **3** of you

  4 to have worked   **5** for adults

  6 to have canceled

B 1 of him   **2** of you   **3** for you

  4 for me   **5** for us   **6** of her

C 1 to be flat   **2** to be

  3 to have been   **4** to have lived

D 1 It was sweet of you to send me flowers.

  2 It was easy for him to remember numbers.

  3 The conference is scheduled to be held in Seoul.

  4 He seems to have been a member of the club last year.

E 1 It was wise of him to admit his mistake.

  2 It is dangerous for them to play in the street.

  3 He seems to have known what I did last summer.

F 1 It is impossible for her to finish a marathon.

  2 It was honest of you to tell the truth.

  3 She seemed to understand the explanation.

  4 Knives are not to be used by children.

UNIT 04 **Infinitives as Object Complements** pp. 28-29

A 1 to be   **2** walking   **3** to agree

  4 to achieve   **5** find   **6** to move

  7 hammer

B 1 to remove   2 go
    3 enter (entering)   4 to wash
    5 to take   6 clean

C 1 screaming   2 stand   3 to prepare
    4 to take   5 buy

D 1 My sister will not allow me to wear her clothes.
    2 The good news made me feel happy.
    3 The doctor told me not to drink or eat anything for two hours.
    4 She heard the boys talk (talking) about her behind the tree.

E 1 I heard somebody call my name.
    2 The police had the man take everything out of his pockets.
    3 I asked the clerk to recommend the most popular model.

F 1 My father does not let me go out after 9 p.m.
    2 I saw a group of dolphins swim (swimming) in the sea.
    3 Many people helped me complete (to complete) this project.
    4 Her poor health caused her to give up her dream.

UNIT 05   Common Structures of Infinitives   pp. 30-31

A 1 To tell   2 rich enough
    3 To make   4 to get
    5 large enough   6 to wear

B 1 엄마는 너무 바빠서 나와 시간을 보낼 수 없다.
    2 이상하게 들리겠지만, 지난밤에 나는 유령을 봤다.
    3 그는 이 상황에서 평정심을 유지할 수 있을 만큼 강인하다.
    4 솔직히 말하면, 그녀가 말한 것이 기억나지 않는다.

C 1 so to speak   2 old enough
    3 tall enough   4 to protect
    5 To be frank with you

D 1 so spicy that I cannot eat it
    2 too young to ride a roller coaster
    3 so hard that she could win the game
    4 old enough to watch those kinds of movies

E 1 This city is not safe enough to walk around in alone.
    2 The movie was too scary for me to watch.
    3 To tell the truth, I have never been to Europe.

F 1 His speech is too difficult for me to understand.
    2 He is wise enough to give advice to his friends.
    3 To do her justice, she is not qualified for the work.
    4 To make matters worse, I missed the last bus.

CHAPTER 06 Gerunds

UNIT 01   Functions & Usage of Gerunds   pp. 32-33

A 1 talking   2 getting   3 his
    4 Climbing   5 not going   6 going
    7 being punished

B 1 looking for   2 his (him)   3 having
    4 Not eating   5 making   6 eating

C 1 being invited   2 my (me) closing
    3 having gotten

D 1 I am not good at making speeches.
    2 Dad does not like my (me) coming home late at night.
    3 Mark enjoyed being photographed by others.
    4 He denied having been married before.

E 1 One of my favorite activities is reading comic books.
    2 She was worried about me being late.
    3 He complained of having been treated poorly.

F 1 Eric enjoys watching the talk show every weekend.
    2 I am proud of having overcome my fears.
    3 Eating too much sugar is not good for your health.
    4 She does not like being blamed by others.

UNIT 02   Gerunds vs. To-infinitives   pp. 34-35

A 1 sleeping   2 to meet   3 writing
    4 eating out   5 complaining

B 1 그는 잃어버린 그의 가방을 찾으려고 노력했다.
    2 Lisa는 시험 삼아 그녀의 방 벽을 파란색으로 칠해 보았다.
    3 나는 회의에 참석할 수 없다고 말하게 되어 유감이다.
    4 나의 남동생은 서랍 속에 열쇠를 넣었던 것을 잊었다.
    5 내가 방에 들어갔을 때 그는 통화하는 것을 멈췄다.

C 1 regretting   2 reading   3 living
    4 to be   5 watching

D 1 She is busy preparing dinner.
    2 We are looking forward to going to your wedding.
    3 All the students agreed to accept the offer.
    4 It seemed that he did not want to spend any money fixing his laptop.

E 1 I tried to carry a lot of luggage at once.
    2 Do you mind my turning off the air conditioner?
    3 Paul remembered traveling to Italy when he was young.

F 1 I feel like going shopping today.
  2 He is used to going to the movies alone.
  3 He forgot to close the window before going out.
  4 She regrets telling lies to her friend.

CHAPTER 07 Participles

UNIT 01 Functions of Participles pp. 36-37

A 1 exciting   2 embarrassed
  3 bored   4 broken
  5 cleaned   6 talking
  7 amazing

B 1 play (playing)   2 carrying
  3 depressed   4 tired
  5 impressed   6 walk (walking)

C 1 dancing   2 hurt
  3 tested   4 stolen
  5 surprising   6 shocked

D 1 Did you see Teddy play (playing) baseball in the park?
  2 Too much homework made me stressed out.
  3 I could feel my dog lick (licking) my right arm.
  4 The water flowing in this brook is from the mountain valley.

E 1 The treasure was hidden in the cave.
  2 This laptop computer has a very confusing manual.
  3 She seemed quite satisfied with the results.
  4 Some people enjoy watching frightening movies.

F 1 The hot weather made me exhausted all day long.
  2 I often read novels written by Jane Austin.
  3 The person standing next to me in the picture is my teacher.

UNIT 02 Participle Clauses pp. 38-39

A 1 Walking   2 Eating
  3 Listening   4 Taking
  5 following   6 having taken

B 1 웃기는 영화를 보면서 나는 긴장을 풀려고 노력했다.
  2 요즘 바쁘기 때문에 나는 쉴 시간이 없다.
  3 금요일에 일을 마친 후 그는 보통 일찍 잠자리에 든다.

4 내가 청소하는 것을 도와주면 네가 비디오 게임을 하게 해 줄게.
  5 그가 정직하다는 것은 인정하지만 나는 여전히 그를 채용할 수 없다.

C 1 Taking   2 Not feeling
  3 Having seen   4 (Being) Made

D 1 Having no car, she goes to work by bus.
  2 Finishing the job training, they went back to America.
  3 Having left Korea in his childhood, he still remembered Korean.

E 1 Having spent a lot of money on the project, I expected a positive outcome.
  2 Having read the book several times, I do not fully understand it.
  3 Getting an F in composition, he had to take the subject again.

F 1 Not knowing them, I kept silent.
  2 Having been stolen, the car has not been found yet.
  3 Having failed the exam, he decided to try again next year.
  4 (Having been) Built a long time ago, this house is very old.

UNIT 03 Various Participle Clauses pp. 40-41

A 1 Frankly speaking   2 Compared with
  3 Strictly speaking   4 Judging from
  5 Considering

B 1 Jenny는 팔짱을 낀 채로 앉아 있었다.
  2 그 배구 선수는 발에 부상을 당한 채로 계속해서 경기했다.
  3 Diane은 불을 켜 둔 채로 잠이 들었다.
  4 그 배우는 많은 사람들이 환호하는 가운데 나타났다.

C 1 It being   2 closed
  3 Speaking of   4 being

D 1 The singer coming on the stage, people applauded.
  2 There being no food in the refrigerator, I went out to buy some.
  3 Her dress being too long, she had it shortened.

E 1 Before eating this soup, add some salt.
  2 Tomorrow being a holiday, all government offices will be closed.
  3 She was waiting for me with her hair blowing in the wind.
  4 Compared with Greek, English is easy to learn.

F 1 Her family being far away, she felt lonely.
　2 He was running with his shoelaces untied.
　3 Considering his health, he should stay home.
　4 Judging from the reviews on the Internet, the movie must be boring.

CHAPTER 08 Comparisons

UNIT 01 Comparisons Using the Positive Degree pp. 42-43

A 1 fast 2 twice 3 as
　4 easy 5 interesting 6 as big
　7 popular

B 1 easily 2 sour as
　3 as expensive 4 as much as
　5 expensive 6 as fast

C 1 as 2 soon 3 not 4 long

D 1 twice as heavy 2 as soon as possible
　3 as well as 4 as old as

E 1 The movie was not as funny as the cartoon.
　2 You should experience as much as possible.
　3 The virus is spreading twice as fast as we thought.

F 1 This road is as bumpy as that road.
　2 Let me know the results as soon as possible.
　3 Most pets cannot live as long as humans.
　4 The download speed on my computer is three times as fast as (faster than) the upload speed.

UNIT 02 Comparisons Using Comparatives pp. 44-45

A 1 longer 2 warmer
　3 much 4 stronger
　5 more valuable 6 the happier
　7 popular

B 1 worse 2 healthier
　3 the more easily 4 more important
　5 larger 6 expensive

C 1 than 2 better
　3 more 4 much

D 1 The new program is superior to the old one.
　2 The results were much better than we had expected.

3 The hotter it gets, the more water people drink.
4 The boy from a small town became more and more famous.

E 1 Life gets more and more complicated.
　2 Jason's popularity is getting higher and higher.
　3 Sue is much more interested in reading than in shopping.
　4 The more coffee I drank, the more awake I was.

F 1 Traffic is much heavier now than two hours ago.
　2 Her speaking skills are getting better and better.
　3 The economic condition of the country is more serious than you know.

UNIT 03 Comparisons Using Superlatives pp. 46-47

A 1 youngest 2 most popular
　3 buildings 4 more intelligent
　5 have ever played

B 1 tallest 2 largest
　3 languages 4 best
　5 most attractive

C 1 This jacket is the more popular of the two.
　2 No other teacher at our school is friendlier than Ms. Gates.
　3 The Nile is one of the longest rivers in the world.
　4 Camels are the most important animals in the desert.

D 1 = larger than any other ocean
　 = No other ocean, is larger
　 = is as large as the Pacific Ocean
　2 = more difficult, any other subject
　 = is more difficult
　 = difficult as math

E 1 Asia is the biggest continent in the world.
　2 He was one of the most unfortunate men in history.
　3 No other thing is as important as your health.

F 1 Tyler is the smartest of all the students.
　2 Montreux is one of the most beautiful cities in Switzerland.
　3 Bungee jumping is the most impressive experience (that) I have ever had.

CHAPTER 09 Conjunctions

UNIT 01 Subordinating Conjunctions pp. 48-49

A 1 before 　　2 Though 　　3 while
　　4 once 　　5 as

B 1 그는 그 주제에 관심이 있었기 때문에 주의 깊게 들었다.
　　2 비록 눈이 많이 오고 있었지만 그녀는 학교에 늦지 않았다.
　　3 만약 네가 똑바로 앉지 않는다면 허리를 다칠 수 있다.
　　4 그는 은퇴하자마자 아내와 여행을 갈 것이다.

C 1 Although 　　2 Unless 　　3 since

D 1 I have to do my homework today as I have plans tomorrow. (As I have plans tomorrow, I have to do my homework today.)
　　2 In case it rains, I will bring an umbrella. (I will bring an umbrella in case it rains.)
　　3 Wash your hands often in order that you can avoid catching a cold. (In order that you can avoid catching a cold, wash your hands often.)

E 1 My mom will be there until my class is over. (Until my class is over, my mom will be there.)
　　2 Remove these boxes so that people can pass by. (So that people can pass by, remove these boxes.)
　　3 Though it was very hot, the children were playing baseball. (The children were playing baseball though it was very hot.)

F 1 When she enters and leaves the building, she does not take the elevator. (She does not take the elevator when she enters and leaves the building.)
　　2 He could not keep his promise because (as, since) he was busy. (Because (As, Since) he was busy, he could not keep his promise.)
　　3 If the price is reasonable, I want to buy these shoes. (I want to buy these shoes if the price is reasonable.)
　　4 Though (Although, Even though) my friends live abroad, we contact one another regularly. (We contact one another regularly though (although, even though) my friends live abroad.)

UNIT 02 Correlative Conjunctions / Indirect Questions pp. 50-51

A 1 either 　　　　2 as well as
　　3 who won 　　　4 both
　　5 whether 　　　6 he left
　　7 neither

B 1 where 　　2 who 　　3 Whether 　　4 if

C 1 Whether 　　　　　2 Neither
　　3 you moved 　　　4 are
　　5 but also 　　　　6 plays
　　7 or

D 1 What do you think he wants to be?
　　2 I wonder why she lied to her parents.
　　3 Neither she nor he likes the class schedule. (Both she and he do not like the class schedule.)
　　4 Can you tell me if (whether) he arrived at the hotel?

E 1 He recycles neither paper nor cans.
　　2 She is both warm-hearted and energetic.
　　3 I am not sure why she fell in love with him.
　　4 I do not know whether this sentence is correct.

F 1 I will make either some pasta or a pizza.
　　2 I am not sure whether (if) you can find a bank.
　　3 I am curious why he explores new places.
　　4 Jeff realized that he was talking too much.

CHAPTER 10 Relatives

UNIT 01 Relative Pronouns pp. 52-53

A 1 whom 　　2 whose 　　3 that
　　4 what 　　5 that 　　6 who

B 1 나는 그때 너무 긴장해서 내가 생각한 것을 잘 표현하지 못했다.
　　2 때로는 당신의 형제나 자매가 당신이 가장 화내는 상대이다.
　　3 나는 방금 네 것과 정확히 같은 코트를 입은 소녀를 보았다.
　　4 저쪽에 선글라스를 쓰고 있는 남자를 봐라.

C 1 The tiger which it grew too big has been sent to a larger zoo.
　　2 Isn't that the woman who she lives across the street from you?
　　3 This is the postcard that my cousin sent me it.
　　4 I thought hard to figure out what I really wanted the thing.
　　5 Sally is my friend whom I often study with her.

D 1 the boy with whom
　　2 which he had lost
　　3 café whose walls are
　　4 The best thing that I have ever done

E 1 The person who came up with the idea was Hank.
2 I know someone whose older brother is a police officer.
3 People who don't exercise at all tend to be less healthy.
4 The chair on which he sat down suddenly broke.

F 1 Helen Keller was an educator who was deaf and blind.
2 Tell me what you need, and I will get it for you.
3 Is there anything that you need?
4 The reporter is interviewing a man whose house was damaged by the flood.

UNIT 02 Relative Adverbs pp. 54-55

A 1 why 2 how 3 where
4 when 5 at which 6 the day

B 1 그들은 그가 왔던 날을 기억하지 못한다.
2 나는 중고 책을 살 수 있는 서점을 찾고 있다.
3 우리는 우리의 기차가 떠나는 시간을 확인해야 한다.
4 이것이 내가 영어 단어를 암기하는 방법이다.
5 내가 살았던 집은 강 근처에 있었다.

C 1 × 2 ○ 3 × 4 ○

D 1 is the place where
2 Spring is the time when
3 The day on which we arrived
4 The reason why she turned down

E 1 This is the house in which Jeff lives.
2 2016 was the year when Christmas fell on a Sunday.
3 Do you know the reason why Sera cried? (Do you know the reason Sera cried? / Do you know why Sera cried?)
4 Do you remember the park where we used to play together?

F 1 Pyeongchang is the city in which the 2018 Winter Olympics were held.
2 Let me show you how you can shut down this computer.
3 Wednesday and Sunday are the days when I clean my room.
4 I left my bag in the restaurant where I had dinner.

UNIT 03 Nonrestrictive Relative Clauses pp. 56-57

A 1 who 2 which 3 where 4 as

B 1 Mia는 내게 비밀 편지를 전달해 달라고 부탁했는데 나는 그것을 즉시 읽었다.

2 나는 살면서 걱정거리가 많았는데 그것들 중 대부분은 일어나지 않았다.
3 꿈이 없는 사람은 아무도 없다.
4 그는 작은 아파트로 이사할 예정인데 많은 사람들이 그곳에 귀신이 산다고 믿는다.

C 1 whose 2 whom 3 which
4 where 5 when

D 1 many of whom visit Hallasan
2 which I could not understand
3 which is why
4 which was very unusual
5 most of which were rotten
6 where I met April
7 when she visited

E 1 She grew up in Germany, which is why she understands German.
2 whom I met at the school gym, is a very talented badminton player
3 You should not eat more food than is needed.
4 I bought ten pairs of socks, one of which had a hole.

UNIT 04 Compound Relatives pp. 58-59

A 1 Whatever 2 whoever
3 Wherever 4 However
5 whichever 6 No matter when

B 1 마지막으로 교실을 떠나는 사람은 누구든 불을 꺼야 한다.
2 그는 내가 그에게 말하고 싶어할 때마다 바쁘다.
3 아무리 작은 과제라고 할지라도 그녀는 그것을 잘하려고 노력한다.
4 그는 내가 제안하는 것은 무엇이든 반대하는 것 같다.

C 1 wherever 2 whoever
3 Whatever 4 Anything

D 1 who wants to go
2 matter how rich you are
3 matter where he happens to be
4 matter what they may say

E 1 Wherever you go, I will follow you.
2 He will kindly give an answer to whoever asks him a question.
3 However hungry she is, she does not eat fast food.
4 Whatever you want is yours.

F 1 Mayor Smith is welcome wherever he goes.
2 I think of him whenever I hear that song.
3 Whatever you do with your friends, return home before 10.

CHAPTER 11 Subjunctive Mood

UNIT 01 Subjunctives — pp. 60-61

A 1 had 2 come
3 would have 4 would
5 stopped 6 give

B 1 did not 2 will
3 would have 4 would not
5 were 6 had been

C 1 had, cannot 2 did not have, could not buy
3 had not been, would have been
4 would not be, stayed up

D 1 If I had a house with a swimming pool, I could swim every day.
2 If I were a famous soccer player, I would be rich.
3 If you had not been busy, I would have asked you to help me.
4 If James had asked me what happened that day, I would have said something.

E 1 If you had studied hard, you could enter the university.
2 If the plane had landed on time, we would not be late for the event.
3 If I had remembered Amy's address, I would have sent her a Christmas card.

F 1 If I were the director, I would not cast the actress.
2 If I had had the book, I would have lent it to you.
3 If he had gone on the camping trip, he would be there with them now.

UNIT 02 I wish/as if/It is time + Subjunctive — pp. 62-63

A 1 were 2 were
3 had not met 4 cleaned
5 had saved

B 1 had not eaten 2 had cooked
3 made 4 made (had made)
5 prepared 6 had chosen

C 1 does not know 2 sang 3 finished
4 had not told 5 were

D 1 He talked as if he had fought with Dick.
2 I wish more people were interested in charity work.
3 It is time she learned a practical skill besides studying.

4 He talked as if he had met the fashion model in person.
5 I wish my grandmother had not passed away.
6 It is high time we finished writing the report.

E 1 I wish I had joined the band with Raina.
2 Aiden described the town as if he had visited it.
3 I wished James had left some pizza for me.
4 Alicia talks as if she read the newspaper article.
5 I wish I knew all the answers to the test questions.

UNIT 03 Implied Subjunctive / Leaving Out *if* — pp. 64-65

A 1 Having 2 To see
3 Otherwise 4 Had

B 1 Working 2 Were I
3 would live (would have lived) 4 Had

C 1 Having been (had he been), would have gotten
2 not been for, could not have achieved
3 see him do magic, would see
4 were

D 1 Had it not been for cell phones, our lives might have been more simple.
2 A good book would give you pleasure as well as information.
3 To talk to him, you would realize he has a good sense of humor.
4 I got caught in a traffic jam. Otherwise, I would have arrived here earlier.
5 Were it not for my teacher's help, I could not finish the project.

E 1 Having been informed of the new policy, we would not have been confused.
2 But for the Internet, people would have difficulty finding information.
3 Without my parents' encouragement, I might have given up on my career.
4 Tom ate a sandwich for breakfast. Otherwise, he would have been hungry in class.

CHAPTER 12 Agreement & Narration

UNIT 01 Number Agreement — pp. 66-67

A 1 has 2 require 3 is
4 Has 5 is 6 is

B 1 많은 학생들이 숙제를 마감 날짜에 제출하는 데 실패했다.
  2 경찰 보고에 따르면 사망자들의 대다수가 영국인이었다고 한다.
  3 지구 표면의 거의 4분의 3이 물로 덮여 있다.
  4 전문가들은 세계의 언어의 수가 미래에 줄어들 것이라고 말한다.

C 1 has   2 knows
  3 were   4 are (were)

D 1 Every parent loves his or her child.
  2 The writer and the environmentalist are planning a charity event.
  3 The number of people who go abroad on vacation is increasing.
  4 All the information was analyzed by the computer.
  5 Creating new products takes a lot of time.
  6 Half a million dollars was donated to the homeless.
  7 Whether you spend your vacation with us is important to me.
  8 The young tend to have a preference for exciting activities.

E 1 Measles was a serious disease in the Middle Ages.
  2 Nine dollars for that hamburger is too expensive.
  3 The rest of the pages are about the author's life.
  4 Some of the water was spilled on the keyboard.
  5 Drinking coffee is what Anne does as soon as she gets up.

UNIT 02 Tense Agreement   pp. 68-69

A 1 opens   2 will   3 rang
  4 wakes   5 took   6 was

B 1 has already left   2 invented   3 was
  4 gets   5 would not   6 broke out

C 1 was suffering   2 had paid   3 travels

D 1 how well I felt
  2 anything that is necessary
  3 started to comb his hair
  4 I have put my phone

E 1 Yesterday I rode my bike to school but walked home later.
  2 Bob cooked a meal for his mother and then did all the dishes.
  3 The scientist proved that the earth is round.
  4 The boys loved the tree house which they had built themselves.

F 1 The train came, but Anna could not find her train ticket.

2 Benjamin Franklin believed (that) honesty is the best policy.
3 I heard (that) Ethan always watches the news on TV before he goes to bed.
4 We know (that) the Korean War was over in 1953.

UNIT 03 Indirect Speech   pp. 70-71

A 1 told   2 if   3 whether
  4 asked me what   5 said   6 to

B 1 might   2 to   3 asked
  4 asked   5 said

C 1 Has   2 did you
  3 Are you   4 do you

D 1 was sitting on his bag then
  2 said (that) World War II began in 1939
  3 checked his email that morning
  4 had come the day before
  5 asked, where she could wash her hands
  6 not to throw trash there
  7 the earth's rotation causes the seasons
  8 they would mind if he opened the window

E 1 The nurse asked me if I could go there the next day.
  2 Holly said (that) there was a fly in her soup.
  3 My mother told me to close the window if it rained.
  4 One of the girls asked me when her turn was.

CHAPTER 13 Sentence Arrangement

UNIT 01 Emphasis, Negation, & Parallel Structure   pp. 72-73

A 1 that   2 snowboarding   3 No
  4 did   5 attends

B 1 어젯밤에 이상한 소리가 나온 것은 바로 천장으로부터였다.
  2 나는 너와 싸울 의사가 전혀 없다.
  3 Nina의 춤은 우아했을 뿐만 아니라 힘이 넘쳤다.
  4 그는 안경을 안 쓰면 정말 다른 사람처럼 보인다.
  5 모든 동물이 생존하는 데 산소를 필요로 하는 것은 아니다.

C 1 no   2 None   3 that   4 did

D 1 finish his homework and then played
  2 Neither of them
  3 must not have any
  4 but because of her personality

E 1 Audrey Hepburn was a kind, beautiful, and passionate person.

2 Eating too much and not exercising at all are harmful to your health.

3 It was I who answered your call a while ago.

4 None of them has any complaints though they were in a difficult situation.

F 1 It is every Friday that my father finishes his work early.

2 Neither of us wanted to apologize first.

3 There is no exception to this grammar rule.

4 I will either go shopping or visit my uncle in the afternoon.

UNIT 02 Apposition, Inversion, & Ellipsis pp. 74-75

A 1 can   2 Here comes   3 that
4 of   5 she was

B 1 우리가 그 게임에서 승리할 것이라는 희망은 없다.

2 정원의 중심에는 아름다운 분수가 있었다.

3 어떤 이들에게는 역사가 지루하다. 다른 이들에게는 (역사가) 재미있다.

4 그는 나를 지나치면서 한마디 말도 하지 않았다.

C 1 did   2 be   3 were
4 did   5 is

D 1 but not eating

2 disappeared the deer

3 nor did I offer it

4 A letter of appreciation

E 1 Here they are!

2 My mom told me to throw away my old toys, but I did not want to.

3 I am a member of the reading club, and so is Barbara.

4 The chances of being hit by lightning in your lifetime are one in 3,000.

F 1 will I make the same mistake

2 It is his habit to hum a song while taking a shower.

3 the roof was a beehive

4 Feminism is the belief that men and women should have equal rights.